This book is
presented to the
Clayton-Liberty
Township Public
Library
by
Gayle Overton

GOOD SPORTS:
A LARGE PRINT
ANTHOLOGY of GREAT
SPORTS WRITING

Vol xing,

Other Anthologies Available in Large Print:

*The Best of My Life: Autobiographies in
     Large Print*
Best-Loved Poems in Large Print
Famous Detective Stories in Large Print
Favorite Animal Stories in Large Print
Favorite Short Stories in Large Print
Favorite Short Stories in Large Print, Volume 2
Great Ghost Stories in Large Print
*A Trail of Memories: The Quotations of
     Louis L'Amour*
Travels in America: A Large Print Anthology
A Treasury of Humor in Large Print
*Senior Sleuths: A Large Print Anthology of
     Mysteries and Puzzlers*

G.K. Hall Large Print Book Series.

Set in 16 pt Plantin.

Library of Congress Cataloging in Publication Data

Good sports: a large print anthology of great sports writing / edited by
     Judith Leet.
          p.   cm.—(G.K. Hall large print book series)
     Large print reprints of previously published articles, including fiction.
     ISBN 0-8161-4235-3
     1. Sports.   2. Large type books.   I. Leet, Judith
[GV707.L37   1990]
796—dc20
                                                                    90-40339

Contents

BACKGROUND

BASEBALL

FISHING

FOOTBALL

EPILOGUE

Editor's Note

Sports is an endlessly popular interest of Americans of every social strata. Americans watch the best athletes on television, participate in sports personally, talk about sports events at great length with friends and strangers, and follow their favorite teams in newsprint each day without fail.

This is the first of a two-volume anthology that assembles a collection of writing on sport by the finest writers, both those who specialize in sportswriting (Paul Gallico, A. J. Liebling, Red Smith, Roger Angell) and those who only occasionally write on sports (John Updike, Joyce Carol Oates, Norman Mailer). All these writers have in common a feeling for language as a means of recreating and interpreting a sports event in ways that many readers will find fresh and compelling.

In this first volume, we have concentrated on just four of the most popular American sports—football, baseball, boxing, and fishing. Tennis, golf, basketball, and other major sporting events will be covered in a second volume. Many selections concentrate on outstanding athletes at the top of their form; other pieces discuss the early development, struggles, and discipline of the young athlete; yet other selections describe the years following the great years—the inevitable decline in strength and reflexes, the retirement from sports, and the changes and new directions after the peak years.

Some pieces discuss the influence of parents and coaches (Vince Lombardi's ability to inspire "mental toughness" in his team; Woody Hayes's idiosyncrasies), the social climate (Joe Louis's role as the first successful black athlete), the tournaments such as Wimbledon, record keeping (and those who break world records), and the professionalization of sports. In these pieces, many facets of sports are analyzed and illuminated; both the newcomer to sports and the sports fan will gain a deeper understanding of the athlete's competitive world from the varied perspectives of these writers.

The reader will contrast the earlier, less high-pressured days of sports when figures such as Knute Rockne (who introduced the forward pass into football), and Babe Ruth were in the headlines with the high-powered, well-paid athletes of today when sports is a big business, often controlled by television considerations. We contrast ever-dependable good sportsmanship of a Chris Evert with those athletes like John McEnroe who are remembered for their temperamental disturbances on the court.

When A. J. Liebling contrasts the fighting styles of Archie Moore, the craftsman, the thinker, with his opponent Rocky Marciano, his dangerously powerful but slow-thinking opponent, sportswriting reaches one of its peak performances.

Sports represents excitement and entertainment, but more than that, it is the admiration the fan feels for those athletes who have developed skills and endurance, both physical and mental, that the rest of us collectively would like to have possessed. But since we are not blessed with these endowments, we do the next best thing, and try to understand what it is like to be a Bill Bradley or a Joe DiMaggio.

I would like to express my appreciation and thanks to Janice Meagher, editor at G.K. Hall, Bill Littlefield, and Renee Shur, for their contributions, particularly their help in choosing the selections in this anthology.

BACKGROUND

TED VINCENT

The Democratic Era of Sport

The development of modern American sports over the last hundred years from local amateur clubs to big professional businesses is here retold by Ted Vincent. In the years after the Civil War, a baseball club was just what it was called, a club, formed by local citizens and managed by local directors, most of whom were not wealthy men. In this early "democratic" era, the wealthy stayed aloof from sports because it was considered in poor taste, a carry-over from puritan disdain of good times and vices, and furthermore it was a risky investment.

All this changed in the recent past when sports became an avenue for creating great wealth for both players and organizations. The era of broad participation was over; the amateur player became a spectator for the highly skilled professional athlete.

During his presidential campaign of 1880 James A. Garfield said in a speech at Lake Chautauqua, New York: "We may divide the whole struggle of the human race into two chapters: first, the fight to get leisure; and then the second fight of civilization—what shall we do with our leisure when we get it?" In 1880 organized sport involving leagues, associations, enclosed stadiums, and substantial coverage in the newspapers was a relatively new phenomenon, only some twenty years old. Most of our modern sports experienced their initial popularity and took organized form at some time between the Civil War and the end of the nineteenth century. The newfound popularity of sport shocked conservative ministers of the Gospel, and was misunderstood as well by powerful business interests, who were slow to see the potential of mass sport for extending their influence.

Compared with today, the distinguishing feature of sport a hundred years ago was that the professional games and contests had not yet been monopolized by corporate wealth, and a fledgling amateur system was not yet under the control of college deans, retired military brass, and corporation executives. The period from the 1860s into the early 1890s was the democratic and pluralist era of American sport, in which a grocer or saloon keeper had as much chance as a millionaire of producing an event that grabbed headlines in the national sporting magazines.

The teams in the early years of professional baseball were group enterprises, and always run by the townspeople. An absentee owner was unthinkable. Baseball clubs were really clubs, with hundreds of members. And when a club became a company, shares of stock were sold to the public, giving a wide range of people a chance to own a piece of "our team." The organizational form for early professional teams is typified in the Philadelphia Athletics of the 1870s, the ancestors of the current Oakland A's and prominent in baseball from the beginning, excepting a few years in the 1890s as

4

a minor operation. For all but one season of the 1870s the Philadelphia Athletics didn't have an individual owner. And the team performed not for a company but for a large membership club. Control changed from year to year through revolving positions on a board of directors and on committees. The officers were ordinary people from Philadelphia. In 1872 the officers of the club were: two liquor dealers, two attorneys, two clerks, a secretary, a livery-stable keeper, a pawnbroker, a sportswriter, two players, and the team manager. Throughout the 1870s the identifiable club officials of the Athletics included only one person of substantial wealth, a Stephen Flannigan, who owned a steamship company.

The input to the popular spectator attractions on the part of the wealthy and powerful was limited for several reasons. They were inhibited by objections from religious and intellectual leaders of the old puritanical gentry, who still pulled weight in public affairs. Sports were a risky financial investment and didn't match the profit potential available in the booming areas of manufacturing, railroads, and banking. Very few baseball teams lasted as did the Philadelphia Athletics; three out of every four professional teams of the nineteenth century went out of business within two years. Those among the wealthy who did go in for sports, the "gentlemen sportsmen," were often nouveaux riches who coveted acceptance by the families of traditional wealth, and felt more acceptable when their amusements were distinct from the popular sports of the masses. The gentlemen sportsmen favored prestigious participatory sports,

5

such as polo, yachting, and tennis, rather than the spectator attractions.

During the democratic era in sports the athletes themselves were often able to do the organizing and promoting. Ordinary fans started teams whose exploits were reported in a sporting press which was developed by similar individuals. *Sporting News* was founded by two telegraphers; *Sporting Life,* by a printer; and the *Police Gazette* was made into a national organ for boxing fans by Richard K. Fox, an immigrant from Ireland who had arrived in this country almost penniless. Top-quality sporting events were not restricted to a few major cities, but enlivened many towns now stereotyped as cultural and sporting wastelands. The distinction between amateur and professional was not clearly drawn, and novices competed against experts. Open competition invited broad participation, as though everyone had a chance to play sandlot ball against a Pete Rose or Reggie Jackson. In track and field, handicap events were common, providing encouragement for the less proficient athletes.

Before the Civil War, organized sporting contests were a rare treat. Durant and Bettmann, in their *Pictorial History of American Sports,* describe the slim pickings for the antebellum sports fan. "Now and then he could take in a ball game or a horse race and, once in a blue moon, a prize fight, if he was willing to risk getting slugged by some hoodlum or having his pocket picked. . . . His comfort wasn't considered at the few sporting events he could attend. There were no stadiums or indoor arenas. He stood on his feet while watching ball games, prize fights and foot races."

6

Americans had been engaged in sports since colonial times, as evidenced in the numerous edicts and diatribes written by Puritans condemning everything from horse racing to deer hunting. However, what passed as athletics in colonial America was along the lines of informal competitions between neighbors to see who was the fastest woodchopper. Missing were the aficionados whose reporting and record keeping turns mere exercise and games into sport. For example, in his history of British sport in the 1700s Montague Shearman cites a report from Virginia concerning a long-jump leap of over 22 feet by the young George Washington. Had there been amateur records, this probably would have been the world's best mark for that century; and had the colonies had a sizable sporting crowd to make a fuss over Washington's leap, we might today speak of the father of our country as our first track and field star.

For fifty years the new nation went without the trappings of a sporting society. Sport seemed a waste of time and out of place in a land of hardworking farmers who had but recently renounced a self-indulgent king and hereditary nobility. The first general sports book published in the United States appears to have been the 1820s volume titled *Children's Amusements: When School Is Over for the Day, the Sprightly Boys Run Off to Play.* Among the accepted play for children the author listed archery, cricket, skating, fives, and various ball games.

An adult sporting world began to take form in the 1830s when grandstands were constructed at racetracks and the first sporting journals appeared.

The growth of sport was quite gradual, however, until the spectacular boom began around the time of the Civil War. Accelerated interest in sport is reflected in the growth of the National Association of Base Ball Players. Founded in 1858 with 25 clubs, the Association had 50 member clubs on the eve of the Civil War. In 1865 there were 97 members, a year later 202, and in 1868 close to 350. By 1869 the *New York Times* estimated that there were over 1,000 clubs, including those operating outside and inside the association; and there were doubtless many additional informal teams playing the game.

The rapid growth of sports in the United States has left scholars perplexed. They mention the effect of urbanization in facilitating the gathering of a crowd; there is discussion of the increase in leisure time produced by the Industrial Revolution; it is shown how improved rail travel sparked intercity competition; the sporting press is seen as capitalizing on the speedy information provided by telegraph companies; and the creation of an advertising industry is shown to have had its impact on the popularity of sport. But the reasons given are too mechanical, and treat sport as one more marketable product in a consumer society. The intensely fraternal motivations of the emerging sporting crowd are overlooked. In the final analysis, one historian admits no answer as to "just why" the boom occurred when it did, while another finds the extent of the sports phenomenon "not easy to explain."

Heroes and teams showered with glory seemed to come out of nowhere. In track and field, new world records were set with ease by the ubiquitous inventors of new events, such as the professional jumping event known as "the run, eight hops and a jump," and the one called "the stand, one hop, two strides, one hop, two strides and a jump"— world record 73'2'. For accomplishments to mean anything there have to be people who will make something out of it. More than athletes were needed to make the abovementioned jumps noteworthy; there was the active cooperation of track fans, whose presence made the event worth recording. The rise of sport is more easily comprehended when fans are credited with more than a passive role. In the formative years of track and field, for example, sponsorship most often came from an ethnic organization, whose members were expected to round up their relatives and friends, so that a big crowd would be on hand when, hopefully, someone would hop, jump, run, throw something, or ride a bicycle to a new world record. The payoff for the club would be a sizable paragraph in the sports page of the next day's newspaper. Reading the story, the club members could feel that they were more than just passive fans taking vicarious thrills. They had rounded up the spectators, who paid the admissions that covered the prize money and attracted the top-rate performer, who in turn set the record that publicized the club and brought in new members.

In every historical period there are the few of economic and social power who seek to dictate cultural taste. Occasionally they fail. In the origins of American sports the control of the elite was temporarily absent; in part because sports was seen as something not to be controlled but to be repressed. A sporting world was being created in a still-puritanical country whose gentry, clergy, and other "respectable" elements had from colonial times condemned sports and frolics as unfit for a hardworking Christian people.

"Society would drop a man who would run around the Common in five minutes," declared the Boston "Brahmin" Oliver Wendell Holmes in 1858. The popular amusements and sports became the preserve of a crowd labeled "the mob" by that venerable journal the *New York Times*. The erudite *Fortnightly Review* wasn't sure who the crowd was, but was certain it was not composed of "men of breeding." The raucous and untamed baseball fans of the period were proudly classified as "the working classes" by Samuel Gompers of the American Federation of Labor; and *Sporting News* termed them "the masses." Henry Chadwick, the dean of American sportswriters, reminisced about the way the prominent dailies rarely mentioned baseball well into the 1860s, and when they did, they "affected sneer and ridicule." Avoided even more thoroughly were sports such as boxing, which one New York gentleman of the day termed "one of the most fashionable abominations of our loafer ridden city." The publishers of the new tabloid "yellow" journals, however, were quick to provide what the gentleman called "the horrid details, with all their disgusting technicalities and vulgar slang."

The urbanization and industrialization of America, begun in the 1850s and greatly accelerated in later decades, created a large mass of people who were not served by traditional spokesmen of culture.

The minister, the banker, the dean of the local academy, and the family of landed wealth had their own version of leisure; at the concert of the string quartet, at the church bazaar, boating on the lake, or attending a lecture about the Australian aborigines or other faraway peoples. The traditional church did not reach out to the new urban dweller; inner-city churches were left with many an empty pew after the old gentry had moved out to the suburbs; only then did the religious leaders discover the virtue of the involved church of the social gospel. The aloof intellectual establishment was nurturing Social Darwinist notions which held the typical worker and his family to be an inferior breed of human being, unqualified to share in the refined cultural and leisure pursuits of the "fittest" classes.

Popular sports were generated from below as one answer to the crying need for organized social activity in the new urban setting. They developed during a time when cities experienced a growth rate of from 100 to 200 percent in a decade. Uprooted populations had a desperate need for new social ties. When people formed an occupational club, ethnic organization, fraternal order, political club, or trade union, they tended to add sports activities as a way of attracting members and solidifying friendships. In the beginning, the majority of baseball clubs were just that—"clubs" of many members, like the Athletics of Philadelphia. Track meets featuring the best athletes were sponsored by such groups as Hibernians, Caledonians, Odd Fellows, and trade unions. The meets were embellished with sack races for the youngsters and special events for the elderly. And when a meet was over, the band started up the music for the evening dance party. High-stakes billiard tournaments stretching out over an entire week provided a sense of purpose for many a pool-hall loafer who was going to be there anyway.

The rise of sport perplexed the critics, who were at a loss to explain what it was that drew the crowds. A hostile reporter at a Madison Square Garden six-day professional walking marathon in 1882 wished he could understand "the peculiar phase of idiocy in the American character" which kept thousands of men and women watching this spectacle well past midnight. Horace Greeley had a tongue-in-cheek explanation "of our public vices." He said they subsisted on rum, and that without liquor, horse racing, gambling halls, and lotteries as well as theaters would wither away. "I don't know of a theatre," said Dwight L. Moody, evangelist king of the 1870s, "that hasn't a bar connected with it, or near it. What is that bar there for? Fallen women go to the theatres, and for no good purpose." During the decades of the rise of sport the per capita liquor consumption almost trebled. There was need of some tranquilizer, some avenue of escape from the tensions of city life, the "splendid chaos" which Rudyard Kipling called Chicago—and having seen it he exclaimed, "I urgently desire never to see it again."

The popularity of spectator sports soared in the aftermath of the Civil War. To put out of their minds the bloody conflict which took a million lives, Americans were throwing away their puritanical inhibitions about amusements—flocking to gaming rooms to have a go with the faro cards, and laughing themselves hoarse at minstrel shows and at the new variety acts called "vaudeville." Theater, sports, and gambling siphoned off the energy of the discharged veterans, then congregating in the cities, creating a bachelor culture of saloons, pool halls, and boardinghouses. "Another Pool Hall on Broadway," headlined the New York *Clipper* on the story of the clutter of billiard parlors, saloons, theaters, dime museums, and the like stretching up from the Bowery toward midtown. The cities were swollen by an ever-increasing stream of immigrants from Europe seeking employment in the new factories and mills. The war veterans who had chosen not to return to their farms and villages were now joined in the city by friends and relatives. From Maine out through Illinois, farms were abandoned by the thousands, and villages stood deserted. A traveler in rural Vermont described the eerie feeling of villages with "abandoned wagonshops, shoeshops, sawmills and other mechanical businesses."

The country had always had its rich and its poor, but outside of the plantation South there had been little precedent in antebellum years for the blatantly obvious class distinctions arising in the burgeoning cities. Whereas in the villages the inns and taverns had served everyone, there were now in the cities separate hotels and separate drinking establishments for the separate classes. Where there had been a village livery stable, there was now in the city the private riding academy for the elite, while the nearest the masses got to riding a horse was watching its backside as they rode the trolley. In rustic America a dinner and dance put on by the best people in town lacked the splendor of a big-city, high-society cotillion held in a huge dance palace with a sixty-piece orchestra. Showing your latest hound dog to a neighbor was certainly not in a class with the Westminster Kennel Show in Madison Square Garden.

The America which Alexis de Tocqueville had described in the 1830s as industrious but plain was turning gaudy as it entered the Gilded Age, which the critic Thorstein Veblen found marked by "conspicuous consumption" and "conspicuous leisure." We can still see its glitter today in the Victorian homes and older office buildings, with their marble staircases and statues in the lobby. Those who had little to flaunt could, at least, find notoriety through identification with the rough and ribald world of public amusements. The more plebeian New Yorkers had their turn at the Garden too. Six-day marathons brought them there in great numbers during the late 1870s and early 1880s. Paying 25 to 50 cents to watch a marathon, a baseball game, or a billiard tournament was the poor folks' way of putting themselves on public display, as the gentlemen and ladies did by attending a Grand Ball, or paying $1.50 to $3.00 to see the great Edwin Booth on the Broadway stage.

One of the more important reasons for the baseball craze was that the teams provided the newly arrived and lonely urban masses a topic around which conversation at the pub could lead to friendships. No history of the early game is complete without mention of the semiliterate fan who could quote all the batting averages and betting odds, and harangue for hours about "our team." The way ball clubs were organized added substance to the "our team" claim. If the fan was not one of the team's club members or stockholders, he was likely to have some of them for friends. The promoters of baseball, well into the 1880s, were typically only a notch above the gate crashers in the sporting crowd.

ANDREW ROONEY

Breaking Sports Records

The most devoted fans have their heads full of the records and statistics of their favorite athletes' performances. But Rooney asks whether athletes of the future can continue to break records, or will they reach some final limits of human strength and endurance? And how tall will the tallest basketball players of the next century grow? Rooney poses questions that arouse our curiosity.

It's hard to guess what sports will be like in fifty or a hundred years. Two race car drivers were killed recently, one of them hit a wall head-on in a car going 187 miles an hour. The car disintegrated and the driver was killed instantly.

At Indianapolis this year, several drivers have qualified for the Indianapolis 500 at speeds of more than 200 miles an hour. Where are we going with records? The average qualifying speed for the Indianapolis 500 this year was 197 miles an hour. In 1970 the average qualifying speed was 167. In 1960 it was 144 and in 1950 it was 131.

My question is this: What will it be in the year 2032? Will it be 300 miles an hour? 400? And if it is, how many drivers will be killed hitting walls head-on?

16

For automobile racing the solution is easy: put a limit on engine size so that racing becomes a contest solely of drivers and mechanics, not cars. But what's going to happen to records in other sports and how are average young athletes going to compete against the supermen we seem to be breeding?

Twenty years ago, Wilt Chamberlain was one of the few seven-foot basketball players around. Today there are fourteen National Basketball Association players at least that tall. A couple of them are heading for eight feet. Every high school has a few players six foot three inches and in college the short fellows who are only six feet tall don't have any better chance of making the team than the Indianapolis driver who only averages 175 miles an hour. The six-footer today isn't tall enough and the 175-mile-an-hour driver is too slow.

My father took me to a track meet at Madison Square Garden when I was young and I watched a man set the world's record in the pole vault at 14'4". Today the record is 19'2".

The sports page of my newspaper last week carried a small-type listing of the results of a high school track meet and I noticed that the boy who finished third in the high jump, cleared the bar at 6'6". Fifty years ago that was the world's record. Today a jumper doesn't win anything if he can't clear 7' and the record is 7'8 ¾".

If the record keeps going up at that rate, approximately one foot every fifty years, does that mean some athlete will be jumping ten feet high in 2082?

The question is: Is there any limit to human

capacity and if there is a limit, what is it? If an athlete can jump ten feet high in a hundred years, will athletes be jumping twenty feet high in five hundred years?

In track and field some of the records can be attributed to better equipment but the basic improvement in every case has been in the athletes themselves. They're bigger, stronger, faster and have more endurance. Football players have gotten heavier and stronger the way basketball players have gotten taller. When a defensive lineman from a good college team gets to the pros weighing only 235 pounds these days, he's made into a line backer because he's too small to play end or tackle.

One of the most encouraging things about all this is that while the human race has never been subjected to any kind of selective breeding, it seems to be improving physically and mentally.

On the other hand, horses have been bred selectively for hundreds of years in an attempt to produce ones that run faster but horses aren't much faster than they ever were. The horse race records at various distances haven't improved anywhere near as dramatically as human records have.

In 1882 the world's record for a man running a mile was 4:21. In 1942 it was 4:04. Today it is down under 3:50.

In 1940 Whirlaway won the Kentucky Derby, a distance of a mile and a quarter, in 2:01. In the past five years it has been run in 2:02 or more.

This is perhaps the strongest case that can be made against racism and Adolf Hitler's kind of superrace theories. It seems the kind of random breeding the human race does, produces a better strain than that produced by scientists or dictators deciding, as horse breeders do, who should breed with whom and who shouldn't breed at all.

If the human race continues to improve as sports records indicate it has, someone in the year 2100 will run the mile in a minute, swim 100 yards in 30 seconds and basketball players will all be ten feet tall.

I'd love to be around to watch but I was probably born a little too early to live to be 180.

JOHN ED BRADLEY
Jock of Ages

A sporting rite of passage as described by John Ed Bradley, sports writer and novelist. He touches upon everyone's recollections of the painful process of growing up, of figuring out how embarrassing things work, and of making or not making the team.

It was at Fontenot and Guidry, a department store in Church Point, Louisiana, that my father bought me my first jockstrap. My great uncle Hugh Guidry ran the store and kept them in boxes hanging on hooks in the underwear department. There were only two sizes, large and extra large, and every one was the same. A pouch that looked like the breathing apparatus of a great fish was sewn onto an elastic waistband and joined at its tapered bottom by two support straps that served to embrace the buttocks.

Because a jockstrap was not the sort of thing you wanted to try on and look at in the tall reflecting glass next to the dressing closets, I put mine on at home in the dark. I pulled down the shades and locked the door and worked it up over my blue jeans, then took off my blue jeans and worked it up over my all-cotton briefs. It was a manly damn thing, a jockstrap was. When I finally managed to work it up over my naked middle, I turned up the radio and danced a manly dance. I did some hot freestyle number. Then I put on a pair of gym trunks and hurried outside. I ran down the street and kicked up gravel in front of Linda Valentine's house. Everything felt good and tight and primal. Later in my room, I practiced taking it on and off in front of a full-length mirror.

My father bought the jockstrap knowing I would be expected to wear one during phys-ed class at the junior high school in Opelousas. It was his way to make the occasion of the purchase as unceremonious as possible, and for that I am eternally grateful. Other boys were less fortunate. I remember one poor creature named Mott who turned up on my eighth-grade softball team. Mott owned an amazing shock of crinkly red hair, but he lacked courage. He spoke English with a clipped Cajun accent and cried when he struck out. He was always striking out, misjudging pop flies, and carrying on in a shameful manner. I liked him for two simple reasons. He was famous for not having known what a jockstrap was and for being dumb enough to believe it was a nose protector.

"You slip it over your face when it's your turn at bat," somebody told Mott the first day of class. We walked him into the bathroom. "Try it on for size," somebody else said. "See how it fits."

It fit perfectly. He had a very small face.

A ninth grader who had been wearing jocks for years threw a toilet-paper roll at poor Mott. He said he was doing his little friend a favor. He said he was breaking in Mott's new nose protector.

21

Mott cried and cried and ran to the PE instructor. "Make them stop," Mott begged. The PE instructor took out his paddle and spanked the accused. When it was over, the ninth grader went off by himself and thought things out. He came back and said, "Mott couldn't carry my damn jockstrap." There were tears in his eyes and a heavy welling of blood in his pimpled cheeks. "You're a no-count sissy, Mott," he said. "You ain't nothing but a sissy."

That was back before they came out with jocks that look like women's nylon panties and ruined everything. Mott transferred to another school and started his life all over again. That was a long time ago.

BASEBALL

RED SMITH

One of a Kind: Babe Ruth

A recollection of some small moments in the life of Babe Ruth that illuminates the authentic character of this deservedly respected athlete. His record of sixty home runs in a season some fans would argue still stands since Roger Maris broke it by hitting more homers in a longer season. Many know about Ruth's special aptitude for batting, but few remember his other formidable talent, as a pitcher, compiling a record that lasted for forty-three years—for the most consecutive scoreless innings in a World Series. Because his batting was more valuable to the team—even though as a pitcher he had had two twenty-game-winning seasons—he was permanently converted into an outfielder.

His strengths in both hitting and pitching lead Red Smith to conclude that Ruth truly deserves his legend. And on top of that, his original and charismatic personality made him invaluable to sportswriters.

Grantland Rice, the prince of sportswriters, used to do a weekly radio interview with some sporting figure. Frequently, in the interest of spontaneity, he would type out questions and answers in advance. One night his guest was Babe Ruth.

"Well, you know, Granny," the Babe read in response to a question, "Duke Ellington said the

Battle of Waterloo was won on the playing fields of Elkton."

"Babe," Granny said after the show, "Duke Ellington for the Duke of Wellington I can understand. But how did you ever read Eton as Elkton? That's in Maryland, isn't it?"

"I married my first wife there," Babe said, "and I always hated the gawdam place." He was cheerily unruffled. In the uncomplicated world of George Herman Ruth, errors were part of the game.

Babe Ruth died 25 years ago but his ample ghost has been with us all summer and he seems to grow more insistently alive every time Henry Aaron hits a baseball over a fence. What, people under 50 keep asking, what was this creature of myth and legend like in real life? If he were around today, how would he react when Aaron at last broke his hallowed record of 714 home runs? The first question may be impossible to answer fully; the second is easy.

"Well, what d'you know!" he would have said when the record got away. "Baby loses another! Come on, have another beer."

To paraphrase Abraham Lincoln's remark about another deity, Ruth must have admired records because he created so many of them. Yet he was sublimely aware that he transcended records and his place in the American scene was no mere matter of statistics. It wasn't just that he hit more home runs than anybody else, he hit them better, higher, farther, with more theatrical timing and a more flamboyant flourish. Nobody could strike out like Babe Ruth. Nobody circled the bases with the same pigeon-toed, mincing majesty.

"He was one of a kind," says Waite Hoyt, a Yankee pitcher in the years of Ruthian splendor. "If he had never played ball, if you had never heard of him and passed him on Broadway, you'd turn around and look."

Looking, you would have seen a barrel swaddled in a wrap-around camel-hair topcoat with a flat camel-hair cap on the round head. Thus arrayed he was instantly recognizable not only on Broadway in New York but also on the Ginza in Tokyo. "Baby Roos! Baby Roos!" cried excited crowds, following through the streets when he visited Japan with an all-star team in the early nineteen-thirties.

The camel-hair coat and cap are part of my last memory of the man. It must have been in the spring training season of 1948 when the Babe and everybody else knew he was dying of throat cancer. "This is the last time around," he had told Frank Stevens that winter when the head of the H. M. Stevens catering firm visited him in French Hospital on West 30th Street, "but before I go I'm gonna get out of here and have some fun."

He did get out, but touring the Florida training camps surrounded by a gaggle of admen, hustlers and promoters, he didn't look like a man having fun. It was a hot day when he arrived in St. Petersburg but the camel-hair collar was turned up about the wounded throat. By this time, Al Lang Stadium had replaced old Waterfront Park where he had drawn crowds when the Yankees trained in St. Pete.

"What do you remember best about this place?" asked Francis Stann of *The Washington Star*.

Babe gestured toward the West Coast Inn,

27

an old frame building a city block beyond the right-field fence. "The day I hit the [adjectival] ball against that [adjectival] hotel." The voice was a hoarse stage whisper; the adjective was one often printed these days, but not here.

"Wow!" Francis Stann said. "Pretty good belt."

"But don't forget," Babe said, "the [adjectival] park was a block back this way then."

Ruth was not noted for a good memory. In fact, the inability to remember names is part of his legend. Yet he needed no record books to remind him of his own special feats. There was, for example, the time he visited Philadelphia as a "coach" with the Brooklyn Dodgers. (His coachly duties consisted of hitting home runs in batting practice.) This was in the late nineteen-thirties when National League games in Philadelphia were played in Shibe Park, the American League grounds where Babe had performed. I asked him what memories stirred on his return.

"The time I hit one into Opal Street," he said.

Now, a baseball hit over Shibe Park's right-field fence landed in 20th Street. Opal is the next street east, just a wide alley one block long. There may not be 500 Philadelphians who know it by name, but Babe Ruth knew it.

Another time, during a chat in Hollywood, where he was an actor in the film *Pride of the Yankees,* one of us mentioned Rube Walberg, a good left-handed pitcher with the Philadelphia Athletics through the Ruth era. To some left-handed batters there is no dirtier word than the name of a good left-handed pitcher, but the Babe spoke fondly:

"Rube Walberg! What a pigeon! I hit 23 home runs off him." Or whatever the figure was. It isn't in the record book but it was in Ruth's memory.

Obviously it is not true that he couldn't even remember the names of his teammates. It was only that the names he remembered were not always those bestowed at the baptismal font. To him Urban Shocker, a Yankee pitcher, was Rubber Belly. Pat Collins, the catcher, was Horse Nose. All redcaps at railroad stations were Stinkweed, and everybody else was Kid. One day Jim Cahn, covering the Yankees for *The New York Sun*, watched two players board a train with a porter toting the luggage.

"There go Rubber Belly, Horse Nose and Stinkweed," Jim said.

Don Heffner joined the Yankees in 1934, Ruth's last year with the team. Playing second base through spring training, Heffner was stationed directly in the line of vision of Ruth, the right fielder. Breaking camp, the Yankees stopped in Jacksonville on a night when the Baltimore Orioles of the International League were also in town. A young reporter on *The Baltimore Sun* seized the opportunity to interview Ruth.

"How is Heffner looking?" he asked, because the second baseman had been a star with the Orioles in 1933.

"Who the hell is Heffner?" the Babe demanded. The reporter should, of course, have asked about the kid at second.

Jacksonville was the first stop that year on the barnstorming trip that would last two or three weeks and take the team to Yankee Stadium by a meandering route through the American bush. There, as everywhere, Ruth moved among crowds. Whether the Yankees played in Memphis or New Orleans or Selma, Alabama, the park was almost always filled, the hotel overrun if the team used a hotel, the railroad depot thronged. In a town of 5,000, perhaps 7,500 would see the game. Mostly the players lived in Pullmans and somehow word always went ahead when the Yankees' train was coming through. At every stop at any hour of the night there would be a cluster of men on the platform, maybe the stationmaster and telegrapher, a section gang and the baggage agent watching the dark sleeping cars for the glimpse of a Yankee, possibly even the Babe.

It was said in those days, probably truly, that receipts from the pre-season exhibitions more than paid Ruth's salary for the year, even when he was getting $80,000, which was substantially more than any other player earned, or any manager or baseball executive. It was more than President Herbert Hoover received, but if this was ever pointed out to Ruth he almost surely did not reply, as the story goes: "I had a better year than he did." He would have been correct, but the Babe was not that well informed on national affairs.

Crowds were to Ruth as water to a fish. Probably the only time on record when he sought to avert a mob scene was the day of his second marriage. The ceremony was scheduled for 6 A.M. on the theory that people wouldn't be abroad then, but when he arrived at St. Gregory's in West 90th Street, the church was filled and hundreds were waiting outside.

A reception followed in Babe's apartment on

Riverside Drive, where the 18th Amendment did not apply. It was opening day of the baseball season but the weather intervened on behalf of the happy couple. The party went on and on, with entertainment by Peter de Rose, composer-pianist, and May Singhi Breen, who played the ukulele and sang.

Rain abated in time for a game next day. For the first time, Claire Ruth watched from a box near the Yankees' dugout, as she still does on ceremonial occasions. Naturally, the bridegroom hit a home run. Rounding the bases, he halted at second and swept off his cap in a courtly bow to his bride. This was typical of him. There are a hundred stories illustrating his sense of theater—how he opened Yankee Stadium (The House That Ruth Built) with a home run against the Red Sox, how at the age of 40 he closed out his career as a player by hitting three mighty shots out of spacious Forbes Field in Pittsburgh, stories about the times he promised to hit a home run for some kid in a hospital and made good, and of course the one about calling his shot in a World Series.

That either did or did not happen in Chicago's Wrigley Field on Oct. 1, 1932. I was there but I have never been dead sure of what I saw.

The Yankees had won the first two games and the score of the third was 4–4 when Ruth went to bat in the fifth inning with the bases empty and Charley Root pitching for the Cubs. Ruth had staked the Yankees to a three-run lead in the first inning by hitting Root for a home run with two on base. Now Root threw a strike. Ruth stepped back and lifted a finger. "One." A second strike, a second upraised finger. "Two." Then Ruth made

31

some sort of sign with his bat. Some said, and their version has become gospel, that he aimed it like a rifle at the bleachers in right center field. That's where he hit the next pitch. That made the score 5–4. Lou Gehrig followed with a home run and the Yankees won, 7–5, ending the series the next day.

All the Yankees, and Ruth in particular, had been riding the Cubs unmercifully through every game, deriding them as cheapskates because in cutting up their World Series money the Chicago players had voted only one-fourth of a share to Mark Koenig, the former New York shortstop who had joined them in August and batted .353 in the last month of the pennant race. With all the dialogue and pantomime that went on, there was no telling what Ruth was saying to Root. When the papers reported that he had called his shot, he did not deny it.

He almost never quibbled about anything that was written. During the 1934 World Series between the Cardinals and Detroit Tigers, *The St. Louis Post-Dispatch* assigned its Washington correspondent, Paul Y. Anderson, to write features. His seat in the auxiliary press box was next to Ruth, a member of the sweaty literati whose observations on the games would be converted into suitably wooden prose by a syndicate ghost-writer. Babe was companionable as usual.

"You see the series here in '28?" he asked.

"No," Anderson said, "was it a good one?"

"That was when I hit three outta here in the last game."

"Gee," Anderson said, "a good day for you, eh?"

"Yeah," Babe said, "I had a good day. But don't forget, the fans had a hell of a day, too."

Paul Anderson was at ease with men as dissimilar as Huey Long, John L. Lewis and Franklin D. Roosevelt but he had never encountered anyone quite like this child of nature. He devoted his story to the bumptious bundle of vanity seated beside him. To his discomfort, a press-box neighbor asked Ruth the next day whether he had read the story. Ruth said sure, though he probably hadn't. "What did you think of it?" the other persisted while Anderson squirmed.

"Hell," Babe said, "the newspaper guys always been great to me."

A person familiar with Ruth only through photographs and records could hardly be blamed for assuming that he was a blubbery freak whose ability to hit balls across county lines was all that kept him in the big leagues. The truth is that he was the complete ballplayer, certainly one of the greatest and maybe the one best of all time.

As a left-handed pitcher with the Boston Red Sox, he won 18 games in his rookie season, 23 the next year and 24 the next before Ed Barrow assigned him to the outfield to keep him in the batting order every day. His record of pitching 29 2/3 consecutive scoreless innings in World Series stood 43 years before Whitey Ford broke it.

He was an accomplished outfielder with astonishing range for his bulk, a powerful arm and keen baseball sense. It was said that he never made a mental error like throwing to the wrong base.

He recognized his role as public entertainer and understood it. In the 1946 World Series the Cardinals made a radical shift in their defense against Ted Williams, packing the right side of the field and leaving the left virtually unprotected. "They did that to me in the American League one year," Ruth told the columnist, Frank Graham. "I coulda hit .600 that year slicing singles to left."

"Why didn't you?" Frank asked.

"That wasn't what the fans came out to see."

Thirteen years after Ruth's death, when another rightfielder for the Yankees, Roger Maris, was threatening the season record of 60 home runs that Babe had set 34 years earlier, I made a small sentimental pilgrimage in Baltimore where the Yankees happened to be playing. The first stop was the row house where the Babe was born. A gracious woman showed visitors through the small rooms. Next came a drink in the neighborhood saloon Babe's father ran when Babe was a boy. Nobody ever came in who remembered the Ruth family, the bartender said. The tour ended at St. Mary's Industrial School, which the wrecker's big iron ball was knocking down.

St. Mary's was Babe's home through most of his boyhood because his parents weren't interested in rearing him. He left the home on Feb. 27, 1914, three weeks after his 19th birthday, to pitch for the Baltimore Orioles of the International League. Jack Dunn, the owner, paid him $600 and sold him late that summer to the Red Sox for $2,900. He was 6-foot-2 and an athlete, thick-chested but not fat. "A big, lummockin' sort of fella," said a waiter in Toots Shor's who had worked in a restaurant near the Red Sox park where young Ruth got sweet on one of the waitresses.

When his hard-pressed employers sold him to the Yankees, he was still a trim young ballplayer who had hit 29 of the Boston club's 32 home runs that season of 1919. He hit an unthinkable 54 in his first New York summer, 59 in his second, and became a god. His waistline grew with his fame, until the legs that nobody had considered spindly began to look like matchsticks and his feet seemed grotesquely small.

He changed the rules, the equipment and the strategy of baseball. Reasoning that if one Babe Ruth could fill a park, 16 would fill all the parks, the owners instructed the manufacturers to produce a livelier ball that would make every man a home-run king. As a further aid to batters, trick pitching deliveries like the spitball, the emery ball, the shine ball and the mud ball were forbidden.

The home run, an occasional phenomenon when a team hit a total of 20 in a season, came to be regarded as the ultimate offensive weapon. Shortstops inclined to swoon at the sight of blood had their bats made with all the wood up in the big end, gripped the slender handle at the very hilt and swung from the heels.

None of these devices produced another Ruth, of course, because Ruth was one of a kind. He recognized this as the simple truth and conducted himself accordingly. Even before they were married and Claire began to accompany him on the road, he always occupied the drawing room on the team's Pullman; he seldom shared his revels after dark with other players, although one year he did take a fancy to a worshipful rookie named Jimmy Reese and made him a companion until management intervened; if friends were not on hand with transportation, he usually took a taxi by himself to hotel or ball park or railroad station. Unlike other players, Ruth was never seen in the hotel dining room or sitting in the lobby waiting for some passerby to discard a newspaper.

St. Louis was one town where he was always met. When the team left St. Louis, his friends would deliver him to the station along with a laundry basket full of barbecued ribs and tubs of home brew. Then anybody—player, coach or press—was welcome in the drawing room to munch ribs, swill the yeasty beer and laugh at the Babe's favorite record on the Babe's portable phonograph. He would play Moran & Mack's talking record, "Two Black Crows," a hundred times and howl at the hundredth repetition: "How come the black horses ate more'n the white horses?" "Search me, 'cept we had more black horses than white horses."

Roistering was a way of life, yet Ruth was no boozer. Three drinks of hard liquor left him fuzzy. He could consume great quantities of beer, was a prodigious eater and his prowess with women was legendary. Sleep was something he got when other appetites were sated. He arose when he chose and almost invariably was the last to arrive in the clubhouse, where Doc Woods, the Yankees' trainer, always had bicarbonate of soda ready. Before changing clothes, the Babe would measure out a mound of bicarb smaller than the Pyramid of Cheops, mix and gulp it down.

"Then," Jim Cahn says, "he would belch. And all the loose water in the showers would fall down."

The man was a boy, simple, artless, genuine and unabashed. This explains his rapport with children, whom he met as intellectual equals. Probably his natural liking for people communicated itself to the public to help make him an idol.

He was buried on a sweltering day in August, 1948. In the pallbearers' pew, Waite Hoyt sat beside Joe Dugan, the third baseman. "I'd give a hundred dollars for a cold beer," Dugan whispered. "So would the Babe," Hoyt said.

In packed St. Patrick's Cathedral, Francis Cardinal Spellman celebrated requiem mass and out in Fifth Avenue thousands and thousands waited to say good-by to the waif from Baltimore whose parents didn't want him.

"Some twenty years ago," says Tommy Holmes, the great baseball writer, "I stopped talking about the Babe for the simple reason that I realized that those who had never seen him didn't believe me."

RUSSELL BAKER

Idylls of the Kid

Russell Baker remembers, when he was a kid on roller skates, the power of radio to conjure up images in his head of Joe DiMaggio—"to create pictures inside my head more spectacular than television can possibly convey." Reflecting on his own passing years since the days of radio, Baker compares the aging DiMaggio seen on colored TV commercials with the ageless black-and-white DiMaggio of movie newsreels. He takes solace in the fact that, whenever he has the yearning, he can still see DiMaggio in his prime covering the outfield with endless grace.

Joe DiMaggio is seventy. His birthday was last Sunday. The papers made nothing of it and I would not have been aware of it if we hadn't seen him Tuesday night doing his Mister Coffee commercial on television. "Joe DiMaggio is old," Harry said.

"Joe DiMaggio can never be old," I said. This is true in a very important unfactual sense. Joe DiMaggio inhabits a world in which I am always eleven years old. In it I always wear corduroy knickers and brown knee-length stockings held up by rubber bands and move around on roller skates.

There is a Philco radio in the parlor. Inside is the voice of Franklin D. Roosevelt.

"That hair is gray," Harry said.

"Joe looks terrific, Harry."

He did, too. The commercial he was doing, of course, was in color. That was all wrong. Joe DiMaggio looks truly natural only in black and white. This is because when I see him he is always nineteen or twenty or some age like that, much older than I on my roller skates but not really old as Carl Hubbell, say, is old.

Hubbell pitches for the New York Giants. So we are talking, obviously, about the age of black and white, and neither Hubbell, who seems old but oh so magically unbeatable with his fabulous screwball, nor DiMaggio, who seems young and gawky, can exist in the age of color.

I see them always where they belong, motionless yet mysteriously and beautifully fluid in grainy black-and-white newspaper pictures on the sports pages of the *Journal American* and the *Daily Mirror*, the papers built for kids, with plenty of comics, full coverage of the electrocutions at Sing Sing, and great action still photos of great achievers, the old great Hubbell, the young great DiMaggio.

"Harry," I said, "Joe DiMaggio cannot be seen authentically on color television. Or on television at all, for that matter. No wonder you think he's old. Did you ever see DiMaggio play on television?"

I certainly never did. A few times I may have seen him swing the bat in one of the grainy black-and-white newsreels accompanying the double-feature bill at the Capitol or Horn movie theaters. This is probably why I often associate Joe DiMaggio with skating up to the Horn to see a Charlie Chan and a Laurel and Hardy.

"Snap out of it," Harry said. "Nobody has seen a Charlie Chan and a Laurel and Hardy on a double bill since Mussolini was in his prime."

"And those were the real Charlie Chans starring Warner Oland," I said, "not the decadent later Charlie Chans with Sidney Toler."

"The truth is," said Harry, "that you, just like me, never saw DiMaggio play anywhere except in a newsreel, so don't give me that malarkey about Joe's gracefulness being too pure to be appreciated by today's ignorant TV audiences."

Harry is a good man, but there is no poetry in him. He is a believer in facts. It has never occurred to him that there might be a wide chasm between fact and truth. The truth of this particular matter is that I can see DiMaggio play whenever the mood is on me.

This is something I owe to radio. By turning on the Philco, besides getting the voice of Franklin D. Roosevelt, I can often get sounds from the Yankee Stadium, sounds with power to create pictures inside my head more spectacular than television can possibly convey.

When I am eleven years old, in corduroy knickers, skimming down Washington Avenue on roller skates, these radio sounds show me Joe DiMaggio loping across a beautiful field of grass in the faraway, exotic Bronx, to haul in the white ball whirling out of the sky. Then I can see Joe stepping into the batter's box, wearing those loose billowing knickers real ballplayers all wore until television spurred them to vanity and vanity drove them to

40

skin-tight double knits, like so many cruising sex objects.

"Harry," I said, "I hope Joe retires before television corrupts the baseball uniform. I'd hate to see him prancing around the diamond like some common, run-of-the-mill uniformed sex object."

The conversation had become pointless, since Harry had gone home in some disgust, leaving me, as he had said at the door, free to "skate up to the Horn and catch the new Mister Moto movie starring Peter Lorre on a double bill with Randolph Scott driving the cattle to Abilene."

Aside from having no poetry in him, Harry also has a weakness for ham-handed sarcasm, but I let it pass and, since my lumbago had me almost prostrate, went early to bed. Next morning Harry, the eternal fact man, phoned early.

"I looked it up. DiMaggio turned seventy on November 25," he said. In corduroy knickers, on roller skates, I said, "Harry, do you think we'll ever make enough money to go to Yankee Stadium sometime and see a game?"

JOHN UPDIKE
Hub Fans Bid Kid Adieu

In this deservedly popular piece, an outstanding writer analyzes an outstanding athlete's extraordinary powers. Both masters in their chosen fields, they need each other: Updike's efforts to get at both Williams's style as a power hitter and his lack of popularity with the fans inspire his most evocative prose. On the other hand, Williams requires Updike's skills to clarify for the reader the baffling, unaccommodating personality he presented to the public during his prime playing years.

As he watches Williams "switching the stick at the pitcher with an electric velocity," Updike has a clarifying revelation as he takes in the last home game of Williams's career: "This man, you realized—and here, perhaps, was the difference, greater than the difference in gifts—really desired to hit the ball."

Fenway Park, in Boston, is a lyric little bandbox of a ballpark. Everything is painted green and seems in curiously sharp focus, like the inside of an old-fashioned peeping-type Easter egg. It was built in 1912 and rebuilt in 1934, and offers, as do most Boston artifacts, a compromise between Man's Euclidean determinations and Nature's beguiling irregularities. Its right field is one of the deepest in

42

the American League, while its left field is the shortest; the high left-field wall, three hundred and fifteen feet from home plate along the foul line, virtually thrusts its surface at right-handed hitters. On the afternoon of Wednesday, September 28th, 1960, as I took a seat behind third base, a uniformed groundkeeper was treading the top of this wall, picking batting-practice home runs out of the screen, like a mushroom gatherer seen in Wordsworthian perspective on the verge of a cliff. The day was overcast, chill, and uninspirational. The Boston team was the worst in twenty-seven seasons. A jangling medley of incompetent youth and aging competence, the Red Sox were finishing in seventh place only because the Kansas City Athletics had locked them out of the cellar. They were scheduled to play the Baltimore Orioles, a much nimbler blend of May and December, who had been dumped from pennant contention a week before by the insatiable Yankees. I, and 10,453 others, had shown up primarily because this was the Red Sox's last home game of the season, and therefore the last time in all eternity that their regular left fielder, known to the headlines as TED, KID, SPLINTER, THUMPER, TW, and, most cloyingly, MISTER WONDERFUL, would play in Boston. "WHAT WILL WE DO WITHOUT TED? HUB FANS ASK" ran the headline on a newspaper being read by a bulb-nosed cigar smoker a few rows away. Williams' retirement had been announced, doubted (he had been threatening retirement for years), confirmed by Tom Yawkey, the Red Sox owner, and at last widely accepted as the sad but probable truth. He was forty-two and had redeemed his abysmal season of 1959 with a

—considering his advanced age—fine one. He had been giving away his gloves and bats and had grudgingly consented to a sentimental ceremony today. This was not necessarily his last game; the Red Sox were scheduled to travel to New York and wind up the season with three games there.

I arrived early. The Orioles were hitting fungos on the field. The day before, they had spitefully smothered the Red Sox, 17–4, and neither their faces nor their drab gray visiting-team uniforms seemed very gracious. I wondered who had invited them to the party. Between our heads and the lowering clouds a frenzied organ was thundering through, with an appositeness perhaps accidental, "You *maaaade* me love you, I didn't wanna do it, I didn't wanna do it. . . ."

The affair between Boston and Ted Williams was no mere summer romance; it was a marriage composed of spats, mutual disappointments, and, toward the end, a mellowing hoard of shared memories. It fell into three stages, which may be termed Youth, Maturity, and Age; or Thesis, Antithesis, and Synthesis; or Jason, Achilles, and Nestor.

First, there was the by now legendary epoch[1] when the young bridegroom came out of the West and announced "All I want out of life is that when I walk down the street folks will say 'There goes the greatest hitter who ever lived.' " The dowagers of local journalism attempted to give elementary deportment lessons to this child who spake as a god, and to their horror were themselves rebuked. Thus began the long exchange of backbiting, bat-flipping, booing, and spitting that has distinguished

44

Williams' public relations.[2] The spitting incidents of 1957 and 1958 and the similar dockside courtesies that Williams has now and then extended to the grandstand should be judged against this background: the left-field stands at Fenway for twenty years have held a large number of customers who have bought their way in primarily for the privilege of showering abuse on Williams. Greatness necessarily attracts debunkers, but in Williams' case the hostility has been systematic and unappeasable. His basic offense against the fans has been to wish that they weren't there. Seeking a perfectionist's vacuum, he has quixotically desired to sever the game from the ground of paid spectatorship and publicity that supports it. Hence his refusal to tip his cap[3] to the crowd or turn the other cheek to newsmen. It has been a costly theory—it has probably cost him, among other evidences of good will, two Most Valuable Player awards, which are voted by reporters[4]—but he has held to it. While his critics, oral and literary, remained beyond the reach of his discipline, the opposing pitchers were accessible, and he spanked them to the tune of .406 in 1941.[5] He slumped to .356 in 1942 and went off to war.

In 1946, Williams returned from three years as a Marine pilot to the second of his baseball avatars, that of Achilles, the hero of incomparable prowess and beauty who nevertheless was to be found sulking in his tent while the Trojans (mostly Yankees) fought through to the ships. Yawkey, a timber and mining maharajah, had surrounded his central jewel with many gems of slightly lesser water, such as Bobby Doerr, Dom DiMaggio, Rudy York, Birdie Tebbetts, and Johnny Pesky. Throughout the

45

late forties, the Red Sox were the best paper team in baseball, yet they had little three-dimensional to show for it, and if this was a tragedy, Williams was Hamlet. A succinct review of the indictment—and a fair sample of appreciative sports-page prose—appeared the very day of Williams' valedictory, in a column by Huck Finnegan in the Boston *American* (no sentimentalist, Huck):

Williams' career, in contrast [to Babe Ruth's], has been a series of failures except for his averages. He flopped in the only World Series he ever played in (1946) when he batted only .200. He flopped in the playoff game with Cleveland in 1948. He flopped in the final game of the 1949 season with the pennant hinging on the outcome (Yanks, 5, Sox, 3). He flopped in 1950 when he returned to the lineup after a two-month absence and ruined the morale of a club that seemed pennant-bound under Steve O'Neill. It has always been Williams' records first, the team second, and the Sox non-winning record is proof enough of that.

There are answers to all this, of course. The fatal weakness of the great Sox slugging teams was not-quite-good-enough pitching rather than Williams' failure to hit a home run every time he came to bat. Again, Williams' depressing effect on his teammates has never been proved. Despite ample coaching to the contrary, most insisted that they *liked* him. He has been generous with advice to any player who asked for it. In an increasingly combative baseball atmosphere, he continued to duck beanballs docilely. With umpires he was gracious to a fault. This courtesy itself annoyed his critics, whom there was no pleasing. And against the ten crucial games (the seven World Series games with the St. Louis Cardinals, the 1948 play-off with the Cleveland Indians, and the two-game series with the Yankees at the end of the 1949 season, when one victory would have given the Red Sox the pennant) that make up the Achilles' heel of Williams' record, a mass of statistics can be set showing that day in and day out he was no slouch in the clutch.[6] The correspondence columns of the Boston papers now and then suffer a sharp flurry of arithmetic on this score; indeed, for Williams to have distributed all his hits so they did nobody else any good would constitute a feat of placement unparalleled in the annals of selfishness.

Whatever residue of truth remains of the Finnegan charge those of us who love Williams must transmute as best we can, in our own personal crucibles. My personal memories of Williams began when I was a boy in Pennsylvania, with two last-place teams in Philadelphia to keep me company. For me, "W'ms, lf" was a figment of the box scores who always seemed to be going 3-for-5. He radiated, from afar, the hard blue glow of high purpose. I remember listening over the radio to the All-Star Game of 1946, in which Williams hit two singles and two home runs, the second one off a Rip Sewell "blooper" pitch; it was like hitting a balloon out of the park. I remember watching one of his home runs from the bleachers of Shibe

Park; it went over the first baseman's head and rose methodically along a straight line and was still rising when it cleared the fence. The trajectory seemed qualitatively different from anything anyone else might hit. For me, Williams is the classic ballplayer of the game on a hot August weekday, before a small crowd, when the only thing at stake is the tissue-thin difference between a thing done well and a thing done ill. Baseball is a game of the long season, of relentless and gradual averaging-out. Irrelevance—since the reference point of most individual contests is remote and statistical—always threatens its interest, which can be maintained not by the occasional heroics that sportswriters feed upon but by players who always *care;* who care, that is to say, about themselves and their art. Insofar as the clutch hitter is not a sportswriter's myth, he is a vulgarity, like a writer who writes only for money. It may be that, compared to such managers' dreams as the manifestly classy Joe DiMaggio and the always helpful Stan Musial, Williams was an icy star. But of all team sports, baseball, with its graceful intermittences of action, its immense and tranquil field sparsely settled with poised men in white, its dispassionate mathematics, seems to me best suited to accommodate, and be ornamented by, a loner. It is an essentially lonely game. No other player visible to my generation concentrated within himself so much of the sport's poignance, so assiduously refined his natural skills, so constantly brought to the plate that intensity of competence that crowds the throat with joy.

By the time I went to college, near Boston, the lesser stars Yawkey had assembled around Williams had faded, and his rigorous pride of craftsmanship had become itself a kind of heroism. This brittle and temperamental player developed an unexpected quality of persistence. He was always coming back— back from Korea, back from a broken collarbone, a shattered elbow, a bruised heel, back from drastic bouts of flu and ptomaine poisoning. Hardly a season went by without some enfeebling mishap, yet he always came back, and always looked like himself. The delicate mechanism of timing and power seemed sealed, shockproof, in some case deep within his frame.[7] In addition to injuries, there was a heavily publicized divorce, and the usual storms with the press, and the Williams Shift— the maneuver, custom-built by Lou Boudreau of the Cleveland Indians, whereby three infielders were concentrated on the right side of the infield.[8] Williams could easily have learned to punch singles through the vacancy on his left and fattened his average hugely. This was what Ty Cobb, the Einstein of average, told him to do. But the game had changed since Cobb; Williams believed that his value to the club and to the league was as a slugger, so he went on pulling the ball, trying to blast it through three men, and paid the price of perhaps fifteen points of lifetime average. Like Ruth before him, he bought the occasional home run at the cost of many directed singles—a calculated sacrifice certainly not, in the case of a hitter as average-minded as Williams, entirely selfish.

After a prime so harassed and hobbled, Williams was granted by the relenting fates a golden twilight. He became at the end of his career perhaps the best *old* hitter of the century. The dividing line falls between the 1956 and the 1957 seasons. In September of the first year, he and Mickey Mantle were contending for the batting championship. Both were hitting around .350, and there was no one else near them. The season ended with a three-game series between the Yankees and the Sox, and, living in New York then, I went up to the Stadium. Williams was slightly shy of the four hundred at-bats needed to qualify; the fear was expressed that the Yankee pitchers would walk him to protect Mantle. Instead, they pitched to him. It was wise. He looked terrible at the plate, tired and discouraged and unconvincing. He never looked very good to me in the Stadium.[9] The final outcome in 1956 was Mantle .353, Williams .345.

The next year, I moved from New York to New England, and it made all the difference. For in September of 1957, in the same situation, the story was reversed. Mantle finally hit .365; it was the best season of his career. But Williams, though sick and old, had run away from him. A bout of flu had laid him low in September. He emerged from his cave in the Hotel Somerset haggard but irresistible; he hit four successive pinch-hit home runs. "I feel terrible," he confessed, "but every time I take a swing at the ball it goes out of the park." He ended the season with thirty-eight home runs and an average of .388, the highest in either league since his own .406, and, coming from a decrepit man of thirty-nine, an even more supernal figure. With eight or so of the "leg hits" that a younger man would have beaten out, it would have been .400. And the next year, Williams, who in 1949 and 1953 had lost batting championships by decimal whiskers to George Kell and Mickey Vernon, sneaked in behind his teammate Pete Runnels and filched his sixth title, a bargain at .328.

In 1959, it seemed all over. The dinosaur thrashed around in the .200 swamp for the first half of the season, and was even benched ("rested," Manager Mike Higgins tactfully said). Old foes like the late Bill Cunningham began to offer batting tips. Cunningham thought Williams was jiggling his elbows;[10] in truth, Williams' neck was so stiff he could hardly turn his head to look at the pitcher. When he swung, it looked like a Calder mobile with one thread cut; it reminded you that since 1954 Williams' shoulders had been wired together. A solicitous pall settled over the sports pages. In the two decades since Williams had come to Boston, his status had imperceptibly shifted from that of a naughty prodigy to that of a municipal monument. As his shadow in the record books lengthened, the Red Sox teams around him declined, and the entire American League seemed to be losing life and color to the National. The inconsistency of the new super-stars—Mantle, Colavito, and Kaline—served to make Williams appear all the more singular. And off the field, his private philanthropy—in particular, his zealous chairmanship of the Jimmy Fund, a charity for children with cancer—gave him a civic presence matched only by that of Richard Cardinal Cushing. In religion, Williams appears to be a humanist, and a selective one at that, but he and the abrasive-voiced Cardinal, when their good works intersect and they appear in the public eye together, make a handsome pair of seraphim.

51

Humiliated by his '59 season, Williams determined, once more, to come back. I, as a specimen Williams partisan, was both glad and fearful. All baseball fans believe in miracles; the question is, how *many* do you believe in? He looked like a ghost in spring training. Manager Jurges warned us ahead of time that if Williams didn't come through he would be benched, just like anybody else. As it turned out, it was Jurges who was benched. Williams entered the 1960 season needing eight home runs to have a lifetime total of 500; after one time at bat in Washington, he needed seven. For a stretch, he was hitting a home run every second game that he played. He passed Lou Gehrig's lifetime total, and finished with 521, thirteen behind Jimmy Foxx, who alone stands between Williams and Babe Ruth's unapproachable 714. The summer was a statistician's picnic. His two-thousandth walk came and went, his eighteen-hundredth run batted in, his sixteenth All-Star Game. At one point, he hit a home run off a pitcher, Don Lee, off whose father, Thornton Lee, he had hit a home run a generation before. The only comparable season for a forty-two-year-old man was Ty Cobb's in 1928. Cobb batted .323 and hit one homer. Williams batted .316 but hit twenty-nine homers.

In sum, though generally conceded to be the greatest hitter of his era, he did not establish himself as "the greatest hitter who ever lived." Cobb, for average, and Ruth, for power, remain supreme. Cobb, Rogers Hornsby, Joe Jackson, and Lefty O'Doul, among players since 1900, have higher lifetime averages than Williams' .344. Unlike Foxx, Gehrig, Hack Wilson, Hank Greenberg, and

Ralph Kiner, Williams never came close to matching Babe Ruth's season home-run total of sixty.[11] In the list of major-league batting records, not one is held by Williams. He is second in walks drawn, third in home runs, fifth in lifetime average, sixth in runs batted in, eighth in runs scored and in total bases, fourteenth in doubles, and thirtieth in hits.[12] But if we allow him merely average seasons for the four-plus seasons he lost to two wars, and add another season for the months he lost to injuries, we get a man who in all the power totals would be second, and not a very distant second, to Ruth. And if we further allow that these years would have been not merely average but prime years, if we allow for all the months when Williams was playing in sub-par condition, if we permit his early and later years in baseball to be some sort of index of what the middle years could have been, if we give him a right-field fence that is not, like Fenway's, one of the most distant in the league, and if—the least excusable "if"—we imagine him condescending to outsmart the Williams Shift, we can defensibly assemble, like a colossus induced from the sizable fragments that do remain, a statistical figure not incommensurate with his grandiose ambition. From the statistics that are on the books, a good case can be made that in the *combination* of power and average Williams is first; nobody else ranks so high in both categories. Finally, there is the witness of the eyes; men whose memories go back to Shoeless Joe Jackson—another unlucky natural—rank him and Williams together as the best-looking hitters they have seen. It was for our last look that ten thousand of us had come.

Two girls, one of them with pert buckteeth and eyes as black as vest buttons, the other with white skin and flesh-colored hair, like an underdeveloped photograph of a redhead, came and sat on my right. On my other side was one of those frowning chestless young-old men who can frequently be seen, often wearing sailor hats, attending ball games alone. He did not once open his program but instead tapped it, rolled up, on his knee as he gave the game his disconsolate attention. A young lady, with freckles and a depressed, dainty nose that by an optical illusion seemed to thrust her lips forward for a kiss, sauntered down into the box seat right behind the roof of the Oriole dugout. She wore a blue coat with a Northeastern University emblem sewed to it. The girls beside me took it into their heads that this was Williams' daughter. She looked too old to me, and why would she be sitting behind the visitors' dugout? On the other hand, from the way she sat there, staring at the sky and French-inhaling, she clearly was *somebody*. Other fans came and eclipsed her from view. The crowd looked less like a weekday ballpark crowd than like the folks you might find in Yellowstone National Park, or emerging from automobiles at the top of scenic Mount Mansfield. There were a lot of competitively well-dressed couples of tourist age, and not a few babes in arms. A row of five seats in front of me was abruptly filled with a woman and four children, the youngest of them two years old, if that. Someday, presumably, he could tell his grandchildren that he saw Williams play. Along with these tots and second-honeymooners, there were Harvard freshmen, giving off that peculiar nervous glow created when a sufficient quantity of insouciance is saturated with enough insecurity; thick-necked Army officers with brass on their shoulders and steel in their stares; pepperings of priests; perfumed bouquets of Roxbury Fabian fans; shiny salesmen from Albany and Fall River; and those gray, hoarse men —taxi drivers, slaughterers, and bartenders—who will continue to click through the turnstiles long after everyone else has deserted to television and tramporamas. Behind me, two young male voices blossomed, cracking a joke about God's five proofs that Thomas Aquinas exists—typical Boston College levity.

The batting cage was trundled away. The Orioles fluttered to the sidelines. Diagonally across the field, by the Red Sox dugout, a cluster of men in overcoats were festering like maggots. I could see a splinter of white uniform, and Williams' head, held at a self-deprecating and evasive tilt. Williams' conversational stance is that of a six-foot-three-inch man under a six-foot ceiling. He moved away to the patter of flash bulbs, and began playing catch with a young Negro outfielder named Willie Tasby. His arm, never very powerful, had grown lax with the years, and his throwing motion was a kind of muscular drawl. To catch the ball, he flicked his glove hand onto his left shoulder (he batted left but threw right, as every schoolboy ought to know) and let the ball plop into it comically. This catch session with Tasby was the only time all afternoon I saw him grin.

A tight little flock of human sparrows who, from the lambent and pampered pink of their faces, could only have been Boston politicians moved toward the plate. The loudspeakers mammothly coughed as someone huffed on the microphone. The ceremonies began. Curt Gowdy, the Red Sox radio and television announcer, who sounds like everybody's brother-in-law, delivered a brief sermon, taking the two words "pride" and "champion" as his text. It began. "Twenty-one years ago, a skinny kid from San Diego, California . . ." and ended, "I don't think we'll ever see another like him." Robert Tibolt, chairman of the board of the Greater Boston Chamber of Commerce, presented Williams with a big Paul Revere silver bowl. Harry Carlson, a member of the sports committee of the Boston Chamber, gave him a plaque, whose inscription he did not read in its entirety, out of deference to Williams' distaste for this sort of fuss. Mayor Collins, seated in a wheelchair, presented the Jimmy Fund with a thousand-dollar check.

Then the occasion himself stooped to the microphone, and his voice sounded, after the others, very Californian; it seemed to be coming, excellently amplified, from a great distance, adolescently young and as smooth as a butternut. His thanks for the gifts had not died from our ears before he glided, as if helplessly, into "In spite of all the terrible things that have been said about me by the knights of the keyboard up there. . . ." He glanced up at the press rows suspended behind home plate. The crowd tittered, appalled. A frightful vision flashed upon me, of the press gallery pelting Williams with erasers, of Williams clambering up the foul screen to slug journalists, of a riot, of Mayor Collins being crushed. ". . . And they *were* terrible

56

things," Williams insisted, with level melancholy, into the mike. "I'd like to forget them, but I can't." He paused, swallowed his memories, and went on, "I want to say that my years in Boston have been the greatest thing in my life." The crowd, like an immense sail going limp in a change of wind, sighed with relief. Taking all the parts himself, Williams then acted out a vivacious little morality drama in which an imaginary tempter came to him at the beginning of his career and said, "Ted, you can play anywhere you like." Leaping nimbly into the role of his younger self (who in biographical actuality had yearned to be a Yankee), Williams gallantly chose Boston over all the other cities, and told us that Tom Yawkey was the greatest owner in baseball and we were the greatest fans. We applauded ourselves lustily. The umpire came out and dusted the plate. The voice of doom announced over the loudspeakers that after Williams' retirement his uniform number, 9, would be permanently retired—the first time the Red Sox had so honored a player. We cheered. The national anthem was played. We cheered. The game began.

Williams was third in the batting order, so he came up in the bottom of the first inning, and Steve Barber, a young pitcher born two months before Williams began playing in the major leagues, offered him four pitches, at all of which he disdained to swing, since none of them were within the strike zone. This demonstrated simultaneously that Williams' eyes were razor-sharp and that Barber's control wasn't. Shortly, the bases were full, with Williams on second. "Oh, I hope he gets held up at third! That would be wonderful," the girl beside me moaned, and, sure enough, the man at bat walked and Williams was delivered into our foreground. He struck the pose of Donatello's David, the third-base bag being Goliath's head. Fiddling with his cap, swapping small talk with the Oriole third baseman (who seemed delighted to have him drop in), swinging his arms with a sort of prancing nervousness, he looked fine—flexible, hard, and not unbecomingly substantial through the middle. The long neck, the small head, the knickers whose cuffs were worn down near his ankles—all these clichés of sports cartoon iconography were rendered in the flesh.

With each pitch, Williams danced down the baseline, waving his arms and stirring dust, ponderous but menacing, like an attacking goose. It occurred to about a dozen humorists at once to shout "Steal home! Go, go!" Williams' speed afoot was never legendary. Lou Clinton, a young Sox outfielder, hit a fairly deep fly to center field. Williams tagged up and ran home. As he slid across the plate, the ball, thrown with unusual heft by Jackie Brandt, the Oriole center fielder, hit him on the back.

"Boy, he was really loafing, wasn't he?" one of the collegiate voices behind me said.

"It's cold," the other voice explained. "He doesn't play well when it's cold. He likes heat. He's a hedonist."

The run that Williams scored was the second and last of the inning. Gus Triandos, of the Orioles, quickly evened the score by plunking a home run over the handy left-field wall. Williams, who had had this wall at his back for twenty years,[13] played the ball flawlessly. He didn't budge. He just stood still, in the center of the little patch of grass that his patient footsteps had worn brown, and, limp with lack of interest, watched the ball pass overhead. It was not a very interesting game. Mike Higgins, the Red Sox manager, with nothing to lose, had restricted his major-league players to the left-field line—along with Williams, Frank Malzone, a first-rate third baseman, played the game—and had peopled the rest of the terrain with unpredictable youngsters fresh, or not so fresh, off the farms. Other than Williams' recurrent appearances at the plate, the *maladresse* of the Sox infield was the sole focus of suspense; the second baseman turned every grounder into a juggling act, while the shortstop did a breathtaking impersonation of an open window. With this sort of assistance, the Orioles wheedled their way into a 4–2 lead. They had early replaced Barber with another young pitcher, Jack Fisher. Fortunately (as it turned out), Fisher is no cutie; he is willing to burn the ball through the strike zone, and inning after inning this tactic punctured Higgins' string of test balloons.

Whenever Williams appeared at the plate— pounding the dirt from his cleats, gouging a pit in the batter's box with his left foot, wringing resin out of the bat handle with his vehement grip, switching the stick at the pitcher with an electric ferocity—it was like having a familiar Leonardo appear in a shuffle of *Saturday Evening Post* covers. This man, you realized—and here, perhaps, was the difference, greater than the difference in gifts—really desired to hit the ball. In the third inning, he hoisted a high fly to deep center. In the

59

fifth, we thought he had it; he smacked the ball hard and high into the heart of his power zone, but the deep right field in Fenway and the heavy air and a casual east wind defeated him. The ball died. Al Pilarcik leaned his back against the big "380" painted on the right-field wall and caught it. On another day, in another park, it would have been gone. (After the game, Williams said, "I didn't think I could hit one any harder than that. The conditions weren't good.")

The afternoon grew so glowering that in the sixth inning the arc lights were turned on—always a wan sight in the daytime, like the burning headlights of a funeral procession. Aided by the gloom, Fisher was slicing through the Sox rookies, and Williams did not come to bat in the seventh. He was second up in the eighth. This was almost certainly his last time to come to the plate in Fenway Park, and instead of merely cheering, as we had at his three previous appearances, we stood, all of us, and applauded. I had never before heard pure applause in a ballpark. No calling, no whistling, just an ocean of handclaps, minute after minute, burst after burst, crowding and running together in continuous succession like the pushes of surf at the edge of the sand. It was a sombre and considered tumult. There was not a boo in it. It seemed to renew itself out of a shifting set of memories as the Kid, the Marine, the veteran of feuds and failures and injuries, the friend of children, and the enduring old pro evolved down the bright tunnel of twenty-two summers toward this moment. At last, the umpire signalled for Fisher to pitch; with the other players, he had been frozen in position. Only Williams had moved during the ovation, switching his bat impatiently, ignoring everything except his cherished task. Fisher wound up, and the applause sank into a hush.

Understand that we were a crowd of rational people. We knew that a home run cannot be produced at will; the right pitch must be perfectly met and luck must ride with the ball. Three innings before, we had seen a brave effort fail. The air was soggy, the season was exhausted. Nevertheless, there will always lurk, around the corner in a pocket of our knowledge of the odds, an indefensible hope, and this was one of the times, which you now and then find in sports, when a density of expectation hangs in the air and plucks an event out of the future.

Fisher, after his unsettling wait, was low with the first pitch. He put the second one over, and Williams swung mightily and missed. The crowd grunted, seeing that classic swing, so long and smooth and quick, exposed. Fisher threw the third time, Williams swung again, and there it was. The ball climbed on a diagonal line into the vast volume of air over center field. From my angle, behind third base, the ball seemed less an object in flight than the tip of a towering, motionless construct, like the Eiffel Tower or the Tappan Zee Bridge. It was in the books while it was still in the sky. Brandt ran back to the deepest corner of the outfield grass, the ball descended beyond his reach and struck in the crotch where the bullpen met the wall, bounced chunkily, and vanished.

Like a feather caught in a vortex, Williams ran around the square of bases at the center of our beseeching screaming. He ran as he always ran out home runs—hurriedly, unsmiling, head down, as if our praise were a storm of rain to get out of. He didn't tip his cap. Though we thumped, wept, and chanted "We want Ted" for minutes after he hid in the dugout, he did not come back. Our noise for some seconds passed beyond excitement into a kind of immense open anguish, a wailing, a cry to be saved. But immortality is nontransferable. The papers said that the other players, and even the umpires on the field, begged him to come out and acknowledge us in some way, but he refused. Gods do not answer letters.

Every true story has an anticlimax. The men on the field refused to disappear, as would have seemed decent, in the smoke of Williams' miracle. Fisher continued to pitch, and escaped further harm. At the end of the inning, Higgins sent Williams out to his left-field position, then instantly replaced him with Carrol Hardy, so we had a long last look at Williams as he ran out there and then back, his uniform jogging, his eyes steadfast on the ground. It was nice, and we were grateful, but it left a funny taste.

One of the scholasticists behind me said, "Let's go. We've seen everything. I don't want to spoil it." This seemed a sound aesthetic decision. Williams' last word had been so exquisitely chosen, such a perfect fusion of expectation, intention, and execution, that already it felt a little unreal in my head, and I wanted to get out before the castle collapsed. But the game, though played by clumsy midgets under the feeble glow of the arc lights, began to tug at my attention, and I loitered in the runway until it was over. Williams' homer had, quite incidentally, made the score 4–3. In the bottom of the ninth inning, with one out, Marlin Coughtry, the second-base juggler, singled. Vic Wertz, pinch-hitting, doubled off the left-field wall, Coughtry advancing to third. Pumpsie Green walked, to load the bases. Willie Tasby hit a double-play ball to the third baseman, but in making the pivot throw Billy Klaus, an ex-Red Sox infielder, reverted to form and threw the ball past the first baseman and into the Red Sox dugout. The Sox won, 5–4. On the car radio as I drove home I heard that Williams, his own man to the end, had decided not to accompany the team to New York. He had met the little death that awaits athletes. He had quit.

[1] This piece was written with no research materials save an outdated record book and the Boston newspapers of the day; and Williams' early career preceded the dawning of my *Schlagballewusstsein* (Baseball-consciousness). Also for reasons of perspective was my account of his beginnings skimped. Williams first attracted the notice of a major-league scout—Bill Essick of the Yankees—when he was a fifteen-year-old pitcher with the San Diego American Legion Post team. As a pitcher-outfielder for San Diego's Herbert Hoover High School, Williams recorded averages of .586 and .403. Essick balked at signing Williams for the $1,000 his mother asked; he was signed instead, for $150 a month, by the local Pacific Coast League franchise, the newly created San Diego Padres. In his two seasons with this team, Williams hit merely .271 and .291, but his style and slugging (23 home runs the second year) caught

the eye of, among others, Casey Stengel, then with the Boston Braves, and Eddie Collins, the Red Sox general manager. Collins bought him from the Padres for $25,000 in cash and $25,000 in players. Williams was then nineteen. Collins' fond confidence in the boy's potential matched Williams' own. Williams reported to the Red Sox training camp in Sarasota in 1938 and, after showing more volubility than skill, was shipped down to the Minneapolis Millers, the top Sox farm team. It should be said, perhaps, that the parent club was equipped with an excellent, if mature, outfield, mostly purchased from Connie Mack's dismantled A's. Upon leaving Sarasota, Williams is supposed to have told the regular outfield of Joe Vosmik, Doc Cramer, and Ben Chapman that he would be back and would make more money than the three of them put together. At Minneapolis he hit .366, batted in 142 runs, scored 130, and hit 43 home runs. He also loafed in the field, jabbered at the fans, and smashed a water cooler with his fist. In 1939 he came north with the Red Sox. On the way, in Atlanta, he dropped a foul fly, accidentally kicked it away in trying to pick it up, picked it up, and threw it out of the park. It would be nice if, his first time up in Fenway Park, he had hit a home run. Actually, in his first Massachusetts appearance, the first inning of an exhibition game against Holy Cross at Worcester, he *did* hit a home run, a grand slam. The Red Sox season opened in Yankee Stadium. Facing Red Ruffing, Williams struck out and, the next time up, doubled for his first major-league hit. In the Fenway Park opener, against Philadelphia, he had a single in five trips. His first home run came on April 23, in that same series with the A's. Williams was then twenty, and played *right* field. In his rookie season he hit .327; in 1940, .344.

[2] See *Ted Williams,* by Ed Linn (Sport Magazine Library), Chapter 6, "Williams vs. the Press." It is Linn's

suggestion that Williams walked into a circulation war among the seven Boston newspapers, who in their competitive zeal headlined incidents that the New York papers, say, would have minimized, just as they minimized the less genial side of the moody and aloof DiMaggio and smoothed Babe Ruth into a folk hero. It is also Linn's thought, and an interesting one, that Williams thrived on even adverse publicity, and needed a hostile press to elicit, contrariwise, his defiant best. The statistics (especially of the 1958 season, when he snapped a slump by spitting in all directions, and inadvertently conked an elderly female fan with a tossed bat) seem to corroborate this. Certainly Williams could have had a truce for the asking, and his industrious perpetuation of the war, down to his last day in uniform, implies its usefulness to him. The actual and intimate anatomy of the matter resides in locker rooms and hotel corridors fading from memory. When my admiring account was printed, I received a letter from a sports reporter who hated Williams with a bitter and explicit immediacy. And even Linn's hagiology permits some glimpses of Williams' locker-room manners that are not pleasant.

[3] But he did tip his cap, high off his head, in at least his first season, as cartoons from that period verify. He also was extravagantly cordial to taxi-drivers and stray children. See Linn, Chapter 4, "The Kid Comes to Boston": "There has never been a ballplayer—anywhere, anytime—more popular than Ted Williams in his first season in Boston." To this epoch belong Williams' prankish use of the Fenway scoreboard lights for rifle practice, his celebrated expressed preference for the life of a fireman, and his determined designation of himself as "The Kid."

[4] In 1947 Joe DiMaggio and in 1957 Mickey Mantle, with seasons inferior to Williams', won the MVP award

because sportswriters, who vote on ballots with ten places, had vengefully placed Williams ninth, tenth, or nowhere at all. The 1941 award to Joe DiMaggio, even though this was Williams' .406 year, is more understandable, since this was also the *annus miraculorum* when DiMaggio hit safely in 56 consecutive games.

[5] The sweet saga of this beautiful decimal must be sung once more. Williams, after hitting above .400 all season, had cooled to .39955 with one doubleheader left to play, in Philadelphia. Joe Cronin, then managing the Red Sox, offered to bench him to safeguard his average, which was exactly .400 when rounded to the third decimal place. Williams said (I forget where I read this) that he did not want to become the .400 hitter with just his toenails over the line. He played the first game and singled, homered, singled, and singled. With less to gain than to lose, he elected to play the second game and got two more hits, including a double that dented a loudspeaker horn on the top of the right-field wall, giving him six-for-eight on the day and a season's average that, in the forty years between Rogers Hornsby's .403 (1925) and the present, stands as unique.

[6] For example: In 1948, the Sox came from behind to tie the Indians by winning three straight; in those games Williams went two for two, two for two, and two for four. In 1949, the Sox overtook the Yankees by winning nine in a row; in that streak, Williams won four games with home runs.

[7] Two reasons for his durability may be adduced. A non-smoker, non-drinker, habitual walker, and year-round outdoorsman, Williams spared his body the vicissitudes of the seasonal athlete. And his hitting was in large part a mental process; the amount of cerebration he devoted to

such details as pitchers' patterns, prevailing winds, and the muscular mechanics of swinging a bat would seem ridiculous, if it had not paid off. His intellectuality, as it were, perhaps explains the quickness with which he adjusted, after the war, to the changed conditions—the night games, the addition of the slider to the standard pitching repertoire, the new cry for the long ball. His reaction to the Williams Shift, then, cannot be dismissed as unconsidered.

[8] Invented, or perpetrated (as a joke?) by Boudreau on July 14, 1946, between games of a doubleheader. In the first game of the doubleheader, Williams had hit three homers and batted in eight runs. The shift was not used when men were on base and, had Williams bunted or hit late against it immediately, it might not have spread, in all its variations, throughout the league. The Cardinals used it in the lamented World Series of that year. Toward the end, in 1959 and 1960, rather sadly, it had faded from use, or degenerated to the mere clockwise twitching of the infield customary against pull hitters.

[9] Shortly, after his retirement, Williams, in *Life*, wrote gloomily of the Stadium, "There's the bigness of it. There are those high stands and all those people smoking—and, of course, the shadows. . . . It takes at least one series to get accustomed to the Stadium and even then you're not sure." Yet his lifetime batting average there is .340, only four points under his median average.

[10] It was Cunningham who, when Williams first appeared in a Red Sox uniform at the 1938 spring training camp, wrote with melodious prescience: "The Sox seem to think Williams is just cocky enough and gabby enough to make a great and colorful outfielder, possibly the Babe Herman type. Me? I don't like the way he stands at the plate. He

bends his front knee inward and moves his foot just before he takes a swing. That's exactly what I do just before I drive a golf ball and knowing what happens to the golf balls I drive, I don't believe this kid will ever hit half a singer midget's weight in a bathing suit."

[11] Written before Roger Maris' fluky, phenomenal sixty-one.

[12] Again, as of 1960. Since then, Musial may have surpassed him in some statistical areas.

[13] In his second season (1940) he was switched to left field, to protect his eyes from the right-field sun.

ROGER KAHN

Ceremonies of Innocence

As a young reporter for the New York Herald Tribune, *Roger Kahn recorded his adventures traveling with the "Jackie Robinson Brooklyn Dodgers." In 1952 and again in 1953, the Dodgers lost the World Series to the Yankees, both times after fierce campaigns, and during these same volatile years, they were the first team to attempt to integrate professional baseball.*

Kahn describes the dominant personalities of the time, including baseball executive Branch Rickey, famous for his deft phrase-making, and the events, the most disturbing of which was the overt and covert racism Jackie Robinson faced both from his teammates and from private citizens when traveling in the South during spring training. When Kahn tried to call his editor's attention to an urgent story, the ongoing nasty discrimination that Robinson was facing, he too came up against disbelief and entrenched opposition.

Wesley Branch Rickey arrived in Brooklyn during World War II fired by two dreams that were to falter. He would build a dynasty to surpass the Yankee empire in the Bronx. He would personally achieve enormous wealth. Rickey became Dodger

69

president after Larry MacPhail responded to the blast of World War II and re-enlisted. MacPhail's Dodgers, assembled under a threat of bankruptcy, could not long endure. Rickey reached Brooklyn thinking in terms of generations, and, as soon as peace came, and manpower stabilized, his Dodgers emerged, formidable, aggressive and enduring. "My ferocious gentlemen," he liked to say. Although Rickey had been banished to Pittsburgh by 1952, every important Dodger pitcher, without exception, had been acquired during his remarkable suzerainty.

Raised on an Ohio farm, Branch Rickey graduated from the University of Michigan, considered becoming a Latin teacher, but chose baseball. Old records indicate that he performed marginally. He caught for the St. Louis Browns and the New York Highlanders—the paleozoic Yankees—doubling as an outfielder. In four years he batted an aggregate .239. Then he managed in St. Louis, moving from the Browns to the Cardinals. He never brought home a team higher than third. Gruff Rogers Hornsby replaced Rickey in 1925 and the Cardinals won the World Series in 1926. Rickey was forty-five that year, and without great distinction. Then he moved into the Cardinal front office and his life turned around. As an executive, Rickey let his intellect run free; broadly, as Henry Ford shaped the future of the business of automobiles, Rickey shaped the future of the game of baseball. It was Rickey who invented the so-called farm system, baseball's production line. He stocked the sources, a half dozen teams, with young, uncertain talent. As their ability allowed, ball players advanced. In one case in twenty-five, a player proved gifted enough for the majors. It was a bloodless procedure, but effective, and presently the Cardinals dominated the National League. Rickey paid execrable salaries—$7,500 a year was high pay. Considering the attrition rate, he had to curb expenses, but Rickey was also a man of principle. He had a Puritan distaste for money in someone else's hands.

In the mid-1940s he bought minor league teams for Brooklyn and the old Latinist, having organized a Dodger farm system, next created a camp where legions of players could be instructed. He chose an abandoned naval air station, four miles west of Vero Beach, Florida, as the training site. There among palms, palmettos, scrub pines and swamp, he made a world. The old Navy barracks, renamed Dodgertown, became spring housing for two hundred athletes. The mess hall now served not navigators but infielders. Outside, Rickey supervised the construction of four diamonds, five batting cages, two sliding pits and numberless pitcher's mounds, everywhere pitcher's mounds. Pitching excited Rickey. It moved him to melodramatics.

At one meeting of the Dodger command, Rickey lifted a cigar and cried, "I have come to the point of a cliff. I stand poised at the precipice. Earth crumbles. My feet slip. I am tumbling over the edge. Certain death lies below. Only one man can save me. *Who is that man?*" This meant that the Dodger bullpen needed help and would someone kindly suggest which minor league righthander should be promoted? It is a tempered irony that Rickey's sure hand failed him where he most wanted sureness. He was unable to produce a great Brooklyn pitching staff.

Pitchers, of all ball players, profit most from competitive intelligence. It is a simple, probably natural thing to throw. A child casts stones. But between the casting child and the pitching major leaguer lies the difference between a boy plunking the piano and an artist performing.

A major leaguer ordinarily has mastered four pitches. The sixty feet six inches that lie between the mound and home plate create one element in a balanced equation between pitcher and batter. No one can throw a baseball past good hitters game after game. The major league pitching primer begins: "Speed is not enough." But a fast ball moves if it is thrown hard enough. Depending on grip, one fast ball moves up and into a righthanded batter. Another moves up and away from him. A few men, like Labine, develop fast balls that sink.

The fast ball intimidates. The curve—"public enemy number one," Chuck Dressen called it —aborts careers. A curve breaks sideways, or downward or at an intervening angle, depending on how it is thrown. Branch Rickey regarded the overhand curve as the best of breaking pitches. An overhand curve, the drop of long ago, breaks straight down, and, unlike flatter curve balls, an overhand curve is equally appalling to righthanded and lefthanded batters. The pure drop, hurtling in at the eyes and snapping to the knees, carried Carl Erskine and Sandy Koufax to strikeout records (fourteen and fifteen) in World Series separated by a decade.

Finally, the technique of major league pitching requires excellent control. Home plate is seventeen inches wide; and a man does best to work the corners. A good technical pitcher throws the baseball at speeds that exceed ninety miles an hour, makes it change direction abruptly and penetrate a target area smaller than a catcher's mitt.

Art proceeds subsequently. The artful pitcher tries never to offer what is expected. Would the batter like a fast ball? Curve him, or, better, throw the fast ball at eye height. Eagerness leads to a wild swing. *Strike one.* Would the batter like another? Now throw that public enemy, down and dirty at the knees. *Strike two.* Now he's on notice for the curve. Hum that jumping fast ball letter-high. That's the pitch he wanted, but not there, not then. Sit down. *Strike three called.* Who's next?

The pitchers are different from the others. They work less often, but when they do, they can hold nothing back. Others cry at a loafing pitcher, "Bend your back. Get naked out there." Action suspends and nine others wait until the pitcher throws. All eyes are on the pitcher, who sighs and thinks. "Ya know," Casey Stengel said about a quiet Arkansan named John Sain, "he don't say much, but that don't matter much, because when you're out there on the mound, you got nobody to talk to." Pitchers are individualists, brave, stubborn, cerebral, hypochondriacal and lonely.

There was so much that Rickey thought that he could do with pitchers. At Vero Beach three plates were crowned with an odd superstructure. This was the strike zone, outlined in string. Pitching through strings, Rickey said, let a man see where his fast ball went. He devised a curve-ball aptitude test. *Hold pitching arm with hand toward*

73

face. Grip ball along seams. Draw arm back fully so that ball touches point of shoulder. Now throw as far as you can. One can throw neither far nor hard. The test humiliates most people, including good major league curve-ball pitchers.

Rickey erred, retrospect suggests, in overestimating the body and in underestimating the insecurity of pitchers. His favorite overhand curve tortures the arm. A line of strain runs from the elbow to the base of the shoulder. An extraordinary number of Rickey's best pitching prospects rapidly destroyed their arms. In trainer's argot, they stripped their gears.

One gentle, soft-featured Nebraskan, Rex Barney, threw overpowering fast balls, although, as Bob Cooke said so often, he pitched as though the plate were high and outside. Rickey led Barney to the strike zone strings at Vero Beach and commanded, "Please pitch with your right eye covered." Presently he said, "Pitch with your left eye covered." After months of test and experiment, Barney was still wild, and now given to periods of weeping. Rickey threw up his hands and ordered Barney to a Brooklyn psychiatrist. Before he reached thirty, Barney became a bartender. Another major talent, Jack Banta, was finished at twenty-five. Ralph Branca won twenty-one games when he was twenty-one years old. He retired to sell insurance at thirty.

Can each failure be laid at Rickey's grave? No more than one can credit Rickey with Duke Snider's 418 home runs. A model Rickey team played magnificently. A model Rickey pitching staff writhed with aching arms and nervous stomachs.

The first flaw laid bare another. Rickey treated newspapermen with condescending flattery, as one might treat stepchildren, recognizing them as an inescapable price one pays for other delights. In Pittsburgh once he invited me to his box. He was then president of the Pirate team that would lose 101 games. "Good you could come," the master began in a hoarse, intimate whisper, placing a hand on my arm. Bushy, graying eyebrows dominated the face. "I have a question on which I'd value your opinion. What do you think of Sid Gordon?"

"Well, he's slowed down, but he's a strong hitter and an intelligent hitter. His arm is fine and he can catch a fly."

Rickey nodded in excessive gratitude. "How would Sid fare at Ebbets Field?" The gnarled hand squeezed my arm. "On an *everyday* basis?"

"He'd belt a few to left."

"And right," Rickey said. "And right. Don't you think he could clear the scoreboard with regularity?"

"Why, yes. I suppose he could."

Rickey winked. "I appreciate your sharing your views. I don't mind telling you I'm concerned about the Dodgers. So many are my ball players. I'm afraid they may not win it, in which case many will blame bad luck, which would not be the entire case. Luck is the residue of design."

As I left, Rickey remarked, "You know, of course, Gordon was born in Brooklyn." His putative design was altruistic. His real intention was to have me urge the Dodgers to buy Gordon in the pages of the *Herald Tribune*. Publicity is the paradigm of salesmanship.

Balancing this deviousness, which hindered reporting, Rickey offered utter mastery of the phrase. His rolling Ohio-Oxonian dialect was a delightful instrument. Were the Pirates going to win the pennant? I asked once. "Ah, a rosebush blooms on the twelfth of May and does it pretty nearly every year. And one day it's all green and the next it's all in flower. I don't control a ball club's development the way nature controls a rosebush." Was his star home run hitter, Ralph Kiner, for sale? "I don't want to sell Ralph, but if something overwhelming comes along, I am willing to be overwhelmed." To what did he attribute the Pirates' poor record? "We are last on merit." Was he himself discouraged? "My father died at eighty-three, planting fruit trees in unpromising soil."

Once away from the days of this year, Rickey could be quite direct, but in the running of current business he was wed to intrigue. By the late 1940s his relationship with Dick Young and the *Daily News* had become catastrophic.

Where Rickey was rotund, classical and Bible Belt, Young was spiky, self-educated and New York. Rickey was shocked by alcoholism, extramarital sex and the word "shit." Young was shocked by Rickey's refusal to attend Sunday games after a week of misleading reporters. A war was inevitable. Its Sarajevo was bad pitching.

Young began baseball writing in 1943, at twenty-five, and very quickly stretched the accepted limits of the beat. He wrote not only about the games but about the athletes, giving each of the players a personality. It was traditional to present athletes as heroes. Newspaper readers learned that Babe Ruth, Lou Gehrig and Grover Cleveland Alexander were grand gentlemen and a credit to the games of baseball and life. Young had heroes—Reese and Campanella—but he fleshed out his cast with heavies. He called Gene Hermanski "a stumbling clown in the outfield." Hermanski responded by shoving Young, a compact five feet seven. But Young would not cower. He loved his job, which "a lot of very rich guys would give an arm to have," and relished the power it provided, and worked at it in original ways. He cultivated some players, argued with others, writing hard stories and soft ones, but always defending his printed words in person. If Young knocked a man on Tuesday, he sought him out on Wednesday. "I wrote what I wrote because I believe it. If you got complaints, let me hear 'em. If you want better stories, win some games."

In time Young came to know the Dodgers better than any other newspaperman and better, too, than many Dodger officials. He sensed when to flatter, when to cajole, when to threaten. As far as any lay reader of instincts can say, Young possessed a preternatural sense of the rhythms and balances of human relations.

Conversations with several Dodgers strengthened Young's harsh conclusion that a number of pitchers lacked heart and, after one losing game in 1948, he composed a polemical lead:

"The tree that grows in Brooklyn is an apple tree and the apples are in the throats of the Dodgers."

There is a nice implicit pun here on Adam's

apple, but the first thrust is Young's thought. Some Dodgers cannot swallow. They are choking.

Branch Rickey had been schooled on a tame sporting press, easy to manipulate. He could not or would not recognize Young as the centurion of a new journalism. He would not even discuss choking frankly. Instead, he expressed private loathing "for *everything* about that man and what he stands for." In public he patronized Young, who above all things would not be patronized. By the time Rickey left Brooklyn in 1950, he was battling Young, Young's boss, and consequently the most widely read newspaper in the United States. In the *Daily News*, Jimmy Powers, the sports editor, identified Rickey as "El Cheapo." Young ghosted Powers' column ten times a year. The *News* would not mention Rickey's manager, Burt Shotton, by name. Instead, Young lanced the bubble of Shotton as genial paterfamilias by giving him the acronym "KOBS." The letters, forged in sarcasm, stood for Kindly Old Burt Shotton. The Dodgers lost because of, won despite, KOBS.

These assaults did not hurt Dodger attendance, but they murdered egos. When Rickey left, and Walter O'Malley became president, his first order of business was to replace KOBS with Dressen. Then O'Malley appointed Emil J. Bavasi, a warm and worldly Roman, as general manager *de facto* (at $17,500), and vice president in charge of Dick Young.

With time, one comes to regret that two such talented men as Rickey and Young fought so bitterly. Neither, I suppose, was faultless, although Rickey, being older, more secure and less tractable, probably warrants more blame. He went to his grave as a babe in public relations.

On the jacket of his ghosted memoir, *The American Diamond*, Rickey is quoted as summing up: "The game of baseball has given me a life of joy. I would not have exchanged it for any other." That's it. That's the old man exactly, still musing on the game and joy at eighty. But the introduction sounds like Rickey, too. Here, seeking a quotation from a man universally appealing, admired and beloved, Rickey began with five maundering lines from Herbert Hoover.

By the time Harold Rosenthal commended me to Dick Young's tutorship, Young and Bavasi had become friends. In addition, Young respected Dressen and enjoyed the attention and machinations of Walter Francis O'Malley. Coincidentally, he had stopped attacking management. "It is not hard to write scoops like Young does," one of the other writers remarked, "after Bavasi feeds the stuff to you." When Young found a few hours for an orientation lecture in Miami on my third day with the team, he angrily mentioned the accusation.

"You do a good job, some guy who can't do a good job says you're cheating. Have you heard that shit? You heard they feed me stuff?" Young was sipping bourbon, which Roscoe McGowen of the *Times*, who at seventy still paid dutiful visits to his mother, suggested did more for longevity than Scotch.

"I heard that, yes."

Young looked into his glass and began cursing.

"I know who told you," he said, "and you're just goddamn dumb enough to believe him."

"Oh, I don't know. I'm not so dumb that I'd say who told me."

Young shook his head. "How the hell did *you* ever get this club anyway? You got pull? What the *fuck* are you doing here? Chrissake. They sent a boy."

"Look. You worry about you and the fucking *News*. I'll worry about the *Tribune*."

"I'll kill you, kid." Young's face went blank. I wanted to escape his scorn, but sat there without words. "First, though," Young said, "I gotta tell you rules. You know baseball? You ever cover a club? You know what to do or did you go to fucking Yale? Doan matter. I'm gonna take another bourbon. Hey. Another Old Crow. You're a good Jewish boy. Your mother read the *Times*. Well, you can forget that fucking paper. Rocco's a helluva man, but that don't mean a fuck. They wouldn't let him write it the right way if he fucking wanted. I'm not so sure he wants. The old *Times* way is no good any more, if it ever was any good. You following me? I'm only gonna do this once."

"The *Times* is a pretty successful paper." I winced as I heard my words. The *Times* is pretty successful. Jackie Robinson runs bases well. Dick Young is a hard man. I sit in this hotel bar, a half dozen thoughts about my brain. Who the hell are you, Young, illiterate bastard, to talk to me like this? You know what I think of the *Daily News?* My grandfather wouldn't let it in our house. It was a Fascist, Jew-baiting paper. People bought the *News* when somebody got raped. They read the details on page four. And, if by mistake they forgot to throw the paper out, they said, "Hey, look. I found it on the subway." Goddamn right Bavasi feeds you stuff. You wanna scoop me, you go ahead and try (but please, don't make me look too bad).

"It'll catch up to the *Times* the way they do things," Young said. His rage was done. "You like the way the *Times* writes baseball?" The storm had ended.

"Not much. No."

"Our paper has four times as many readers; not brokers and bank presidents, but you know what Lincoln said. *'He made so many of them.'* "

I quoted a *Times* lead I had been reading all my life: "The Yankees drew first blood yesterday and then had it spilled all over them as . . ."

"Yeah," Young said.

The son of a bitch, I thought, doesn't even give points for quoting.

"See, that was maybe okay a long time ago. Not now. I'm gonna tell you how it got to be now, once, like I say. You listening? Shit. You ain't drinking, so you must be listening. There's a lot of games in a season."

"One hundred fifty-four."

"Wrong. You're forgetting fucking spring training and playoffs and World Series. The number changes. It's always, like I said, a lot. Now you're gonna write the games most of the time. Nothing you can do about that and it ain't bad. But anytime, you hear me, *anytime* you can get your story off the game you got to do it. Because that's unusual and people read unusual things. Fights. Bean balls. Whatever. Write them, not the game."

"But most of the time you do write the games."

"That's right, and when you do, you forget the *Times*. They tell you the score, but your real fan knows the score already. When you got to write the game, the way you do it is: 'In yesterday's 3–2 Dodger victory, the most interesting thing that happened was . . .' Get that? Someone stole two bases. Someone made a horseshit pitch. Dressen made a mistake. Whatever the hell. Not just the score. Tell 'em fucking why or make them laugh. Hey. Gimme another bourbon."

Into the heavy silence, I sent forth: "Young's two rules of sportswriting." What he had articulated among curses and assaults was his credo, and a man like Dick Young, who has been hurt by life and who lives behind rings of fortification, is pained on yielding up a credo. It is like a birth. As a laboring woman, he had cried out. Now to his splendid, terse analysis of his job and mine, I had said, in condescension, "Young's two rules."

"There's a third rule, kid."

"What's that?"

"Don't be so fucking sure."

"Hey, Dick. That's goddamn good."

"It isn't mine."

"What do you mean?"

"That rule was made by a *New York Times* sportswriter whose favorite lead—you know, about the blood—you were just making fun of."

After Miami, the Dodgers rode chartered buses to Tampa, where the team played five exhibition games, then joined the Boston Braves, their foils for an agonizing, lucrative journey through the South. In 1952 apartheid flowered in what Stanley Woodward called the American hookworm belt. Blacks attended separate schools, patronized separate restaurants, drank at separate water fountains, relieved themselves at separate urinals, watched baseball from separate sections of the grandstand, bought Cokes at separate soft-drink concessions and, at the end of the wearying way, were eulogized in black churches and interred in cemeteries for colored only. "We like our nigras," said white people who described themselves as moderates. "They like us. We all like the way things are. Say, y'all oughta heah 'em sing."

That time seems simpler than today, but mostly because the past always seems simpler when its wars are done. Jackie Robinson was a focus. At big, dark Number 42, forces converged: white hatred for his black pride, for his prophetic defiance and simply for his color, contested with black hope, the same black hope which Southern whites said did not exist. *Man, a little music and some coins is all them pickaninnies want.*

Before anything else, however, Robinson was used commercially. His visit to a Southern city stirred scuffles for reserved seats among whites. Black crowds lined up early on the morning of each game, struggling for places in the narrow colored section (reserved seats not available). When you barnstormed the South with the Robinson Dodgers, you always covered sold-out games. And if you were inclined toward economics, you realized that Jack was doing something other than reordering baseball. He was earning his annual salary, which never exceeded $40,000, before the season began.

We boarded Pullmans in St. Petersburg. The Dodgers and the Braves leased private cars and a roomette became one's movable home. We all dozed on the Pullman sleepers, ate in the Pullman diners and drank in Pullman club cars. The players would shower in ball park clubhouses. Reporters shared the toilet next to a hotel press room, which the Dodgers rented in each town at a day rate of $6 or $8.

After winning an exhibition from Cincinnati in Tampa, the team thundered into the dining car at St. Petersburg. "Players first," cried Lee Scott, the traveling secretary. He was a slight, fastidious man with a pencil-line mustache. "They worked hard. Let the workers eat first."

Ignoring Scott, Young, who had worked hard, joined Carl Furillo. The two talked intensely over shrimp cocktail. At another table Robinson sat with Erskine. At a third Campanella ate beside Labine. Although I did not know it then, Robinson had ordered the blacks "spread out. Don't sit together at one table. Mix it up. Eat with the white guys. You all sit at one table, you look like a spot."

I obeyed Lee Scott and drank and read, and ate with a man from the New York *Post*, and went to bed, but not to sleep. Our train was a world (I thought) free and independent in the racist South. If you chose to draw the shades, you could pretend that there was no racist South. Certain older reporters did just that. Hell, a ball game was a ball game anywhere, wasn't it? And afterward the club bought beer. Then there were cards. On a barnstorming trip you could play poker very late every night for two straight weeks. Other reporters, including Young, had seen the South before. They accepted apartheid with a brief, angry grunt, the way they accepted a cramped press box, or a sinewy steak. Hurtling due west, our train transversed the Florida panhandle. It was odd, I thought. We wrote about the games, the players and the prospects. But, here in a wounding land, no one would report or could report the horror all about—racism. It was legal, even controlled, to be sure, but outside my roomette window stirred nameless, unreasoning racial hate threatening then as it threatens now to shatter the country. I wish I could figure a way, I thought, punching at a tiny Pullman pillow, to get beyond the ball games and to get the real story into the paper.

There was a glue factory in Mobile, someone said. Whatever, the clear morning smelled. We rode taxis out of the railyards to the Admiral Semmes Hotel and breakfasts and showers. Fairly clean, at one o'clock I hailed a taxi along with Bill Roeder, a reserved, round-faced man of thirty, who composed airy pieces for the New York *World-Telegram*.

"Ball park," Roeder said.

"Hartwell Field?" the driver asked. He turned, showing a square face and spectacles.

"How many ball parks do you have?" Roeder said.

"Oh, we got plenty," said the driver, starting the cab. "Say, you guys goin' out to see the coal?" Roeder and I sat in separate silences. "We comin' to where I grew up," the driver said. He turned into a street of gnarled trees and clapboard homes. "Coal now. The coal is taking over. How do you like that? Where I grew up there's all these fucking cannibals."

"All right," Roeder said.

"We got to stop these cannibals 'fore they eat us. Gonna be a lotta cannibals out today, see that nigger Robinson."

"Just drive, will you?" Roeder said.

"Does this happen all the time?" I said.

Roeder stared sullen out the window. After a while, a green wooden grandstand rose in front of us. "You get out," Roeder said. "I'll pay him."

"Fucking niggers want to take over baseball, too," said the driver.

"Go on ahead," Roeder said. In a minute I heard the driver shout. Roeder had paid the meter but withheld a tip. That was our social protest, emancipation through nontipping. We'll straighten out this country yet, I thought. And if we meet a kleagle, you know what? I'm not going to buy him a drink. Surely I *wanted* to protest, but I rejoiced in the luxury of sportswriting and, instead of ripping the meter out of the cab, or citing John Stuart Mill or doing something wise, I hurried away from the taxi to see how Hartwell Field looked, and where the press box was, and whether Western Union facilities would be satisfactory.

Most of the old grandstand was reserved for whites. It was crowded, but not yet full. Two strips, at the end of each foul line, were open to blacks. The black humanity of Mobile stood and squatted and bent and sat wedged two to a seat.

Twenty minutes before game time workmen rigged ropes from the black sections to the outfield. Armed Mobile police and Alabama troopers took patrol positions. Then the cattle car of a stand was opened and the black mass spilled onto the field. The people ran. There was no reason to run. There was ample space for everyone behind the ropes. But they ran in jubilation and relief, and as they hurried, the black mass diffused and ceased to be a mass and became individual men and women who were running, and who wore bright red and yellow and green. Someone in a yellow shirt was limping. A woman was carrying a baby and leading a small boy. These were people and that was a hard thing to face, and rather than face it I asked Young what the ruling would be on balls hit into the black crowd.

"Double."

"Getting a two-base hit in every inning." In a needling little game we composed parodies of the hoary lead, "scoring in every inning."

"Wordy," Young said.

"Doubling in every inning."

"Better."

Jackie Robinson was the third man to bat. Vern Bickford's first pitch to him broke wide, and when the scoreboard showed "ball one," the blacks, who ringed the entire outfield, cheered in triumph. Robinson fouled the next pitch, hopping in an awkward follow-through. A roar went up from the whites. In the end, to a *tutti* of enthusiasm and disappointment, Robinson hit a short fly to left. He played an unimportant role in this exhibition. Both teams used other blacks. But to the crowd, Sam Jethroe and Roy Campanella were ball players who happened to be colored. Then there was Robinson, the threatening, glorious black.

"Does that bother you?" I asked at dusk, as our sealed train moved slowly on a single track among low pine trees.

"What?" Robinson said.

"That noise about everything you do and the way the fans get pushed around."

"If I let *that* shit bother me," he said without emotion, "I wouldn't be here."

"I mean—"

"Gotta play cards," Robinson said.

But one way or another, Robinson always answered a question. At Pelican Field in New Orleans we began to chat while he threw with Pee Wee Reese along the third-base line. "Writers think I should thank them when they do a good story about me," Robinson said, "but aren't they just doing their job?"

"You get on a writer when he knocks you."

"That's right." Robinson moved about as he caught. "If I think he's wrong, I blast him. Why shouldn't I?"

"Well . . ."

A cry rose from the stands and at once defined the scene. Robinson whirled. "Goddamnit no," he shrieked. "Don't cheer those goddamn bastards. Don't cheer. Keep your fucking mouths shut." A barrier was coming down at Pelican Field. One small section of unoccupied seats in the white section was being opened to blacks. White policemen had opened the gates and the blacks were cheering in joy.

"Stupid bastards," Robinson screamed. "You got it coming. You're only getting what's coming. Don't cheer those bastards, you stupid bastards. Take what you got coming. Don't cheer."

He threw down his glove and walked in a little circle.

"You come to catch, Jack?" Reese shouted.

"Shit," Robinson said, and picked up his glove and resumed warming up.

In a minute he walked into the dugout and slumped down by himself. "I'm sure it doesn't mean a damn, Jack," I said, "but I just want you to know I think that racist shit is a disgrace."

"Then write it."

"I will."

"You'll be the first."

"This must be hell," I said to Jackie Robinson.

"Never been there."

"I mean knowing that you can't get off the train, that if we had to stop overnight in any one of these towns, you wouldn't have a place to stay."

"Are you kidding?" Robinson's high voice grew shrill. "Any town down here, any one, I could be a guest of the most successful Negro family—the lawyer, the banker, the doctor. I could be their house guest. I'm not stuck like you. I don't need any fucking salesmen's hotel."

Sportswriters reigned at the salesmen's hotels. The Jeff Davis with its Urban Room in Montgomery. The Biltmore ("Lions Meet Here") in hilly Nashville. And the Read House, where Broad and Chestnut intersect in Chattanooga (package store, meeting rooms, pets limited).

I found Chuck Dressen in a suite at the Read,

sitting on a flowered sofa, sipping a Scotch and black cherry soda. It was almost noon. "I want to talk about pitching," I said.

"Was you in an incubator?"

"No. Not that I know of."

"Well, if a pitcher is a incubator baby, he can't go nine. The incubator weakens 'em. Ya didn't know that, did you? College ain't nothing in this business, kid. Ya wanna drink, kid, ya drink, doncha?"

"I've got to write."

"It's good to take one, 'fore you write, ain't it, Jake?"

A coach had been sitting at the rainy window. "Yep," Jake Pitler said. He was fifty-eight, Jewish and retained, some said, primarily to absent himself on Yom Kippur, publicizing Dodger Semitism without hurting the starting line-up. Now Pitler moved quickly and made a Scotch and soda. "Ya oughta try it with black cherry, kid."

"I'd better stick to just plain soda."

"There's tricks to this game," Dressen said. "Ya can't just worry about the next play. Ya gotta worry about two plays, or three." Dressen was a short and thick-bodied man full of hypotheses and advice. He had been born in Decatur, Illinois, in 1898, the son of a railroad man, and played for the Staleys, the professional football team that evolved into the Chicago Bears, and after that major league baseball. By reputation he was a man of shrewdness, a master stealer of signs and a grand tactician. "You get blowed, kid?" he said.

"No. No. I don't know anybody here."

"Well, don't do it. Don't get yourself blowed.

Getting blowed makes you sweat in hot weather. You can't do the job, pitching or writin' good stories, when it's hot if you let them go down on you."

"I didn't know that."

"And watch out for pickpockets, right, Jake?"

"Right, Chuck."

"At the 1933 World's Fair in Chicago, a pickpocket damn near got my dough. Now me, I got small nuts, but even so I felt his hand. I got small nuts but sensitive. Right, Jake? Whoop. Yep. Goodbye, Dolly Gray." Dressen whistled and winked.

"I wanted to ask about pitching."

"Too many incubators and too many guys that get blowed."

"It's kind of hard to write that in the paper, Chuck."

"What? Whoop? Yup. I see what ya mean."

"Well?"

"Water seeks its own level," Dressen said.

So my grandmother had told me once in Brooklyn. Chuck Dressen had a small pinched face. He began to remind me of my grandmother.

"Charlie's goddamn right," Pitler said.

"Ya pitch 'em and pitch 'em," Dressen said, "and they eliminate theirselves. The pitchers eliminate theirselves and the hitters seek their level like water."

"Charlie's right," Jake Pitler said.

"Water seeks its own level," Dressen said. "A .220 hitter will hit .220 if you play him long enough and a .320 hitter will hit .320."

"Like Stan Musial," I said.

91

"Aah, Musial," Dressen said. "I gotta way to pitch to Musial."

"How?"

"A slow curve. That's public enemy number one. The curve. A slow curve breakin' in on Musial tit-high."

"Have you tried it?"

"Nah."

"Why not?"

"The pitchers won't listen to what I say."

"Who's your best pitcher?"

"Newcombe, but the Army got him."

"Who would you say is your best ball player?"

Dressen winked. He had small eyes that darted.

"Not to write," I said. "I'm just asking, Chuck."

"Not to write?"

"I heard you promise," Pitler said.

"Robi'son," Dressen said, "is the best ball player I ever managed, anywhere."

"Color doesn't matter?"

"Lookit," Dressen said. "I know about that Klan. I don't go to church, but my folks was Catholics and them Klan bastards burned crosses where I grew up. I never got much schoolin', but I know a lot of things. Now on this team there's some guys, they don't like Robi'son, or none of 'em. But that don't mean shit because we're gonna win the pennant and when they see it's Robi'son getting them World Series money, he's gonna look awful white awful fast."

We had another drink and I asked about Joe Black, who had pitched well that day in Mobile. "Might," Dressen said. "Dunno. Ain't afraid. College guy. Maybe. Does he get blowed? Dunno. Maybe in relief."

There was no privacy with the team and very few secrets. That night on the Pullman rolling toward Virginia Joe Black hailed me from his roomette. "Hey, man. Sit down. Ya wanna talk a little? I used to teach in school. I'm not a dummy. Hey. How you like the South?"

Black was six feet three and very dark, with fine features and a bull neck. "How do *you* like the South?" I said.

Black grinned. "I can't tell you," he said. "They won't let me in."

"You take your family to Vero Beach?"

"That's what I mean," Black said. "There aren't any colored in Vero Beach. They got a whole separate town for colored, called Gifford. You been to Gifford? No? I don't believe that town has running water."

Black looked out the window. The train was hurrying through bare Piedmont Hills. Spring had not advanced beyond Tennessee. "Hey," Black said, gazing with large, soft eyes, "am I gonna make this club?"

"How do I know?"

"You talked to Number 7."

"That's right."

"He like that game in Mobile? Six good innings. Hey. I can give better than that. And I'll protect them. And I don't walk many. And I hum it pretty good. You know what Campy says, 'Ah hums that pea.' "

I put a hand on Joe's huge arm. "I'll see if I can

find out a little more," I said. "You really want to make this ball club, don't you?"

Black dropped his drawl. "If I could express myself as well as Shakespeare," he said, "I still couldn't tell you how much."

The team split in St. Louis, after a smooth ride down the Alton Line. A chartered bus carried the whites to the Chase Hotel, a comfortable and seemingly gracious white-stone building, where the room clerks greeted us by name. The blacks rode black taxis to the Hotel Adams. "It doesn't bother me," Robinson said. "I get treated like a hero at the Adams. They give me anything I want there. *Anything.*" (Two years later when the Chase agreed to accept Negroes, provided "they eat in their rooms," certain blacks rejected these conditions. Robinson said the terms were acceptable; it was a wedge anyway. Presently hotel officials lifted all barriers and someone told Robinson that he should consider himself as just another guest. After that the other blacks followed. When Robinson said he didn't want the Chase, he spoke in the voice of wounded pride.)

Still in first place, the team won a night game from the Cardinals, and at one the next afternoon, Robinson telephoned me and said, "It's started again."

"What's started?"

"The Cardinals have started racial shit. I've been in the league for seven years and I don't think I have to put up with it any more." The night before, while Robinson played second, several players in the St. Louis dugout continually shouted

94

"Nigger." Someone else yelled, "Hey, porter, git my bag." Another phrase he had heard was "black bastard." Finally, Robinson said someone, he didn't know who, had held up a pair of baseball shoes, shouting, "Here, boy. Here, boy. Shine."

"I've got to write that."

"That's what I thought you'd say. I think if people knew what was going on, they'd want it stopped."

I hung up and dialed the Cardinal office and asked for Ed Stanky, an old hero. In 1945, Stanky, a mediocre hitter, drew 148 bases on balls. He battled and won games and once, on accepting an award from baseball writers, he said, "Thank you for recognizing my intangibles." He was a poor boy from Philadelphia, hard-eyed, Polish and bright.

"What's on your mind?" he said. "You need an early story?"

"I got an early story. I want to check it."

"A newspaperman checking out a story. What are you, some kind of Bolshevik?"

"I'm trying to be fair."

"I'm just kidding you," Stanky said. "Go ahead."

I told him Robinson's accusations.

Silence.

"What I'm asking, Ed, is did this really happen?"

After another pause, Stanky said, "I heard nothing out of line."

"Are you denying it?"

"I was right there," Stanky said. His voice was rising. "I'm telling you I was there and I

95

heard nothing out of line. And you can quote me."

"Okay. I'm just trying to get both sides."

"Will I see you tonight?"

"Sure."

"Don't let yourself become Robinson's little bobo," Stanky said. "That's free advice."

I wrote a conventional story in which I quoted Robinson's charge and Stanky's denial and tried to give each equal space. I telephoned the piece to the paper, then joined Clem Labine in the lobby. "I was in the bullpen," Labine said. "I couldn't hear what was going on in the dugouts. But nobody was talking about stuff like that later. I don't think it's much of a story anyway." Clem clenched his right fist and considered his forearm. "Look," he said, "maybe if someone called me a French-Catholic bastard, I'd tell him to go fuck himself. I wouldn't come crying to you."

"It's not the same thing."

"Why?"

"Because in Mississippi they're not lynching French-Catholic bastards, only niggers." Labine winced and then he nodded.

At the ball park, I reported Stanky's denial to Robinson, as he was getting ready to take batting practice. He made a circular gesture, and his strong, black hands come to rest on the gray uniform shirt. "Do I need publicity? Do I want racial unrest? I wouldn't have told you what I told you if it wasn't true."

With a sudden stab, I understood. Stanky had played me for a fool. I had followed the textbook maxim, consulting both sides (but been lax in gathering neutral opinion) as if there were two sides. I had been misled. Now the first edition of the *Herald Tribune* was on the streets of New York, circulating my misleading story.

In the dusk I charged toward the St. Louis clubhouse and Stanky's office, angry, confused and in a queer sense hurt. A St. Louis newspaperman lounged in Stanky's office. "Well," Stanky announced. "Here comes Robi'son's li'l bobo."

He was sitting behind his desk, a square man, with strong arms and burning eyes. A bat rack stood in one corner of his office. I stopped beside it.

"Are Robi'son's feelings hurt?" Stanky said. "Are they black and blue?" I could not speak.

"Don't you get it?" Stanky said. *"Black* and blue."

"I get it." My voice was high. "I want to clear up that matter of last night."

"It's all cleared up," Stanky said.

"Robinson swears he heard those things."

"I was right there," Stanky said, "and I heard nothing out of line. I heard 'black bastard.' I don't happen to consider that out of line." He half-rose in his chair. His lips and the bridge of his nose had gone pale.

"What?"

" 'Black bastard' and 'nigger' are not out of line," Stanky said. He was standing up, ready. I grabbed a bat. If he charged, I was going to use a bat. Or try to use a bat. I was going to club at an old idol. Suddenly Stanky grinned. "Maybe you aren't Robi'son's bobo. Maybe you're Charlie

97

Dressen's. That's all right. Don't take it all so serious."

Later in the high press box, I typed a substitute story very quickly:

"Ed Stanky, manager of the St. Louis Cardinals, today confirmed charges by Jackie Robinson. . . ." I recounted what happened and filed a story, feeling that if I had been naïve in the afternoon, I was enterprising by night. The scoop would reform no bigots, but at the least it would discomfit some. And it would set down the record accurately.

The press box rose in tiers. White reporters sat in the front row. The few Negro sportswriters were confined to the rear. Now, I trotted up the stairs, going from white to black, wreathed in virtue, and fetched myself a beer. I was not thinking of the segregated press box or of the pennant race, when the teleprinter by my side began to clatter:

NOTE TO KAHN: HERALD TRIBUNE WILL NOT BE A SOUNDING BOARD FOR JACKIE ROBINSON. WRITE BASEBALL, NOT RACE RELATIONS. STORY KILLED. SOL ROOGOW, NIGHT SPORTS EDITOR.

By the conclusion of this mortifying trip, June had arrived, the Dodgers narrowly held first place and it was time to sail further on the voyage with *Ulysses*, as navigated in the Grand Army Plaza section of Brooklyn by Olga Kahn. Come rain, come losing streak, come headache, come relief, on Wednesdays, when in town I read. These nights, begun with a formal opening statement and concluded with coffee, had shown us Stephen

Dedalus rising, teaching, walking, Leopold Bloom meditating and lunching, but in an ambiance of humorless intensity I had not yet grown as fond of *Ulysses* as I was of *Portrait*.

"Good evening, Professor," said Gordon Kahn at the door of the old apartment. He led me through a foyer. "Your mother's on the phone. Why can't they get a bigger lead?"

"Furillo isn't hitting."

We reached the living room. My father sank into his red Cogswell chair. "It's nonsense," he said, "when some boob describes Furillo as 'The Rock.' He always throws to the right base. There's something there."

"He doesn't have much actual learning."

"And Dressen. It isn't fair to patronize him. He's doing an excellent job."

"Yeah."

"Managing a baseball team is one of those things that looks easy when someone else does it."

"Look. You know what happened in one town last trip? The team was losing, 5 to 2. They go out on the field in the last of the eighth, and Dressen says, 'Hold 'em, fellers. I'll think of something.' "

Gordon Kahn's eyes showed shock. I wanted that. I had no stomach to be quizzed on my bobbling of the Robinson story or on the *Herald Tribune*'s sudden censorship.

"Were you on the field to hear that?"

"Reese told me."

"Has it occurred to you that Reese might want to manage?"

"Boy. Absolutely wrong. You don't know the club at all."

99

"Ah," said Olga, returning from the telephone. "The chapter tonight is about Hamlet and simply full of puns." She was carrying the red-covered Modern Library *Ulysses*. "In Dublin on June 16, 1904, it is two o'clock in the afternoon." She slipped onto her chair, a flowered wingback. "The scene symbolizes the classic Scylla and Charybdis."

"Don't oversimplify human relationships," Gordon said.

"What's that?" Olga cried.

"He's talking to me," I said from the blue couch.

"About *Ulysses?*"

"About Dressen."

Olga said, "Oh, dear," looked upward and began: " 'Urbane, to comfort them, the Quaker librarian purred: And we have, have we not, those priceless pages of *Wilhelm Meister?* A great poet on a great brother poet . . .' "

"I think that's enough, for this evening," Gordon said mildly after two hours of communal reading.

"Yes," Olga said. "We all know Joyce believed that in *Hamlet,* the ghost, not the prince, was Shakespeare himself. Coffee is waiting."

"If he wasn't kidding," I said.

"Who?" Olga said.

"Joyce."

"Joyce didn't kid," Gordon said. "Is there a good game this week? I haven't seen one in some time."

"Tomorrow," I said. My mind flew between England and Ireland. Shakespeare as a ghostly father.

My father's basso drew me back to Brooklyn. "Thursday is bad. How about Saturday?"

"Phillies." I wondered whether Al Laney knew if Joyce were kidding.

"Declining team," my father said.

"Dad, the way it works is that two games a week are damn good. Two are fair. Three are one-sided." My own guess was that Joyce was serious.

"Well, then."

"Do you want to sit behind first or watch the pitching?" What was the difference which one truly was Shakespeare? I thought. Joyce had looked at genius as a genius. That was the exciting thing. "We'll have a drink afterward," I said at last unthinking to my father.

The Saturday game was one-sided, but not with the weight of Dodger power. The team's pitching collapsed and the Phils won easily, 9 to 3, enabling me to start my story during the eighth inning. Twenty minutes after Andy Pafko flied to short right center field for the final out, I joined my father in a deserted section near first base. We had sat there together fifteen years before. "Come on up to the press room," I said.

He rose, a Pall Mall dropping a quarter inch of ash. "The pitchers couldn't keep the ball low," he said. "In a ball park this size you have to keep the ball low."

"I know. They call that wild high."

"I certainly wouldn't suggest that this is a great team."

"Nobody looks good getting beat by six."

We walked toward the elevator that rose in the southwestern corner of Ebbets Field. Dressen was waiting at the elevator gate. His small eyes rolled about. His lower jaw twitched.

"So this is your boy," he said, after I made introductions.

"Yes, sir," Gordon Kahn said. He beamed and ashes fell.

"I take good care of him. Ya gotta watch these young guys." Dressen winked at my father. "But I set you straight," Dressen said to me. "Ain't that right?"

Fellatio equals perspiration, I remembered. "You're a helluva head counselor, Chuck."

"Aaah," Dressen said, pleased, and the elevator arrived.

We rode up silently, my father and Dressen eye to eye. As we entered the press room, Gordon said, "I'm sorry the game didn't turn out more satisfactorily, Mr. Dressen."

"Huh?" Charlie said. "The way them cocksuckers played? The fuckers din' deserve to win. They played like pansies. Shit. Know what I fuckin' mean?"

My father nodded solemnly. Dressen started gulping his Scotch and White Rock black cherry. I whispered to my father, "I'm sorry about the language. He's a little, uh, coarse."

"Nonsense," my father said, his deep voice overloud. "I can tell at once that he's an intelligent man."

ROGER ANGELL
The Interior Stadium

In this final essay from his first book on baseball,
The Summer Game, *Roger Angell meditates on
America's obsession with sports, on what he calls its
"excessive excessiveness," and on his own special obsession, baseball. Daydreaming about baseball—sending
great hitters and pitchers of different generations against
one another in imaginary fantasy games—is one of his
specialties. Another is writing about and characteriz-
ing the virtues of great players and great games. For
example, in Angell's description of Yastrzemski in 1967,
he pinpoints for the reader the momentousness of the
occasion when this truly outstanding athlete comes
through in the clutch—"in a situation where all hope
rests on him."*

Sports are too much with us. Late and soon, sitting and watching—mostly watching on television
—we lay waste our powers of identification and enthusiasm and, in time, attention as more and more
closing rallies and crucial putts and late field goals
and final play-offs and sudden deaths and world
records and world championships unreel themselves
ceaselessly before our half-lidded eyes. Professional
leagues expand like bubble gum, ever larger and
thinner, and the extended sporting seasons, now

bunching and overlapping at the ends, conclude in exhaustion and the wrong weather. So, too, goes the secondary business of sports—the news or non-news off the fields. Sports announcers (ex-half-backs in Mod hairdos) bring us another live, exclusive interview in depth with the twitchy coach of some as yet undefeated basketball team or with a weeping (for joy) fourteen-year-old champion female backstroker, and the sports pages, now almost the largest single part of the newspaper, brim with salary disputes, medical bulletins, franchise maneuverings, All-Star ballots, drug scandals, close-up biogs, after-dinner tributes, union tactics, weekend wrap-ups, wire-service polls, draft-choice trades, clubhouse gossip, and the latest odds. The American obsession with sports is not a new phenomenon, of course, except in its current dimensions, its excessive excessiveness. What *is* new, and what must at times unsettle even the most devout and unselective fan, is a curious sense of loss. In the midst of all these successive spectacles and instant replays and endless reportings and recapitulations, we seem to have forgotten what we came for. More and more, each sport resembles all sports; the flavor, the special joys of place and season, the unique displays of courage and strength and style that once isolated each game and fixed it in our affections, have disappeared somewhere in the noise and crush.

Of all sports, none has been so buffeted about by this unselective proliferation, so maligned by contemporary cant, or so indifferently defended, as baseball. Yet the game somehow remains the same, obdurately unaltered and comparable only with itself. Baseball has one saving grace that distinguishes it—for me, at any rate—from every other sport. Because of its pace, and thus the perfectly observed balance, both physical and psychological, between opposing forces, its clean lines can be restored in retrospect. This inner game—baseball in the mind—has no season, but it is best played in the winter, without the distraction of other baseball news. At first, it is a game of recollections, recapturings, and visions. Figures and occasions return, enormous sounds rise and swell, and the interior stadium fills with light and yields up the sight of a young ballplayer—some hero perfectly memorized—just completing his own unique swing and now racing toward first. See the way he runs? Yes, that's him! Unmistakable, he leans in, still following the distant flight of the ball with his eyes, and takes his big turn at the base. Yet this is only the beginning, for baseball in the mind is not a mere returning. In time, this easy summoning up of restored players, winning hits, and famous rallies gives way to reconsiderations and reflections about the sport itself. By thinking about baseball like this—by playing it over, keeping it warm in a cold season—we begin to make discoveries. With luck, we may even penetrate some of its mysteries. One of those mysteries is its vividness—the absolutely distinct inner vision we retain of that hitter, that eager base runner, of however long ago. My father was talking the other day about some of the ballplayers he remembered. He grew up in Cleveland, and the Indians were his team. Still are. "We had Nap Lajoie at second," he said. "You've heard of him. A great big broad-shouldered fellow but a beautiful fielder. He was a rough customer. If he didn't like an umpire's call, he'd give him a faceful of tobacco juice. The shortstop was Terry Turner—a smaller man, and blond. I can still see Lajoie picking up a grounder and wheeling and floating the ball over to Turner. Oh, he was quick on his feet! In right field we had Elmer Flick, now in the Hall of Fame. I liked the center fielder, too. His name was Harry Bay, and he wasn't a heavy hitter, but he was very fast and covered a lot of ground. They said he could circle the bases in twelve seconds flat. I saw him get a home run inside the park—the ball hit on the infield and went right past the second baseman and out to the wall, and Bay beat the relay. I remember Addie Joss, our great right-hander. Tall, and an elegant pitcher. I once saw him pitch a perfect game. He died young."

My father has been a fan all his life, and he has pretty well seen them all. He has told me about the famous last game of the 1912 World Series, in Boston, and seeing Fred Snodgrass drop that fly ball in the tenth inning, when the Red Sox scored twice and beat the Giants. I looked up Harry Bay and those other Indians in the *Baseball Encyclopedia,* and I think my father must have seen that inside-the-park homer in the summer of 1904. Lajoie batted .376 that year, and Addie Joss led the American League with an earned run average of 1.59, but the Indians finished in fourth place. 1904. . . . Sixty-seven years have gone by, yet Nap Lajoie is in plain view, and the ball still floats over to Terry Turner. Well, my father is eighty-one now, and old men are great rememberers of the distant past.

But I am fifty, and I can also bring things back: Lefty Gomez, skinny necked and frighteningly wild, pitching his first game at Yankee Stadium, against the White Sox and Red Faber in 1930. Old John McGraw, in a business suit and a white fedora, sitting lumpily in a dark corner of the dugout at the Polo Grounds and glowering out at the field. Babe Ruth, wearing a new, bright yellow glove, trotting out to right field—a swollen ballet dancer, with those delicate, almost feminine feet and ankles. Ruth at the plate, uppercutting and missing, staggering with the force of his swing. Ruth and Gehrig hitting back-to-back homers. Gehrig, in the summer of 1933, running bases with a bad leg in a key game against the Senators; hobbling, he rounds third, closely followed by young Dixie Walker, then a Yankee. The throw comes in to the plate, and the Washington catcher —it must have been Luke Sewell—tags out the sliding Gehrig and, in the same motion, the sliding Dixie Walker. A double play at the plate. The Yankees lost the game; the Senators go on to a pennant. And, back across the river again, Carl Hubbell. My own great pitcher, a southpaw, tall and elegant. Hub pitching: the loose motion; two slow, formal bows from the waist, glove and hands held almost in front of his face as he pivots, the long right leg (in long, peculiar pants) striding; and the ball, angling oddly, shooting past the batter. Hubbell walks gravely back to the bench, his pitching arm, as always, turned the wrong way round, with the palm out. Screwballer.

Any fan, as I say, can play this private game, extending it to extraordinary varieties and possibilities in his mind. Ruth bats against Sandy Koufax or Sam McDowell. . . . Hubbell pitches to Ted Williams, and the Kid, grinding the bat in his fists, twitches and blocks his hips with the pitch; he holds off but still follows the ball, leaning over and studying it like some curator as it leaps in just under his hands. Why this vividness, even from an imaginary confrontation? I have watched many other sports, and I have followed some—football, hockey, tennis—with eagerness, but none of them yields these permanent interior pictures, these ancient and precise excitements. Baseball, I must conclude, is intensely remembered because only baseball is so intensely watched. The game forces intensity upon us. In the ballpark, scattered across an immense green, each player is isolated in our attention, utterly visible. Watch that fielder just below us. Little seems to be expected of him. He waits in easy composure, his hands on his knees; when the ball at last soars or bounces out to him, he seizes it and dispatches it with swift, haughty ease. It all looks easy, slow, and, above all, safe. Yet we know better, for what is certain in baseball is that someone, perhaps several people, will fail. They will be searched out, caught in the open, and defeated, and there will be no confusion about it or sharing of the blame. This is sure to happen, because what baseball requires of its athletes, of course, is nothing less than perfection, and perfection cannot be eased or divided. Every moment of every game, from first pitch to last out, is measured and recorded against an absolute standard, and thus each success is also a failure. Credit that strikeout to the pitcher but also count it against the batter's average; mark this run unearned, because the left fielder bobbled the ball for an instant and a runner moved up. Yet, faced with this sudden and repeated presence of danger, the big-league player defends himself with such courage and skill that the illusion of safety is sustained. Tension is screwed tighter and tighter as the certain downfall is postponed again and again, so that when disaster does come—a half-topped infield hit, a walk on a close three-and-two call, a low drive up the middle that just eludes the diving shortstop—we rise and cry out. It is a spontaneous, inevitable, irresistible reaction.

Televised baseball, I must add, does not seem capable of transmitting this emotion. Most baseball is seen on the tube now, and it is presented faithfully and with great technical skill. But the medium is irrevocably two-dimensional; even with several cameras, television cannot bring us the essential distances of the game—the simultaneous flight of a batted ball and its pursuit by the racing, straining outfielders, the swift convergence of runner and ball at a base. Foreshortened on our screen, the players on the field appear to be squashed together, almost touching each other, and, watching them, we lose the sense of their separateness and lonesome waiting.

This is a difficult game. It is so demanding that the best teams and the weakest teams can meet on almost even terms, with no assurance about the result of any one game. In March 1962, in St. Petersburg, the World Champion Yankees played for the first time against the newborn New York Mets—one of the worst teams of all time—

in a game that each badly wanted to win; the winner, to nobody's real surprise, was the Mets. In 1970, the World Champion Orioles won 108 games and lost 54; the lowest cellar team, the White Sox, won 56 games and lost 106. This looks like an enormous disparity, but what it truly means is that the Orioles managed to win two out of every three games they played, while the White Sox won one out of every three. That third game made the difference—and a kind of difference that can be appreciated when one notes that the winning margin given up by the White Sox to all their opponents during the season averaged 1.1 runs per game. Team form is harder to establish in baseball than in any other sport, and the 162-game season not uncommonly comes down to October with two or three teams locked together at the top of the standings on the final weekend. Each inning of baseball's slow, searching time span, each game of its long season is essential to the disclosure of its truth.

Form is the imposition of a regular pattern upon varying and unpredictable circumstances, but the patterns of baseball, for all the game's tautness and neatness, are never regular. Who can predict the winner and shape of today's game? Will it be a brisk, neat two-hour shutout? A languid, error-filled 12–3 laugher? A riveting three-hour, fourteen-inning deadlock? What other sport produces these manic swings? For the players, too, form often undergoes terrible reversals; in no other sport is a champion athlete so often humiliated or a journeyman so easily exalted. The surprise, the upset, the total turnabout of expectations and reputations—these are delightful commonplaces of baseball. Al Gionfriddo, a part-time Dodger outfielder, stole second base in the ninth inning of the fourth game of the 1947 World Series to help set up Lavagetto's game-winning double (and the only Dodger hit of the game) off the Yankees' Bill Bevens. Two days later, Gionfriddo robbed Joe DiMaggio with a famous game-saving catch of a 415-foot drive in deepest left field at Yankee Stadium. Gionfriddo never made it back to the big leagues after that season. Another irregular, the Mets' Al Weis, homered in the fifth and last game of the 1969 World Series, tying up the game that the Mets won in the next inning; it was Weis's third homer of the year and his first ever at Shea Stadium. And so forth. Who remembers the second game of the 1956 World Series—an appallingly bad afternoon of baseball in which the Yankees' starter, Don Larsen, was yanked after giving up a single and four walks in less than two innings? It was Larsen's *next* start, the fifth game, when he pitched his perfect game.

There is always a heavy splash of luck in these reversals. Luck, indeed, plays an almost predictable part in the game; we have all seen the enormous enemy clout into the bleachers that just hooks foul at the last instant and the half-checked swing that produces a game-winning blooper over second. Everyone complains about baseball luck, but I think it adds something to the game that is nearly essential. Without it, such a rigorous and unforgiving pastime would be almost too painful to enjoy.

No one, it becomes clear, can conquer this impossible and unpredictable game. Yet every player tries, and now and again—very rarely—we see a man who seems to have met all the demands, challenged all the implacable averages, spurned the mere luck. He has defied baseball, even altered it, and for a time at least the game is truly his. One thinks of Willie Mays, in the best of his youth, batting at the Polo Grounds, his whole body seeming to leap at the ball as he swings in an explosion of exuberance. Or Mays in center field, playing in so close that he appears at times to be watching the game from over the second baseman's shoulder, and then that same joyful leap as he takes off after a long, deep drive and runs it down, running so hard and so far that the ball itself seems to stop in the air and wait for him. One thinks of Jackie Robinson in a close game—any close game—playing the infield and glaring in at the enemy hitter, hating him and daring him, refusing to be beaten. And Sandy Koufax pitching in the last summers before he was disabled, in that time when he pitched a no-hitter every year for four years. Kicking swiftly, hiding the ball until the last instant, Koufax throws in a blur of motion, coming over the top, and the fastball, appearing suddenly in the strike zone, sometimes jumps up so immoderately that his catcher has to take it with his glove shooting upward, like an infielder stabbing at a bad-hop grounder. I remember some batter taking a strike like that and then stepping out of the box and staring back at the pitcher with a look of utter incredulity—as if Koufax had just thrown an Easter egg past him.

Joe DiMaggio batting sometimes gave the same impression—the suggestion that the old rules and dimensions of baseball no longer applied to him and that the game had at last grown unfairly easy. I saw DiMaggio once during his famous hitting streak in 1941; I'm not sure of the other team or the pitcher—perhaps it was the Tigers and Bobo Newsom—but I'm sure of DiMaggio pulling a line shot to left that collided preposterously with the bag at third base and ricocheted halfway out to center field. That record of hitting safely in fifty-six straight games seems as secure as any in baseball, but it does not awe me as much as the fact that DiMadge's old teammates claim they *never* saw him commit an error of judgment in a ball game. Thirteen years and never a wrong throw, a cutoff man missed, an extra base passed up. Well, there was one time when he stretched a single against the Red Sox and was called out at second, but the umpire is said to have admitted later that he blew the call.

And one more for the pantheon: Carl Yastrzemski. To be precise, Yaz in September of the 1967 season, as his team, the Red Sox, fought and clawed against the White Sox and the Twins and the Tigers in the last two weeks of the closest and most vivid pennant race of our time. The presiding memory of that late summer is of Yastrzemski approaching the plate, once again in a situation where all hope rests on him, and settling himself in the batter's box—touching his helmet, tugging at his belt, and just touching the tip of the bat to the ground, in precisely the same set of gestures—and then, in a storm of noise and pleading, swinging violently and perfectly . . . and hitting. In the last two weeks of that season, Yaz batted .522—twenty-three hits for forty-four appearances:

113

four doubles, five home runs, sixteen runs batted in (RBIs). In the final two games, against the Twins, both of which the Red Sox *had* to win for the pennant, he went seven for eight, won the first game with a homer, and saved the second with a brilliant, rally-killing throw to second base from deep left field. (He cooled off a little in the World Series, batting only .400 for seven games and hitting three homers.) Since then, the game and the averages have caught up with Yastrzemski, and he has never again approached that kind of performance. But then, of course, neither has anyone else.

Only baseball, with its statistics and isolated fragments of time, permits so precise a reconstruction from box score and memory. Take another date—October 7, 1968, at Detroit, the fifth game of the World Series. The fans are here, and an immense noise—a cheerful, 53,634-man vociferosity—utterly fills the green, steep, high-walled box of Tiger Stadium. This is a good baseball town, and the cries have an anxious edge, for the Tigers are facing almost sure extinction. They trail the Cardinals by three games to one, and never for a moment have they looked the equal of these defending World Champions. Denny McLain, the Tigers' thirty-one-game winner, was humiliated in the opener by the Cardinals' Bob Gibson, who set an all-time Series record by striking out seventeen Detroit batters. The Tigers came back the next day, winning rather easily behind their capable left-hander Mickey Lolich, but the Cardinals demolished them in the next two games, scoring a total of seventeen runs and again brushing McLain aside; Gibson has now

114

struck out twenty-seven Tigers, and he will be ready to pitch again in the Series if needed. Even more disheartening is Lou Brock, the Cards' left fielder, who has already lashed out eight hits in the first four games and has stolen seven bases in eight tries; Bill Freehan, the Tigers' catcher, has a sore arm. And here, in the very top of the first, Brock leads off against Lolich and doubles to left; a moment later, Curt Flood singles, and Orlando Cepeda homers into the left-field stands. The Tigers are down 3–0, and the fans are wholly stilled.

In the third inning, Brock leads off with another hit—a single—and there is a bitter overtone to the hometown cheers when Freehan, on a pitchout, at last throws him out, stealing, at second. There is no way for anyone to know, of course, that this is a profound omen; Brock has done his last damage to the Tigers in this Series. Now it is the fourth, and hope and shouting return. Mickey Stanley leads off the Detroit half with a triple that lands, 2 inches fair, in the right-field corner. He scores on a fly. Willie Horton also triples. With two out, Jim Northrup smashes a hard grounder directly at the Cardinal second baseman, Javier, and at the last instant the ball strikes something on the infield and leaps up and over Javier's head, and Horton scores. Luck! Luck twice over, if you remember how close Stanley's drive came to falling foul. But never mind; it's 3–2 now, and a game again.

But Brock is up, leading off once again, and an instant later he has driven a Lolich pitch off the left-field wall for a double. Now Javier singles to left, and Brock streaks around third base toward home. Bill Freehan braces himself in front of the plate, waiting for the throw; he has had a miserable Series, going hitless in fourteen at bats so far and undergoing those repeated humiliations by the man who is now racing at him full speed—the man who must surely be counted, along with Gibson, as the Series hero. The throw comes in chest high on the fly from Willie Horton in left; ball and base runner arrive together; Brock does not slide. Brock does not slide, and his left foot, just descending on the plate, is banged away as he collides with Freehan. Umpire Doug Harvey shoots up his fist: out! It is a great play. Nothing has changed, the score is still 3–2, but everything has changed; something has shifted irrevocably in this game.

In the seventh inning, with one out and the Tigers still one run shy, Tiger manager Mayo Smith allows Lolich to bat for himself. Mickey Lolich has hit .114 for the season, and Smith has a pinch hitter on the bench named Gates Brown, who hit .370. But Lolich got two hits in his other Series start, including the first homer of his ten years in baseball. Mayo, sensing something that he will not be able to defend later if he is wrong, lets Lolich bat for himself, and Mickey pops a foolish little fly to right that falls in for a single. Now there is another single. A walk loads the bases, and Al Kaline comes to the plate. The noise in the stadium is insupportable. Kaline singles, and the Tigers go ahead by a run. Norm Cash drives in another. The Tigers win this searching, turned-about, lucky, marvelous game by 5–3.

Two days later, back in St. Louis, form shows its other face as the Tigers rack up ten runs in the third inning and win by 13–1. McLain at last has his Series win. So it is Lolich against Gibson in the finale, of course. Nothing happens. Inning after inning goes by, zeroes accumulate on the scoreboard, and anxiety and silence lengthen like shadows. In the sixth, Lou Brock singles. Daring Lolich, daring the Tiger infielders' nerves, openly forcing his luck, hoping perhaps to settle these enormous tensions and difficulties with one more act of bravado, he takes an excessive lead off first, draws the throw from Lolich, breaks for second, and is erased, just barely, by Cash's throw. A bit later, Curt Flood singles, and, weirdly, he, too, is picked off first and caught in a rundown. Still no score. Gibson and Lolich, both exhausted, pitch on. With two out in the seventh, Cash singles for the Tigers' second hit of the day. Horton is safe on a slow bouncer that *just* gets through the left side of the infield. Jim Northrup hits the next pitch deep and high but straight at Flood, who is the best center fielder in the National League. Flood starts in and then halts, stopping so quickly that his spikes churn up a green flap of turf; he turns and races back madly, but the ball sails over his head for a triple. Disaster. Suddenly, irreversibly, it has happened. Two runs are in, Freehan doubles in another, and, two innings later, the Tigers are Champions of the World.

I think I will always remember those two games —the fifth and the seventh—perfectly. And I remember something else about the 1968 Series when it was over—a feeling that almost everyone seemed to share: that Bob Gibson had not lost that last game and the Cardinals had not lost the Series.

Certainly no one wanted to say that the Tigers had not won it, but there seemed to be something more that remained to be said. It was something about the levels and demands of the sport we had seen—as if the baseball itself had somehow surpassed the players and the results. It was the baseball that won.

Always, it seems, there is something more to be discovered about this game. Sit quietly in the upper stand and look at the field. Half close your eyes against the sun so that the players recede a little and watch the movements of baseball. The pitcher, immobile on the mound, holds the inert white ball, his little lump of physics. Now, with abrupt gestures, he gives it enormous speed and direction, converting it suddenly into a line, a moving line. The batter, wielding a plane, attempts to intercept the line and acutely alter it, but he fails; the ball, a line again, is redrawn to the pitcher, in the center of this square, the diamond. Again the pitcher studies his task—the projection of his next line through the smallest possible segment of an invisible seven-sided solid (the strike zone has depth as well as height and width) 60 feet and 6 inches away; again the batter considers his even more difficult proposition, which is to reverse this imminent white speck, to redirect its energy not in a soft parabola or a series of diminishing squiggles but into a beautiful and dangerous new force, of perfect straightness and immense distance. In time, these and other lines are drawn on the field; the batter and the fielders are also transformed into fluidity, moving and converging, and we see now that all movement in baseball is a convergence toward fixed points—the pitched ball toward the plate, the thrown ball toward the right angles of the bases, the batted ball toward the as yet undrawn but already visible point of congruence with either the ground or a glove. Simultaneously, the fielders hasten toward that same point of meeting with the ball, and both the base runner and the ball, now redirected, toward their encounter at the base. From our perch, we can sometimes see three or four or more such geometries appearing at the same instant on the green board below us and, mathematicians that we are, can sense their solution even before they are fully drawn. It is neat, it is pretty, it is satisfying. Scientists speak of the profoundly moving aesthetic beauty of mathematics, and perhaps the baseball field is one of the few places where the rest of us can glimpse this mystery.

The last dimension is time. Within the ballpark, time moves differently, marked by no clock except the events of the game. This is the unique, unchangeable feature of baseball and perhaps explains why this sport, for all the enormous changes it has undergone in the past decade or two, remains somehow rustic, unviolent, and introspective. Baseball's time is seamless and invisible, a bubble within which players move at exactly the same pace and rhythms as all their predecessors. This is the way the game was played in our youth and in our fathers' youth, and even back then—back in the country days—there must have been the same feeling that time could be stopped. Since baseball time is measured only in outs, all you have to do is succeed utterly; keep hitting, keep the rally alive, and you have defeated time. You remain forever young. Sitting in the stands, we sense this, if only dimly. The players below us—Mays, DiMaggio, Ruth, Snodgrass—swim and blur in memory, the ball floats over to Terry Turner, and the end of this game may never come.

BOXING

JOYCE CAROL OATES
On Boxing

In this overview of the psyches of various champion fighters, Joyce Carol Oates scrutinizes the necessarily dual nature of a fighter, how the seemingly nonviolent person in daily life can transform himself into a deadly fighter in the ring. She points to Jake LaMotta who believed he deserved to die (convinced he had murdered someone during a robbery) and fearlessly welcomed punishment in the ring, and to vicious Sonny Liston, convicted of armed robbery, who took boxing lessons while serving time in the penitentiary. On the other hand Floyd Patterson, considered an essentially nonviolent man, once helped an opponent with his mouthpiece.

She recalls the "killer instinct" of Dempsey who most spectators felt wanted nothing less than to kill his opponent and Dempsey's "disdain for strategies of self-defense." But the "killer instinct" of present-day fighters is now far more tightly controlled by the early interference of referees, leading to what some call the feminization *of the sport.*

We fighters understand lies. What's a feint?
What's a left hook off the jab?
What's an opening? What's thinking one thing
and doing another . . . ?

—José Torres,
former light-heavyweight champion of the world

One of the primary things boxing is about is lying. It's about systematically cultivating a double personality: the self in society, the self in the ring. As the chess grandmaster channels his powerful aggressive impulses onto the game board, which is the world writ small, so the "born" boxer channels his strength into the ring, against the Opponent. And in the ring, if he is a good boxer and not a mere journeyman, he will cultivate yet another split personality, to thwart the Opponent's game plan vis-à-vis *him*. Boxers, like chess players, must think on their feet—must be able to improvise in mid-fight, so to speak.

(And surely it is championship chess, and not boxing, that is our most dangerous game—at least so far as psychological risk is concerned. Megalomania and psychosis frequently await the grand master when his extraordinary mental powers can no longer be discharged onto the chessboard.)

After his upset victory against WBC junior welterweight Billy Costello in August 1985 the virtually unknown "Lightning" Lonnie Smith told an interviewer for *The Ring* that his model for boxing was that of a chess game: boxing is a "game of control, and, as in chess, this control can radiate in circles *from* the center, or in circles *toward* the center . . .

124

The entire action of a fight goes in a circle; it can be little circles in the middle of the ring or big circles along the ropes, but always a circle. The man who wins is the man who controls the action of the circle." Smith's ring style against Costello was so brazenly idiosyncratic—reminiscent at moments of both Muhammad Ali and Jersey Joe Walcott—that the hitherto undefeated Costello, known as a hard puncher, was totally demoralized, outclassed, outboxed. (As he was outfought some months later by a furious Alexis Arguello, who "retired" Costello from the ring.)

Cassius Clay/Muhammad Ali, that most controversial of champions, was primarily a brilliant ring strategist, a prodigy in his youth whose fast hands and feet made him virtually impossible for opponents to hit. What joy in the young Ali: in the inimitable arrogance of a heavyweight who danced about his puzzled opponents with his gloves at waist level, inviting them to hit him—to try it. (What joy, at any rate, in the Ali of films and tapes, even if in somber juxtaposition to the Ali of the present time, overweight, even puffy, his speech and reactions slowed by Parkinson's disease.) It was the young boxer's style when confronted with a "deadly" puncher like Sonny Liston to simply out-think and -maneuver him: never before, and never since, has a heavyweight performed in the ring with such style—an inimitable combination of intelligence, wit, grace, irreverence, cunning. So dazzlingly talented was Ali in his youth that it wasn't clear whether in fact he had what boxers call "heart"—the ability to keep fighting when one has been hurt. In later years, when Ali's speed was diminished, a new and more complex, one might say a greater, boxer emerged, as in the trilogy of fights with Joe Frazier, the first of which Ali lost.

Sugar Ray Leonard, the most charismatic of post-Ali boxers, cultivated a ring style that was a quicksilver balance of opposites, with an overlay of street-wise, playful arrogance (reminiscent, indeed, of Ali), and, for all Leonard's talent, it was only in his most arduous matches (with Hearns and Durán) that it became clear how intelligently ferocious a boxer he really was. Losing once to Durán, he could not lose a second time: his pride would not allow it. Just as pride would not allow Leonard to continue boxing when he suspected he had passed his peak. (Though at the time of this writing Leonard has publicly declared that he wants to return for one major match: *he* is the only man who knows how to beat Marvin Hagler. A matter of ego, Leonard says, as if we needed to be told.)

The self in society, the self in the ring. But there are many selves and there are of course many boxers —ranging from the shy, introverted, painfully inarticulate Johnny Owen (the Welsh bantamweight who died after a bout with Lupe Pintor in 1979) to the frequently manic Muhammad Ali in his prime (Ali whom Norman Mailer compared to a six-foot parrot who keeps screaming at you that he is the center of the stage: "Come here and get me, fool. You can't, 'cause you don't know who I am"); from the legendary bluster of John L. Sullivan to the relative modesty of Rocky Marciano and Floyd Patterson. (Patterson, the youngest man to win the heavyweight title, is said to have been a nonviolent person who once helped an opponent pick up his mouthpiece from the canvas. "I don't like to see blood," Patterson explained. "It's different when I bleed, that doesn't bother me because I can't see it." He was no match physically or otherwise for the next heavyweight champion, Sonny Liston.) For every boxer with the reputation of a Roberto Durán there are surely a dozen who are simply "nice guys"—Ray Mancini, Milton Mc-Cory, Mark Breland, Gene Hatcher, among many others. Before he lost decisive matches and began the downward trajectory of his career the young Chicago middleweight John Collins was frequently promoted as a veritable split personality, a "Dr. Jekyll/Mr. Hyde" of the ring: the essential (and surely disingenuous) question being, How can a nice courteous young man like you turn so vicious in the ring? Collins's answer was straightforward enough: "When I'm in the ring I'm fighting for my life."

It might be theorized that fighting activates in certain people not only an adrenaline rush of exquisite pleasure but an atavistic self that, coupled with an instinctive sort of tissue-intelligence, a neurological swiftness unknown to "average" men and women, makes for the born fighter, the potentially great champion, the *unmistakably* gifted boxer. An outlaw or non-law self, given the showy accolade "killer instinct." (Though to speak of instinct is always to speak vaguely: for how can "instinct" be isolated from the confluence of factors—health, economic class, familial relations, sheer good or bad luck—that determine a life?) You know the boxer with the killer instinct when the crowd jumps

127

to its feet in a ground swell of delirium in response to his assault against his opponent, no matter if the opponent is the favorite, a "nice guy" no one really wants to see seriously injured.

There is an instinct in our species to fight but is there an instinct to *kill?* And would a "born" killer have the discipline, let alone the moral integrity, to subordinate himself to boxing's rigors in order to exercise it? Surely there are easier ways: we read about them in the daily newspaper. That the fighter, like the crowd he embodies, responds excitedly to the sight of blood—"first blood" being a term from the days of the English Prize Ring —goes without saying; but there are often fight fans shouting for a match to be stopped at the very zenith of the action. My sense of the boxing crowd in a large arena like Madison Square Garden is that it resembles a massive wave containing counter-waves, counter-currents, isolated but bold voices that resist the greater motion toward ecstatic violence. These dissenters are severely critical of referees who allow fights to go on too long.

(I seem to recall my father urging a fight to be stopped: "It's over! It's over! What's the point!" Was it Marciano battering an opponent into submission, or Carmen Basilio? Kid Gavilan? A long time ago, and in our home, the bloody match broadcast over television, hence sanitized. One cannot really imagine the impact of blows on another man's head and body by way of the television screen in its eerily flattened dimensions . . .)

Granted these points, it is nonetheless true that the boxer who functions as a conduit through which the inchoate aggressions of the crowd are

128

consummated will be a very popular boxer indeed. Not the conscientious "boxing" matches but the cheek-by-jowl brawls are likely to be warmly recalled in boxing legend: Dempsey-Firpo, Louis-Schmeling II, Zale-Graziano, Robinson-LaMotta, Pep-Saddler, Marciano-Charles, Ali-Frazier, most recently Hagler-Hearns. Sonny Liston occupies a position *sui generis* for the very truculence of his boxing persona—the air of unsmiling menace he presented to the Negro no less than the white world. (Liston was arrested nineteen times and served two prison terms, the second term for armed robbery.) It may be that former champion Larry Holmes saw himself in this role, the black man's black man empowered by sheer bitterness to give hurt where hurt is due. And, for a while, the Rastafarian Livingstone Bramble, whose vendetta with Ray Mancini seems to have sprung from an unmotivated ill will.

The only self-confessed murderer of boxing distinction seems to have been the welterweight champion Don Jordan (1958–60) who claimed to have been a hired assassin as a boy in his native Dominican Republic. "What's wrong with killing a human?" Jordan asked rhetorically in an interview. "The first time you kill someone, you throw up, you get sick as a dog . . . The second time, no feeling." According to his testimony Jordan killed or helped to kill more than thirty men in the Dominican Republic, without being caught. (He seems in fact to have been in the hire of the government.) After Jordan and his family moved to California he killed a man for "personal" reasons, for which crime he was sent to reform school, aged fourteen: "I burned a man like an animal . . . I staked him to the ground. I wired his hands and his arms, and I put paper around him and I burnt him like an animal. They said, 'You are mentally sick.' " In reform school Jordan was taught how to box: entered the Golden Gloves tournament and won all his matches, and eventually competed in the Olympics, where he did less well. Under the aegis of the Cosa Nostra he turned professional and his career, though meteoric, was short-lived.

In Jake LaMotta's autobiography *Raging Bull* LaMotta attributes his success as a boxer—he was middleweight champion briefly, 1949–51, but a popular fighter for many years—to the fact that he didn't care whether he was killed in the ring. For eleven years he mistakenly believed he had murdered a man in a robbery, and, unconfessed, yet guilty, wanting to be punished, LaMotta threw himself into boxing as much to be hurt as to hurt. His background parallels Rocky Graziano's—they were friends, as boys, in reform school—but his desperation was rather more intense than Graziano's (whose autobiography is entitled *Somebody Up There Likes Me:* a most optimistic assumption). LaMotta said in an interview: "I would fight anybody. I didn't care who they were. I even wanted to fight Joe Louis. I just didn't care . . . But that made me win. It gave me an aggression my opponents never saw before. They would hit me. I didn't care if I got hit." When LaMotta eventually learned that his victim had not died, however, his zest for boxing waned, and his career began its abrupt decline. By way of LaMotta's confession and the film based fragmentarily on it, *Raging Bull*, LaMotta has entered boxing folklore: he is the flashy gutter fighter whose integrity will allow him to throw only one fight (in an era in which fights were routinely thrown), done with such ironic disdain that the boxing commission suspends his license.

Traditionally, boxing is credited with changing the lives of ghetto-born or otherwise impoverished youths. It is impossible to gauge how many boxers have in fact risen from such beginnings but one might guess it to be about 99 percent—even at the present time. (Muhammad Ali is said to have been an exception in that his background was not one of desperate poverty: which helps to account, perhaps, for Ali's early boundless confidence.) Where tennis lessons were offered in some youth centers in the Detroit area, many years ago, boxing lessons were offered in Joe Louis's and Ray Robinson's neighborhood—of course. To what purpose would poor black boys learn tennis? LaMotta, Graziano, Patterson, Liston, Hector Camacho, Mike Tyson— all learned to box in captivity, so to speak. (Liston, a more advanced criminal than the others, began taking boxing lessons while serving his second term for armed robbery in the Missouri State Penitentiary.) Boxing is the moral equivalent of war of which, in a radically different context, William James spoke, and it has the virtue—how American, this virtue!—of making a good deal of money for its practitioners and promoters, not all of whom are white.

Indeed, one of the standard arguments for *not* abolishing boxing is in fact that it provides an outlet for the rage of disenfranchised youths, mainly black or Hispanic, who can make lives for themselves by way of fighting one another instead of fighting society.

The disputable term "killer instinct" was coined in reference to Jack Dempsey in his prime: in his famous early matches with Jess Willard, Georges Carpentier, Luis Firpo ("The Wild Bull of the Pampas"), and other lesser known boxers whom he savagely and conclusively beat. Has there ever been a fighter quite like the young Dempsey?— the very embodiment, it seems, of hunger, rage, the will to do hurt; the spirit of the Western frontier come East to win his fortune. The crudest of nightmare figures, Dempsey is gradually refined into an American myth of comforting dimensions. The killer in the ring becomes the New York *restaurateur*, a business success, "the gentlest of men."

Dempsey was the ninth of eleven children born to an impoverished Mormon sharecropper and itinerant railroad worker in Colorado who soon left home, bummed his way around the mining camps and small towns of the West, began fighting for money when he was hardly more than a boy. It was said in awe of Dempsey that his very sparring partners were in danger of being seriously injured —Dempsey didn't like to share the ring with anyone. If he remains the most spectacular (and most loved) champion in history it is partly because he fought when boxing rules were rather casual by our standards; when, for instance, a boxer was allowed to strike an opponent as he struggled to his feet—

132

as in the bizarre Willard bout, and the yet more bizarre bout with Luis Firpo, set beside which present-day heavyweight matches like those of Holmes and Spinks are minuets. Where aggression has to be cultivated in some champion boxers (Tunney, for example) Dempsey's aggression was direct and natural: in the ring, he seems to have wanted to kill his opponent. The swiftness of his attack, his disdain for strategies of defense, endeared him to greatly aroused crowds who had never seen anything quite like him before.

(Dempsey's first title fight, in 1919, against the aging champion Jess Willard, was called at the time "pugilistic murder" and would certainly be stopped in the first round—in the first thirty seconds of the first round—today. Badly out of condition, heavier than the twenty-four-year-old Dempsey by seventy pounds, the thirty-seven-year-old Willard put up virtually no defense against the challenger. Though films of the match show an astonishing resilient, if not foolhardy, Willard picking himself up off the canvas repeatedly as Dempsey knocks him down, by the end of the fight Willard's jaw was broken, his cheekbone split, nose smashed, six teeth broken off at the gum, an eye was battered shut, much damage done to his lower body. Both boxers were covered in Willard's blood. Years later Dempsey's estranged manager Kearns confessed, perhaps fraudulently, that he had "loaded" Dempsey's gloves—treated his hand tape with a talcum substance that turned hard as concrete when wet.)

It was Dempsey's ring style—swift, pitiless, always direct and percussive—that changed American boxing forever. Even Jack Johnson appears stately by contrast.

So far as "killer instinct" is concerned Joe Louis was an anomaly, which no biography of his life— even the most recent, the meticulously researched *Champion—Joe Louis, Black Hero in White America* by Chris Mead—has ever quite explained. If, indeed, one can explain any of our motives, except in the most sweeping psychological and sociological terms. Louis was a modest and self-effacing man outside the ring, but, in the ring, a machine of sorts for hitting—so (apparently) emotionless that even sparring partners were spooked by him. "It's the eyes," one said. "They're blank and staring, always watching you. That blank look—that's what gets you down." Unlike his notorious predecessor Jack Johnson and his yet more notorious successor Muhammad Ali, Joe Louis was forced to live his "blackness" in secret, if at all; to be a *black* hero in *white* America at the time of Louis's coming-of-age cannot have been an easy task. Louis's dead-pan expression and his killer's eyes were very likely aspects of the man's strategy rather than reliable gauges of his psyche. And his descent into mental imbalance—paranoia, in particular—in his later years was surely a consequence of the pressures he endured, if not an outsized, but poetically valid, response to the very real scrutiny of others focused upon him for decades.

One of the most controversial of boxing legends has to do with the death of Benny "Kid" Paret at the hands of Emile Griffith in a welterweight match in Madison Square Garden in 1962. According to the story Paret provoked Griffith at their weigh-in by calling him *maricón* (faggot), and was in effect killed by Griffith in the ring that night. Recalling the event years later Griffith said he was only following his trainer's instructions—to hit Paret, to hurt Paret, to keep punching Paret until the referee made him stop. By which time, as it turned out, Paret was virtually dead. (He died about ten days later.)

Though there are other boxing experts, present at the match, who insist that Paret's death was accidental: it "just happened."

At the present time boxing matches are usually monitored by referees and ringside physicians with extreme caution: a recent match between welterweights Don Curry and James Green was stopped by the referee because Green, temporarily disabled, had lowered his gloves and *might have been hit*; a match between heavyweights Mike Weaver and Michael Dokes was stopped within two minutes of the first round, before the luckless Weaver had time to begin. With some exceptions—the Sandoval-Canizales and the Bramble-Crawley title fights come most immediately to mind—referees have been assuming ever greater authority in the ring so that it sometimes seems that the drama of boxing has begun to shift: not will X knock out his opponent, but will the referee stop the fight before he can do so. In the most violent fights the predominant image is that of the referee hovering at the periphery of the action, stepping in to embrace a weakened or defenseless man in a gesture of paternal solicitude. This image carries much emotional power—not so sensational as the killing blow but suggestive, perhaps, that the ethics of the ring have evolved to approximate the ethics of everyday life. It is as if, in mythical terms, brothers whose mysterious animosity has brought them to battle are saved—absolved of their warriors' enmity—by the wisdom of their father and protector. One came away from the eight-minute Hagler-Hearns fight with the vision of the dazed Hearns, on his feet but not fully conscious, saved by referee Richard Steele from what would have been serious injury, if not death—considering the extraordinary ferocity of Hagler's fighting that night, and the personal rage he seems to have brought to it. ("This was war," Hagler said.) The fight ends with Hearns in Steele's embrace: tragedy narrowly averted.

Of course there are many who disdain such developments. It's the *feminization* of the sport, they say.

PAUL GALLICO

Jack Dempsey

The young sportswriter Paul Gallico, looking for some colorful material for the Daily News, *challenged the champion Jack Dempsey to a practice round while covering Dempsey's training camp in 1923. Dempsey, who had a reputation for dangerous cruelty in the ring, responded good-naturedly and did Gallico the favor of taking him on. Although the round turned out as expected, Gallico's ingenuity at turning up a story delighted his boss, and he was shortly thereafter promoted to sports editor. As this event had a momentous impact on his life, Gallico assures the reader the knockout blow, the split lip, and bloody nose were well worth it.*

In this retrospective piece on Dempsey's life and times, Gallico portrays one of the great athletes of the twenties and describes several of his heart-stopping fights.

During my thirteen-year tenure at the sports desk of the *Daily News*, I saw Jack Dempsey fight only four times. In those four bouts he was defeated twice and in the other two, which he won by knockouts, each time he came close to being knocked out himself.

Yet, of all the fighters I have ever known and

137

heavyweight champions I have seen in action, Dempsey still rules over my imagination as the greatest, most exciting and dramatic.

And here again you must not think I am trying to say that fighters then were better or harder hitters than ours of today, and perhaps Sonny Liston would have made mincemeat of Dempsey (or perhaps not?). My story is that in addition to being the heavyweight champion of the world, Jack Dempsey was a tremendous personality, one of the most engaging and arresting in the entire realm of what we considered the giants of sports of the 1920s.

And, for that matter, he still is. The old magic still clings to him as it did in the years back, even long after his retirement. I had the most astonishing example of this when I visited him in April 1964 at his restaurant on Broadway in the fifties. The place was packed at the luncheon hour with visitors from out of town. The great majority of them were middle-aged women who must have been little girls, or infants in arms back in the twenties, Dempsey's heyday.

One would have thought that his customers would have been drawn largely from the old-timers among the men who remembered him as the hero of their youth, and would visit him to shake his hand and hear him say, "Well, hello there! How's my old pal from Ashtabula?"

But no, the place was filled instead with clucking hens who were there, I suspect, not because of what Dempsey once was, but for what he still is today, a virile, male animal with a powerful attraction for the female sex.

He was always a spectacular person with an extraordinarily dynamic aura, and I was aware of this from the very first when I knew him as a young man.

When he entered a crowded room or enclosure, such as a gathering after a football game, or a World Series, suddenly there was no one else but Jack Dempsey there. All others, celebrity, star, champion, or ex-champion faded into insignificance before the amazing magnetism of this dark-haired, dark-visaged man with the lithe, panther-like movements and the quick, friendly smile. He was never less than twelve feet tall.

He overshadowed his era, which stretched roughly from July 4, 1919, when he knocked out Jess Willard, until 1932, when he retired for the last time. He served as creator, actor, villain, and hero in a thrilling human story whose excitement and import extended far beyond prize fighting. At the end he became inextricably enmeshed with another engrossing, true-to-life melodrama, that of his successor and the man who dethroned him, Gene Tunney.

It may be difficult for this generation to understand how involved all of us were at one time or another, in some way, with the Dempsey story and how many people, men, women, and children, who never even came near to a prize ring or an arena, or ever saw a gloved blow struck, were influenced by him and felt the impact of his individuality, his rise and his fall. . . .

In the days of Jem Mace, Tom Cribb, Sayres, Heenan, Molineaux, and similar bare-knuckle fighters who performed for Beau Brummel and other Regency dandies and British sports, the occupation with the prize ring was largely an excuse for the exchange of wagers and a kind of clinical interest in how long men could last in fights that went on for as many as seventy, eighty, or a hundred rounds. A round terminated when one or the other, or both, of the battlers hit the turf, either knocked or thrown down. Certain professional bullies enjoyed aristocratic patronage but concern for them, their characters, or their lives there was none, and in this they resembled the paid gladiators of ancient times. It was the immediate outcome of the match that mattered and not the participants, or how they might be affected.

It was not until 1892, when Gentleman Jim Corbett, a speedy, dapper, trimly muscled Fancy Dan, knocked out the beefy, beery, hitherto unbeatable heavyweight champion of the world, John L. Sullivan, that it was first suspected that there might be a dramatic tale in the personality and background of the fighter himself. Thereafter the combination of legalized boxing following upon World War I, the removal of much of the social ostracism connected with its earlier and more sordid days, and the appearance upon the scene of men who not only had stories but who also *were* stories, and lived them right out in the glaring spotlight of increased newspaper publicity, inaugurated the most flourishing and thrilling era in the entire history of fist fighting.

At one championship prize fight, when the challenger was knocked to the floor, I heard and saw a sportswriter arise in his Working Press seat and scream at the dazed and stricken man writhing on the canvas, "Stay down, you tin-canning son-of-a-bitch!"

Here was a moment of pure and personal identification. For the fallen man had never worked any harm upon the sportswriter. They were not personal enemies. But the writer loved and admired the champion and was anathematizing and putting the gypsy curse on his opponent, so that the man he idolized might win. And in some respect the writer was even the champion himself, a hairsbreadth away from victory and no doubt saying to himself, as so many fighters have and do when they have managed to tip their adversaries over with a blow—"Stay down, you son-of-a-bitch!"

If a hardened sportswriter could find himself prey to such violent emotions and uncontrolled outbursts, what about the public, fed day in and day out upon newspaper stories pertaining to their favorites, written by the same inspired and adulating reporters?

The feeling of knowing the heavyweight champion of the world intimately, his virtues, his failings, his strength and his weakness, over a long period of time helped to draw the greatest crowds in the history of the prize ring to see him perform. There was more newspaper space to devote to these characters in those times, and more reason for allotting it, since the interest in such a man as Dempsey was constant and usually at fever heat. The result of this was that when he went into battle there was more than a title at stake. The human being whom we either loved or detested, admired or despised, was entering a kind of public ordeal and we simply had to be there, either in person or by the proxy of our newspapers or radio.

And whether or not one approved of prize fights, Jack Dempsey in association with his clever, cunning manager and alter ego, Jack Kearns, created the dramatic image of the perfect pugilist and more than this, he was Jack the Giant Killer who tumbled into the dust men who outsized and outweighed him.

My old friend will kill me for this, but he was a man of extraordinary beauty as well as virility, and if this is not the word, you, who remember him as he was in his prime, find me a better one. It was beauty in the sense of perfect proportion and the rugged, glowering visage of Lucifer, the Dark Angel; his hair blue-black, his eyes dark and snapping, the mouth cruel and determined, the chin stubborn. In his face was the best of two handsome races, the Celt and the American aborigine. His father was a West Virginia mountain man with some Choctaw blood. From his mother he inherited a Cherokee strain.

Dempsey's body was magnificently put together, trim, tapered at the waist, smoothly muscled, nothing of the bruiser or strong man about the frame or biceps, very little indeed to indicate the destroyer he was. In fact, when matched against some of the giants of the game he looked like a lightweight.

Into the ring with him he carried a swelling truculence that surged up from deep inside him somewhere, exploding into unimaginable violence which found an echo in the aggressiveness lurking in every male. It was this link between the at-

142

tacker on the platform and the spectators that brought the crowd roaring to its feet, experiencing vicariously this unquenchable ferocity as a personal catharsis.

Dempsey, like many champions, was not always popular because of two main issues, neither of which was valid. One was his record in World War I and the other his alleged avoidance of a Negro heavyweight challenger by the name of Harry Wills.

Regarding the affair of World War I, there was a dark shadow behind Dempsey, like Mephisto at the elbow of Dr. Faustus. His name was Jack Kearns, manager. Kearns had not nursed and raised a million-dollar heavyweight championship prospect to be a target for something a boxer couldn't block—shot and shell. And so he put him into a shipyard and gave him a riveter's gun, instead of a khaki uniform and a rifle.

This was indeed naughty and reprehensible but the blame must rest upon Kearns and not on Dempsey. The former was never exactly a sweet-smelling article except when, as was his habit, he dowsed himself with *eau de cologne*. He was devious, untruthful, unscrupulous, but quick-witted, and everything else that a great manager of a prize fighter ought to be.

In his early days Dempsey was completely untutored and ignorant, not only in the ways of the prize ring, but of the world as well. Kearns who, from the very beginning of their association, was getting him more money for bouts than he ever dreamed existed, seemed a super brain to him and he was content to put himself wholly into his

hands. Whenever Dempsey was asked about anything he would say invariably, "Talk to Kearns.
He's the doctor," from which Kearns eventually
derived his nickname, "Doc."

If the Doc made an egregious error with the
shipyard business, it must be remembered that
right up to our actual involvement in World War
I we were singing a popular song entitled, "I
Didn't Raise My Boy To Be A Soldier," which
largely expressed the national sentiment until replaced by the trumpet call of George M. Cohan's
"Over There!" We were pacifist, constantly quoting George Washington's strictures against becoming involved in foreign wars, and a large part of
the population was pro-German as well.

Neither Kearns and certainly not the naïve
Dempsey were bright enough to guess that within
a year those same moms who had not raised their
boys to be soldiers would turn into female, recruiting harpies, harrying young men into uniform and
chanting lays about what we were going to do to
Kaiser Bill. The truth was that there was not an
ounce of beagle in Dempsey ever. He was no more
afraid of being a soldier than he was of being a
fighter, as he proved when, in World War II, as
a Commander in the U.S. Coast Guard on an
inspection tour in the Pacific, he jumped ship to
mingle in the desperate struggle for Okinawa.

It was unforgivably stupid of the otherwise clever
Kearns so to damage the image of his meal-ticket.
For had he permitted Dempsey to enlist, his charge
would probably have faced no dangers greater than
that of becoming an athletic or boxing instructor
in some soldier camp. And yet even this piece of

idiocy could be turned into gold in those postwar days. For when Tex Rickard matched Dempsey with the Frenchman Georges Carpentier at Boyle's 30 Acres in Jersey City in 1921, the result was the first million-dollar gate in the history of prize fighting. As a matter of fact, so many wanted to see Dempsey the villain get his from hero Carpentier, that the gate was only two hundred thousand short of *two* million dollars.

Ringwise it was a gross mismatch, Carpentier being little more than a heavy middleweight. But in those days the scenario was the magnet that drew record crowds to the box office. Once the bell rang, Dempsey threw away the script and dealt romance a body blow by knocking the Frenchman kicking in four rounds, after having received and weathered only one serious right-hand punch from his lighter opponent.

What price, then, Kearns' error? Dempsey's share of this gate was close to a third of a million dollars.

It was equally ridiculous to charge that Dempsey was afraid to defend his title against Harry Wills. Black and white was a political football then, as it is now, though for different reasons. We, who have lived comfortably and pleasurably under the long reign of Joe Louis and now are subjects of heavyweights Sonny Liston and Cassius Clay (whichever one happens to have possession of the ball at the moment) cannot imagine how nervous and squeamish we were then at the thought of another Negro heavyweight champion. This was due perhaps in part to the unfortunate behavior of white and black during the tenure of Jack Johnson from 1908 to 1915. I remember in my boyhood days a period of national idiocy when every up-and-coming Caucasian heavyweight was dubbed a White Hope.

Again the facts are that Dempsey was no more afraid of fighting Harry Wills than he was of fighting anyone else. Actually Tex Rickard never wanted to promote a Dempsey-Wills fight and when pressure of public opinion, whipped up by newspaper criticism, forced Kearns to sign Dempsey for a Wills bout, William Muldoon, then chairman of the New York State Athletic Commission, forbade the fight. No one behaved normally or sensibly during this curious period, but it was Dempsey who was wrongly pilloried.

I saw and met Dempsey for the first time during the summer of 1923 when, as a raw cub reporter from the sports department, I was sent to Saratoga Springs to write some color stories on his training camp. I braced him one hot afternoon on the porch of his cottage to ask him whether he would spar a round with me to enable me to write a story about it. I remember how he looked, not quite as tall as I, clad in an old, gray sweater, still crinkle-nosed then, three days' growth of beard, with his curiously high-pitched voice and body always restless and moving.

Much has been written about Dempsey in his heyday, about his viciousness, his cruelty, and the killer in him, but the truth is that he was basically a good-hearted man. It was a kindly act for him to consent, on the eve of an important defense of his title, to take on an unknown reporter in order that he might not fail in his assignment; one, incidentally, who stood an inch and a half taller and outweighed him by ten pounds.

You might not consider it a kindness to deal out a split lip, a bloody nose, and a knockout, left hook to the chin to a tyro, but it is results that count, and the ten seconds I spent unconscious on the canvas were the turning point of my career. For so amused was Captain Patterson by the affair that shortly afterward he made me sports editor and gave me a daily column to write. It was also one of the few instances when Dempsey stood out against his manager, for Kearns, who was absent at my first meeting with Jack, when the champion agreed to take me on, was furious when he heard of the proposed bout. He pointed out the risk that Dempsey was taking of a possible injury at the hands of one who might be a ringer. I was at the time unknown, weighed a fit 195 pounds, having just graduated from the captaincy of the Columbia crew, and even looked something like a fighter, a resemblance which ended abruptly when the first Dempsey hook bounced off my chin. Dempsey's reply was to the effect that he had agreed to take me on and that he did not go back on his word.

The first fight in which I ever saw Dempsey engage was that tremendous, heart-stopping brawl at the Polo Grounds in New York City on the night of September 14, 1923, against Luis Angel Firpo, which was rightly called the Battle of the Century, for nothing like it has been seen since for thrills, chills, and pure animal savagery, unleashed over a period of three minutes and fifty-eight seconds. In this uninhibited contest there was revealed a barbarity that echoed the earliest battles of primitive man or the awful, slashing, death struggle of wild beasts hidden in the depths of some jungle. Indeed, the giant Firpo had been nicknamed and likened to a wild bull and if this was so, Dempsey was the tiger attacking for the kill.

In that opening round, which surpassed even the one at Toledo in which Dempsey wrecked the huge Willard, Firpo was knocked down six times and Dempsey twice; the latter once at the beginning for no count, by the first punch thrown by Firpo, and the second time near the close, when he was swept completely from the ring by the Argentine's blind rush and clubbing right. Pushed back onto the platform by sportswriters (more in self-defense than in an attempt to aid him), he made it to his feet before "ten" and then, though stunned and no more than semi-conscious, was carrying the fight to the giant when the bell ended the most thrilling first round in the history of the prize ring. In his corner Dempsey was still half out; he didn't know what round it was, what day of the week, or what town he was in either. Yet he rose at the bell with renewed fury to drop Firpo twice more, the last time for the full count.

This was Dempsey's great appeal to us all, the sustained pugnacity that swept him from his corner, heedless of defense, to slug, punch, and batter until his opponent no longer remained before him. In the heat of battle the niceties of ring comportment went by the board. Often many of the blows he sprayed from his weaving, cat-like crouch were low. Against Firpo, half-maddened by battle lust, he stood over the fallen challenger when he

148

knocked him down, instead of retiring to a corner for the count, and slugged him again when he had barely regained his feet. And once even stood behind him and hit him on the rise. The referee, himself stunned by the fury of the fight in which he found himself involved, let Dempsey get away with it.

No one at that time could guess that these actions would one day cost Dempsey the regaining of his lost world's championship, when failure to heed the rule to go to a neutral corner resulted in the famous Chicago long count when he had Gene Tunney on the floor, knocked out, in their second fight, only to have him recover and come on to win.

But no one ever heard William Harrison Dempsey ask for quarter either, or complain of a low punch. After the Chicago affair he admitted that what happened had been his own fault and that was the end of it.

During that great, rambunctious decade Dempsey appeared in one million-dollar extravaganza after another; the heavy in one, hero and leading man in the next. We have seen how he was cast as the villain against Georges Carpentier. He was hero again, and Jack-the-Giant-Killer, against Firpo, who outweighed him by twenty-two pounds and towered over him as well. Yet, when he entered the ring for his title defense against Gene Tunney at Philadelphia, it was Tunney, the underdog, the ex-Marine of World War I, who was cast in the role of leading man. The publicists had revived not only the war-time charges against Dempsey, but the equally untrue bill that he had avoided Harry Wills, his most persistent Negro challenger.

At the end of the ten rounds in which Tunney staggered the experts and the spectators by out-boxing Dempsey, battering one side of his face to a pulp and taking his title away from him, it needed only a single gesture to turn the tables of popularity. Back in the hotel that night his wife, the glamorous motion picture star Estelle Taylor, asked, "What happened, Ginsberg?" (her pet name for him). Dempsey grinned a crooked smile with the good side of his face and said, "Honey, I forgot to duck." The nation took the beaten villain to its heart, loved him again, and dubbed him hero. We were that naïve and that fickle.

Hero, Dempsey remained then, through the night he fought ex-sailor Jack Sharkey to earn his return bout with champion Gene Tunney. It was another million-dollar gate, a crowd of 75,000, and of this maybe there were probably no more than five thousand souls who wanted to see Sharkey win.

In this bout Dempsey came within an ace of being destroyed in the first round, in which Sharkey dealt out such punishment that Jack was barely able to wobble to his corner at its end. But it was another one of those battles so characteristic of the times, when it was the story that mattered; the ex-champion making his comeback.

It seemed that Dempsey could hardly survive another round, yet he did and subsequent ones as well, managing to regain sufficient strength to indulge in several of his exploratory probes to test out just how much character boxing had built into his opponent. In the seventh round he found out. Sharkey applied to the referee for help, foolishly dropping his hands and turning his head to the arbiter to complain of the low punches, thus offering Dempsey a gratis shot at his wide-open chin. Gratefully accepting the invitation, Dempsey left-hooked him into the ten-second oblivion and won the fight. Nobody gave a damn that night whether Dempsey's punches were high or low. Dempsey was our boy. He won!

And hero he remained up to and through the famous Battle of the Long Count in Chicago, where for all of Tunney's boxing skill, he set the crowd of 105,000 partisans aflame with excitement when, in the seventh round, like the Dempsey of old, he slugged Tunney to the floor and then threw away certain victory with his old habit of standing over his opponent. The precious seconds ticked away while Referee Dave Barry kept motioning him to a neutral corner until he obeyed, enabling Tunney's superb recuperative powers to take effect. And thereafter during the rest of that round and Tunney's equally famous back-pedaling flight to victory, the final affecting image was created of the old mauler whose aging, tired legs had failed him, stopping in mid-ring, a look of contempt on his face, motioning with his gloved hands for Tunney to stop running and come in and fight.

Dempsey retired after this battle of September 1927 but was persuaded to begin a comeback tour which started during the summer of 1931 and which ended exactly a year later. During this tour he met some 175 opponents, sometimes taking on three and four a night, and knocked out over a hundred of them. This was perhaps his most remarkable achievement. None of these were heavyweights of note, or had been heard of before, but alone for a thirty-six-year-old fighter to bounce that much beef onto the canvas in a year must be accredited as sensational. In 1932 he took on a fair-to-middling heavyweight, Kingfish Levinsky, and when he was outpointed by him, listened to the message of lost speed and hung up his gloves for good—a man rich, respected, and loved to this day.

For after all, his was one of the first of the great American sports success stories. He had fulfilled every requirement of the legend, having come up the hard way, a poor boy from the rough mining camps and clapboard ranching towns of the Far West to become a giant killer and a millionaire.

But he did more than just fulfill our romantic notions; he provided a reflection of what we hoped was our own masculinity and imagined prowess when it came to "upping" to another male and letting him have it. In the safe haven of the mind we were Dempseys all, dark destroyers against whose flying fists no man could stand. Jack, who believed that the best defense was attack, along with his willingness to take three to give one, dealt a considerable blow to the theory of the Manly Art of Self-Defense, whose greatest exponent was his twice-conqueror, Gene Tunney. But it was in the end the image of Dempsey which nurtured our aggressions and stoked our imaginations with the destructive and explosive bursts of punches he fired against the giants of the ring and which have never been forgotten.

Who, in our times, would not have wanted to be like Jack Dempsey?

CHRIS MEAD
Champion—Joe Louis

No one can now write about Joe Louis, the great heavyweight champion—some say the greatest of them all—without dealing with the status of the black athlete in America of the thirties. Louis fought at a time when blacks were wholly excluded from professional baseball and in large part from college football. (Georgia Tech refused to play Michigan unless Michigan removed its one black player from the squad.)

As a formidable athlete, Joe Louis commanded all sorts of attention from the press, thereby becoming a promising model of success for young blacks to emulate. And as World War II approached, he became the public symbol of American democracy taking on, in his fights with Max Schmeling, the representative of Fascist Germany. Louis conducted himself impeccably as a sportsman and athlete under these symbolic burdens, and set a standard of excellence that would allow the next generation of black athletes gradually to break the race barriers to the major sports. In his later life Louis suffered from financial problems and failing health, attributable to brain damage from his years of fighting.

Joe Louis's death, like so much of his life, was a media event. Newspapers, television, and radio marked Louis's passing with headlines, interruptions in regular programming, and phrases reserved for the famous—"Perhaps the greatest boxer of all time," "A great champion who restored integrity to boxing," "A man who, despite all his misfortunes, maintained his dignity and class." The words echoed an earlier generation of writers and broadcasters who had called Louis a "credit to his race."

Running through these obituary notices was a thread of condescension that wrapped Louis's memory in a cocoon of white warmth. Louis had become a pathetic figure, writers praised him without full respect because he had squandered his money and gone a little crazy in the end.

These tributes belittled a giant. Louis was the first black American to achieve lasting fame and popularity in the twentieth century. When he began to box professionally in 1934, there were no blacks who consistently appeared in white newspapers, no blacks who occupied positions of public prominence, no blacks who commanded attention from whites. Historians recognize W. E. B. DuBois and A. Philip Randolph as the most important black leaders of the 1930s; white Americans of that era would have been hard pressed to recognize their names, still less their faces. DuBois and Randolph simply did not appear in white newspapers.

A few black entertainers—Bojangles Robinson, Paul Robeson, Louis Armstrong—occasionally made the back pages of the white press. No black athlete since Jack Johnson, the first black heavy-

154

weight champion of the world, had really made an impression on the white public, and the impression Johnson had made was entirely negative. Major league baseball was for whites only. Southern college football teams often refused to play northern teams with black players. Blacks had begun to make a breakthrough in track and field during the 1932 Olympics. No one had noticed.

By September 1935, after Louis had knocked out two former heavyweight champions in four months, the American public started to acknowledge him as the best fighter in the world. Louis became a sensation. Stories about his fights, his past, his training routine, his hobbies and personal habits, appeared in sports pages around the country. By 1936, Damon Runyon could write, "It is our guess that more has been written about Louis in the past two years than about any living man over a similar period of time, with the exception of Lindbergh."

The enormous popular interest in Louis was due in large part to his boxing skill. The United States was already undergoing the sports revolution that continues today; great athletes received more publicity than most statesmen or artists. But Louis was more interesting than any other athlete the white public could imagine. Louis was an anomaly: he was black. The way white sportswriters wrote about Louis revealed how novel it was for a black to reach a position of prominence. White journalists, including the best and most sophisticated writers of the day, constantly wrote about Louis's color. Nor were they satisfied with simply identifying him as a "Negro." They gave Louis alliterative nicknames like "the brown bomber," "the dark destroyer," "the tan tornado," "the sepia slugger." They patronized him, stereotyped him, quoted him in darkie dialect, said he had "pin-cushion lips," implied that he was stupid and lazy, called him a "jungle killer." This was not critical comment; it was routinely included in even the most rapturous stories about the emerging champion.

Because Louis was the only black in the white world of fame and fortune, he became the symbol of his race to both blacks and whites. To blacks, Louis was the greatest of a pitifully small pantheon of heroes. Every time he stepped into the ring against a white opponent, Louis refuted theories of white superiority. Louis's victories touched off late-night celebrations in the black neighborhoods of northern cities. Extra details of white policemen watched, half indulgently, half uneasily, as thousands of blacks rejoiced in the streets.

Many people sensed that Louis was a symbol of his race to whites as well as to blacks. Black preachers and white sportswriters lectured Louis on his responsibility: the white public judged a whole people by his actions. That added up to a lot of pressure on a shy, uneducated young man, and the legacy of Jack Johnson compounded the pressure. Johnson had openly flouted the conventions of segregated America twenty years earlier by defeating white opponents and marrying white women.

With the help of a cooperative press, Louis and his managers carefully constructed a "well-behaved" public image. Louis bought his mother a house, modestly downplayed his victories, complimented his white opponents, and married a black "girl" of good family.

At first, the white press mixed patronizing and artificial praise of Louis's behavior with racist stereotypes. But as time went on, Louis won more and more acceptance. He began to relax with reporters and won a more human image. Louis lost his reputation for invincibility in 1936 when he suffered his first professional loss, to Max Schmeling of Germany. Louis won the heavyweight title from James J. Braddock in 1937, then defended his title in a rematch against Schmeling in 1938. Schmeling was the great white hope only of Nazi Germany. The American people embraced Joe Louis, a black, as their representative. In his greatest fight, Louis knocked out Schmeling in the first round. The war with Germany that followed confirmed the fight in America's collective memory as a symbolic defeat of Nazism and racism.

World War II whitewashed Louis in a wave of patriotism. He cheerfully entered the army, and risked his title twice in charity bouts for army and navy relief. The army used Louis as grist for the war propaganda mills, a symbol of U.S. unity, racial tolerance, and willingness to serve. Louis went on morale-boosting tours for the army throughout the war, fighting exhibitions in the United States, Alaska, and Europe. Just as Louis's "good behavior" as a boxer had reassured the white public, his patriotism and loyalty reassured whites who had wondered, at least to themselves, whether a people scorned by their country would nevertheless fight for it.

After the war, the white press's treatment of

Louis changed. The alliterative nicknames disappeared, save the standard "brown bomber" and "dark destroyer." White journalists rarely identified him as a Negro; stereotyped references declined. Important newspapers praised Louis in editorials, and the praise had a more sincere and less condescending ring. The press found a word for Louis that would describe him for the rest of his life, and after—"dignity."

Louis retired for the first time in 1949. Of the forty-three men he had fought before the war, only one had been black. Now both leading contenders for his crown, Joe Walcott and Ezzard Charles, were black. Two years earlier, Jackie Robinson had become the first black to play in the major leagues. Louis had broken the ground. He had opened sports to blacks and made athletics a cutting edge of the civil rights movement.

Even after beating Louis once, Schmeling knew Louis was a dangerous and talented fighter. Schmeling expected Louis to fight cautiously, to be defensive against a man who had already knocked him out once. But an angry and inspired Louis would be an unknown quantity. And Schmeling knew where that anger and inspiration would come from. He got it just right in his memoirs:

Joe Louis, who yesterday had been celebrated by the colored population of Harlem as the exponent of an underprivileged class, was suddenly the symbol of freedom and equal rights of all men and races against the Nazi threat. Soon it also trickled through that someone had also said to Louis himself that I wanted to demonstrate in the coming fight the superiority of whites over Negroes. Joe, the Negro, found himself unwittingly in the role of a national hero, of all Americans.

It was a role that America had never before accorded to a black, and Louis accepted it without making too much of this surprising turn of events. In a ghosted article syndicated nationwide on the day of the fight, he said:

Tonight I not only fight the battle of my life to revenge the lone blot on my record, but I fight for America against the challenge of a foreign invader, Max Schmeling. This isn't just one man against another or Joe Louis boxing Max Schmeling; it is the good old U.S.A. versus Germany.

It is important to note, however, that even on the eve of a fight in which most Americans were rooting for him to defeat the symbol of Nazi Germany, Americans honored Joe Louis more as a symbol than as a man. As a boxer, his quality was still in question; many American sportswriters thought Schmeling would win. Some southern reporters, like O. B. Keeler of the *Atlanta Journal* and Bob Jones of the *Richmond Times-Dispatch*, were rooting for Schmeling.

June 22, 1938, was a Wednesday. Carl Nelson, Louis's bodyguard, woke the heavyweight champion of the world at nine A.M. Louis left for New

York City at ten, in a car with Jack Blackburn, Julian Black, John Roxborough, and Nelson, escorted by three state troopers. The car pulled up in front of the New York Boxing Commission's office at eleven. A crowd of people and newsreel cameras were waiting. Louis wore a light suit without a tie, a polka-dot scarf, a white hat with a black band around the base of the crown, and dark sunglasses with two small, perfect circles for lenses. This invisible man walked between two walls of spectators into the commission's office with slow, easy strides.

Inside, Louis stripped down to boxing shorts for the weigh-in. Schmeling was there, also in shorts. Reporters and photographers wearing suits surrounded the two athletes, staring, snapping pictures, taking notes, occasionally calling out something to Louis or Schmeling. The two fighters nodded to each other, not speaking. Schmeling weighed in at 193, Louis at 198½.

Louis spent the afternoon at a friend's apartment. At three he ate a salad and a steak, then went for a walk along the Harlem River with Blackburn and his friend Freddie Wilson. "How you feel, Joe?" Wilson asked Louis.

"I'm scared."

"Scared?" Wilson asked.

"Yeah, I'm scared I might kill Schmeling tonight," Louis said.

Louis and his party drove to Yankee Stadium at seven. "There were cops wherever you looked," Louis recalled. "When we got to the stadium, you could hardly get in. . . . Going up, we didn't

160

laugh much. Nobody made jokes. It was an important fight."

In his dressing room at Yankee Stadium, less than three hours before the most important fight of his life, Joe Louis went to sleep. Blackburn, Roxborough, Black, and the rest of Louis's entourage waited, talking softly so as not to wake their fighter. Night fell. Outside, members of the Non-Sectarian Anti-Nazi League distributed leaflets calling for a boycott of German goods. Communists handed out leaflets asking the fans to give three cheers for Louis and to boo Schmeling. Over 70,000 people walked into Yankee Stadium, filling the grandstand and bleachers that overlooked the baseball field, milling around on the infield before taking their seats in the neat rows of folding chairs that stretched away from the ring on all sides. Cigarette smoke hung in the muggy air.

At nine P.M., Blackburn woke Louis. Mike Jacobs stepped into the dressing room and said, "Joe, I told these folks you're gonna knock that German out. Don't make a sucker out of me, and make it a quick knockout." Blackburn taped Louis's hands, a familiar, soothing ritual for both of them. Blackburn stretched the tape diagonally across Louis's palms and then straight across the knuckles, curling Louis's fingers into a half fist. Blackburn said, "Keep cool. It's going to be all right." Louis watched Blackburn work, occasionally flexing his fingers to test the bandages and to feel the tape against his hands. He told Blackburn, "In three rounds, Chappie. If I don't have Schmeling knocked out, you better come in and get me, because after that, I'm through."

161

Blackburn said, "No, it's all right. You can go fifteen rounds." But Louis had no intention of letting the fight go the limit. He would either knock Schmeling out early or exhaust himself trying.

Usually Louis shadowboxed for ten minutes before a fight. This night he shadowboxed for half an hour, until it was time to go into the ring. His arms cut the air, with no opponent there to measure their speed and power, with no fans there to watch save his friends, the men who had invested in him, and the trainer who had taught him to throw those punches better than any man in the world.

When he was through, Louis put on a flannel robe and a blue silk robe over it. The champion and his handlers walked to the door of the dressing room. An escort of uniformed policemen surrounded them and led them to the ring.

In the other dressing room Max Schmeling was nervous, unusually so. He heard the cheers from the crowd as the fans caught sight of Louis, a noise that built as Louis entered the ring. Schmeling left his dressing room and walked to the ring in the middle of a police escort. The crowd applauded, but fans on the infield threw banana peels, cigarette packs, and paper cups at Schmeling as he passed. Schmeling covered his head with a towel to protect himself. Once he reached the ring policemen formed a square inside the ropes to block any more thrown objects.

Max Machon left Schmeling to go over to Louis's corner and watch as Louis put on his gloves. Doc Casey, an American who had worked Schmeling's corner for years as a second, had been so shocked by the prefight hysteria that he did not go into the ring with Schmeling. The New York Boxing Commission had banned Schmeling's manager, Joe Jacobs, from the ring because of his connection with Tony Galento, a boxer temporarily out of favor with the commission. In the middle of a sea of people, Schmeling felt lonely.

Over the radio Clem McCarthy told seventy million listeners this was "the greatest fight of our generation." Ring announcer Harry Balogh introduced Jim Braddock, Jack Sharkey, and Max Baer, all former heavyweight champions, all Louis knockout victims. The crowd booed. Balogh introduced the fighters. The crowd cheered both men but cheered louder for Louis.

Referee Arthur Donovan called the two fighters to the center of the ring for instructions. With a sixth sense, Donovan said, "I don't want anybody from your corners sticking his head through the ropes during this fight. It may cause serious trouble." The fighters went back to their corners, and the ring emptied. Louis danced and punched the air. As he waited for the bell, Louis moved up and down on his toes and hitched up his trunks. He looked anxious. Sweat shone on his brown skin.

In the other corner Max Schmeling stood still, arms hanging at his sides, and stared at Louis. Schmeling hadn't shaved. His black, shaggy eyebrows stood out on his face. Max Machon stood outside the ropes on the ring apron, his left hand patting Schmeling's arm, talking to his fighter. Machon was four or five inches shorter than Schmeling. He wore baggy gray trousers and a white long-sleeved shirt. A white towel hung around his neck. Just before the fight began, Machon dropped his arm from Schmeling's shoulder and looked across the ring at Louis. Machon looked back at Schmeling, then turned away as the bell rang.

Schmeling walked out quickly to meet Louis and wiped his brow with his right hand. The two fighters circled each other, heads and shoulders bobbing in quick jerks. Schmeling used the same stance he had in their first fight, leaning backward with his left hand up and his right cocked near his chin. Schmeling backed two steps away, and Louis followed. Louis jabbed, popping Schmeling's greased hair up, jabbed again, and dropped his shoulder for a left hook that landed to Schmeling's face. Schmeling leaned in, Louis pushed him back and threw a short left uppercut that Schmeling ducked, and they broke. Schmeling brushed his forehead with his right glove, leaned back, and waved his left out at Louis. Schmeling backed toward the ropes. Louis suddenly flew at Schmeling, feinting with his right hand, jump stepping with his left foot and throwing a left hook from the waist that went around Schmeling's right hand and landed on the side of Schmeling's head.

Schmeling leaned forward into Louis, gloves covering both sides of his head, and Louis bent down to meet him head to head in a clinch. Louis rose up with a right uppercut that Schmeling partially blocked, then rocked Schmeling back with a left and drove the German into the ropes with a right cross. Louis followed with a straight left that caught Schmeling in the eye and a right to the head,

164

Schmeling ducking with the punch and leaning into Louis.

Louis leaned back and threw a left hook that Schmeling ducked. Schmeling put out his left arm fully extended, as if to push Louis away. Louis ducked under it and leaned forward, backing Schmeling into the ropes, and threw a left just as Schmeling threw his first punch of the night, a weak right. Louis followed with an overhand right. Schmeling ducked, covered up, and leaned down, still trapped against the ropes.

The fighters clinched. Louis tried to work Schmeling's body in tight with a right that Schmeling blocked. Schmeling leaned into Louis with his head and shoulders and brought his right around Louis's arms but could not reach Louis's side with it. Louis tried another right in tight, leaned away and missed with a left hook, and they broke.

Louis immediately jabbed, then pulled his left hand back very high and ducked away, anticipating a right from Schmeling. Schmeling just jabbed weakly with his left, tickling Louis's chest. Louis jabbed, jabbed again, and crossed with a right to Schmeling's face. Schmeling clinched again. Louis pushed him away with both hands, and as Schmeling went backward, his mouth opened, and his eyebrows arched in reflexive fear. Schmeling raised his right hand in front of his face, glove open, with the thumb sticking out, but quickly backed away and resumed his stance.

Louis moved in on Schmeling again, jabbed to Schmeling's face, pulled back for a left hook that Schmeling blocked, but followed with a quick overhand right that landed solidly, driving Schmeling's head down. Schmeling clinched again. Max Machon was yelling, "Move, Max, move!" Louis pushed Schmeling away, and again Schmeling's right hand came up reflexively before he settled back into his stance.

Schmeling leaned away from Louis with an anxious look on his face. Schmeling pawed the air twice with his left. Louis pushed Schmeling's left hand away with his right and dropped down for a big left hook that Schmeling ducked, but now Schmeling was against the ropes. Louis leaned forward with the momentum of his blow, and the two fighters bent over at the waist, their heads and shoulders locked together, gloves up around their chins. Louis tried a right uppercut that Schmeling blocked, landed a weak left to Schmeling's face, drove his left solidly into Schmeling's face again, and threw an overhand right from the shoulder that won the fight. Schmeling blacked out, staggering backward, arms flailing out to catch his balance. Schmeling caught the top strand of the ropes with his right hand and held on, acting only on instinct now.

With Schmeling turned sideways to him and leaning on the ropes, Louis tried to hold Schmeling's chin in place with his left but was unable to reach Schmeling's face with a right hand, Schmeling somehow warding him off with his left arm. Louis drove a left into the middle of Schmeling's stomach. Schmeling bent over and stumbled but hung onto the rope with his right hand. Louis swung a left hook for the head, but Schmeling ducked back against the ropes, turning his body away from Louis, exposing his left side. Louis stuck out his left for Schmeling's chin, as if to hold it in place or get the range for his next punch, and threw a roundhouse right that went under Schmeling's left arm and landed on the side of Schmeling's back. The punch was so powerful that it broke two vertebrae. Schmeling screamed in pain, his mouth opening in a circle, but Louis closed Schmeling's mouth quickly with a left to the body and a left to the head, then an overhand right to the head, a left hook, and an overhand right. Schmeling leaned into the ropes and held on to them with both hands. Another left hook and overhand right made Schmeling's knees buckle; he would have gone down, but his chin caught on the top rope.

Referee Donovan stepped in and pushed Louis away, giving Schmeling a standing count. Schmeling turned, his right hand still on the top strand of the ropes, his left arm and elbow pressing against his side where Louis had hit him. Schmeling moved forward and tried to resume his stance but could not raise his left arm. Donovan hesitated and stopped counting at two. Schmeling was out on his feet and could not take advantage of the full count. The pause in the action was so brief that few spectators understood what was happening.

Louis rushed at Schmeling and threw a left-right combination that snapped Schmeling's head sideways. Schmeling fell forward and rolled over on his back, then rolled on his side. Referee Donovan nearly ran Louis to a neutral corner, but when he turned back to Schmeling, the German was already on his feet. Donovan forgot to wipe the resin from Schmeling's gloves.

Louis approached Schmeling again, and Schmeling ducked on rubbery legs. Louis stood him up with a left hook to the head and dropped Schmeling to his hands and knees with a right cross. Schmeling got up immediately, just as Donovan was beginning to lead Louis to a neutral corner. This time Donovan remembered to wipe Schmeling's gloves on his shirtfront. Schmeling looked over Donovan's shoulder at Louis, who was bouncing up and down, waiting for the referee to get out of the way. Donovan dropped Schmeling's gloves, and once more Schmeling tried to get into his stance. Louis jabbed to get the range, pushed away Schmeling's outstretched left with his right, and threw a left jab to the face, a right to Schmeling's damaged left side, a left hook and a right cross, and Schmeling fell.

Max Machon threw a white towel into the ring. Arthur Donovan led Louis to a neutral corner, where Louis waited in his usual pose, hands on top of the ropes on either side of the corner post. Donovan picked up the towel and threw it on the ropes; there it hung perfectly folded on the middle strand. New York boxing rules did not allow a fighter's corner to surrender. Only the referee could stop the fight.

In the center of the ring, Max Schmeling pushed himself up with his arms, his legs curled under him. Schmeling got to his hands and knees, tried to stand up on his right foot, failed, and went back to his knees. Donovan stood over Schmeling and picked up the count from the official timekeeper. Clem McCarthy growled to the radio audience, "The count is five. Five . . . six . . . seven . . . eight."

Max Machon ran into the ring, afraid the Americans would maim his friend. The crowd had been yelling at full volume for over a minute. Donovan pushed Machon away. Donovan knew Schmeling could not continue. Confused and hurried, with Louis's handlers rushing him from the other side of the ring, as surprised by what had happened as the crowd, Donovan quickly waved his arms over Schmeling. Donovan had stopped the fight before the count reached ten. Official result: technical knockout, at 2:04 of the first round. Donovan lifted Schmeling under the armpits and got Schmeling up on his feet. Donovan's left arm cradled Schmeling's head until Max Machon led the beaten fighter away.

After the fight Schmeling's dressing room was quiet. Schmeling told the NBC radio audience: "Ladies and gentlemen I have not much to say. I very sorry, but, I won't make any excuse, but I get such a terrible hit, the first hit I get in the left kidneys, I was so paralyzed I couldn't even move. And then after it was all over, you know." Schmeling's trainer, Max Machon, and his American manager, Joe Jacobs, claimed that Louis had hit Schmeling with an illegal kidney punch—a foul. Under the pressure of reporters' questions, Schmeling, still befuddled from the beating he had taken, also said he had been fouled. Schmeling got dressed, and an ambulance took him to Polyclinic Hospital.

Louis, as always, remained calm, and his joy

was understated. One of the many reporters who crowded around the champion in his dressing room described him as shy. Still quiet and a little uneasy around writers, Louis announced, "I'm sure enough champion now." *Life* magazine quoted Louis's recollections of the body punch that had hurt Schmeling so badly: "I just hit him, tha's all. I hit him right in the ribs and I guess maybe it was a lucky punch but man, did he scream! I thought it was a lady in the ringside cryin'. He just screamed, tha's all." Louis tried to describe his feelings after his greatest victory. "Something of a relief, I guess, I don't know. But I feel better about being champion." A reporter asked Louis if he would fight Schmeling again. "What for?" Louis replied. "Didn't I just beat him?"

In a two-minute capsule, the second Louis-Schmeling fight epitomized the qualities that made Joe Louis a great boxer. When he climbed into the ring against Schmeling, Louis faced all the pressures of an athletic championship and more. Having lost to Schmeling before, the fight would decide whether Louis would be rated a success or an also-ran; it was the crucible of his career. Moreover, he carried all the hopes of his race into a fight against the symbol of militant racism. If Louis had lost, he would have been criticized as a boxer and derided as another losing Negro. Few human beings face tests like that the Schmeling fight posed for Louis, a single event that will decide whether a life's work will be a success or a failure, with no second chances and the whole world watching. Louis was only twenty-four, and he was not the sort of man who lay awake nights thinking of all these things. It was an accident that his personal test was fraught with historic significance. Nevertheless, vibrating with the moment like some sublime tuning fork, Joe Louis tapped his sense of self, his courage, self-control, and his physical talent and performed heroically.

A. J. LIEBLING

Ahab and Nemesis:
Marciano and Moore

A stylish sportswriter, A. J. Liebling here contrasts the radically opposite strategies of fighters Rocky Marciano and Archie Moore in their 1955 confrontation at Yankee Stadium. Moore, the fighter with superior technique and intelligence takes on the younger champion Marciano, who has brute and often wildly inaccurate power as his principal weapon—but power to spare. With understated wit, Liebling pokes fun at Marciano's lack of finesse and limited knowledge of the art of boxing and admires Moore's polished, if doomed, craftsman's approach. In his entertaining analysis, Liebling interprets this fight as a compelling match between an obsessed, courageous Ahab and a white whale, and as usual, Ahab is the loser.

Back in 1922, the late Heywood Broun, who is not remembered primarily as a boxing writer, wrote a durable account of a combat between the late Benny Leonard and the late Rocky Kansas for the lightweight championship of the world. Leonard was the greatest practitioner of the era, Kansas just a rough, optimistic fellow. In the early rounds Kansas messed Leonard about, and Broun was profoundly disturbed. A radical in politics, he was a conservative in the arts, and Kansas made him think of Gertrude Stein, *Les Six,* and nonrepresentational painting, all novelties that irritated him.

"With the opening gong, Rocky Kansas tore into Leonard," he wrote. "He was gauche and inaccurate, but terribly persistent." The classic verities prevailed, however. After a few rounds, during which Broun continued to yearn for a return to a culture with fixed values, he was enabled to record, "The young child of nature who was challenging for the championship dropped his guard, and Leonard hooked a powerful and entirely orthodox blow to the conventional point of the jaw. Down went Rocky Kansas. His past life flashed before him during the nine seconds in which he remained on the floor, and he wished that he had been more faithful as a child in heeding the advice of his boxing teacher. After all, the old masters did know something. There is still a kick in style, and tradition carries a nasty wallop."

I have often thought of Broun's words in the years since Rocky Marciano, the reigning heavyweight champion, scaled the fistic summits, as they say in *Journal-Americanese,* by beating Jersey Joe Walcott. The current Rocky is gauche and inaccurate, but besides being persistent he is a dreadfully severe hitter with either hand. The predominative nature of this asset has been well stated by Pierce Egan, the Edward Gibbon and Sir Thomas Malory of the old London prize ring, who was less preoccupied than Broun with ultimate implications. Writing in 1821 of a milling cove named Bill Neat, the Bristol Butcher, Egan said, "He possesses a requisite above all the art that *teaching* can achieve for any boxer; namely, *one hit* from his right hand, given in proper distance, can gain a victory; but three of them are positively enough to dispose of a giant." This is true not only of Marciano's right hand but of his left hand, too—provided he doesn't miss the giant entirely. Egan doubted the advisability of changing Neat's style, and he would have approved of Marciano's. The champion has an apparently unlimited absorptive capacity for percussion (Egan would have called him an "insatiable glutton") and inexhaustible energy ("a prime bottom fighter"). "Shifting," or moving to the side, and "milling in retreat," or moving back, are innovations of the late eighteenth century that Rocky's advisers have carefully kept from his knowledge, lest they spoil his natural prehistoric style. Egan excused these tactics only in boxers of feeble constitution.

Archie Moore, the light-heavyweight champion of the world, who hibernates in San Diego, California, and estivates in Toledo, Ohio, is a Brounian rather than an Eganite in his thinking about style, but he naturally has to do more than think about it. Since the rise of Marciano, Moore, a cerebral and hyper-experienced light-colored pugilist who has been active since 1936, has suffered the pangs of a supreme exponent of *bel canto* who sees himself crowded out of the opera house by a guy who can only shout. As a sequel to a favorable review I wrote of one of his infrequent New York appearances, when his fee was restricted to a measly five figures, I received a sad little note signed "The most unappreciated fighter in the world, Archie Moore." A fellow who has as much style as Moore tends to overestimate the intellect—he develops

174

the kind of Faustian mind that will throw itself against the problem of perpetual motion, or of how to pick horses first, second, third, *and* fourth in every race. Archie's note made it plain to me that he was honing his harpoon for the White Whale.

When I read newspaper items about Moore's decisioning a large, playful porpoise of a Cuban heavyweight named Nino Valdes and scoop-netting a minnow like Bobo Olson, the middleweight champion, for practice, I thought of him as a lonely Ahab, rehearsing to buck Herman Melville, Pierce Egan, and the betting odds. I did not think that he could bring it off, but I wanted to be there when he tried. What would *Moby Dick* be if Ahab had succeeded? Just another fish story. The thing that is eternally diverting is the struggle of man against history—or what Albert Camus, who used to be an amateur middleweight, has called the Myth of Sisyphus. (Camus would have been a great man to cover the fight, but none of the syndicates thought of it.) When I heard that the boys had been made for September 20, 1955, at the Yankee Stadium, I shortened my stay abroad in order not to miss the Encounter of the Two Heroes, as Egan would have styled the rendezvous.

In London on the night of September 13, a week before the date set for the Encounter, I tried to get my eye in for fight-watching by attending a bout at the White City greyhound track between Valdes, who had been imported for the occasion, and the British Empire heavyweight champion, Don Cockell, a fat man whose gift for public suffering has enlisted the sympathy of a sentimental people. Since Valdes had gone fifteen rounds with Moore

175

in Las Vegas the previous May, and Cockell had excruciated for nine rounds before being knocked out by Marciano in San Francisco in the same month, the bout offered a dim opportunity for establishing what racing people call a "line" between Moore and Marciano. I didn't get much of an optical workout, because Valdes disposed of Cockell in three rounds. It was evident that Moore and Marciano had not been fighting the same class of people this season.

This was the only fight I ever attended in a steady rainstorm. It had begun in the middle of the afternoon, and, while there was a canopy over the ring, the spectators were as wet as speckled trout. "The weather, it is well known, has no terrors to the admirers of Pugilism of Life," Egan once wrote, and on his old stamping ground this still holds true. As I took my seat in a rock pool that had collected in the hollow of my chair, a South African giant named Ewart Potgieter, whose weight had been announced as 22 stone 10, was ignoring the doctrine of apartheid by leaning on a Jamaican colored man who weighed a mere 16 stone, and by the time I had transposed these statistics to 318 pounds and 224 pounds, respectively, the exhausted Jamaican had acquiesced in resegregation and retired. The giant had not struck a blow, properly speaking, but had shoved downward a number of times, like a man trying to close an overfilled trunk.

The main bout proved an even less grueling contest. Valdes, eager to get out of the chill, struck Cockell more vindictively than is his wont, and after a few gestures invocative of commiseration, the fat man settled in one corner of the ring as heavily as suet pudding upon the unaccustomed gastric system. He had received what Egan would have called a "ribber" and a "nobber," and when he arose it was seen that the latter had raised a cut on his forehead. At the end of the third round, his manager withdrew him from competition. It was not an inspiring occasion, but after the armistice eight or nine shivering Cubans appeared in the runway behind the press section and jumped up and down to register emotion and restore circulation. *"Ahora Marciano!"* they yelled. "Now for Marciano!" Instead of being grateful for the distraction, the other spectators took a poor view of it. "Sit down, you chaps!" one of them cried. "We want to see the next do!" They were still parked out there in the rain when I tottered into the Shepherd's Bush underground station and collapsed, sneezing, on a train that eventually disgorged me at Oxford Circus, with just enough time left to buy a revivifying draught before eleven o'clock, when the pubs closed. How the mugs I left behind cured themselves I never knew. They had to do it on Bovril.

Because I had engagements that kept me in England until a few days before the Encounter, I had no opportunity to visit the training camps of the rival American Heroes. I knew all the members of both factions, however, and I could imagine what they were thinking. In the plane on the way home, I tried to envision the rival patterns of ratiocination. I could be sure that Marciano, a kind, quiet, imperturbable fellow, would plan to go after Moore and make him fight continuously until he tired enough to become an accessible target. After that he would expect concussion to accentuate exhaustion and exhaustion to facilitate concussion, until Moore came away from his consciousness, like everybody else Rocky had ever fought. He would try to remember to minimize damage to himself in the beginning, while there was still snap in Moore's arms, because Moore is a sharp puncher. (Like Bill Neat of old, Marciano hits at his opponent's arms when he cannot hit past them. "In one instance, the arm of Oliver [a Neat adversary] received so paralyzing a shock in stopping the blow that it appeared almost useless," Egan once wrote.) Charlie Goldman would have instructed Marciano in some rudimentary maneuver to throw Moore's first shots off, I felt sure, but after a few minutes Rocky would forget it, or Archie would figure it out. But there would always be Freddie Brown, the "cut man," in the champion's corner to repair superficial damage. One reason Goldman is a great teacher is that he doesn't try to teach a boxer more than he can learn. What he had taught Rocky in the four years since I had first seen him fight was to shorten the arc of most of his blows without losing power thereby, and always to follow one hard blow with another—"for insurance" —delivered with the other hand, instead of recoiling to watch the victim fall. The champion had also gained confidence and presence of mind; he has a good fighting head, which is not the same thing as being a good mechanical practitioner.

"A *boxer* requires a *nob* as well as a *statesman* does a HEAD, coolness and calculation being essential to *second* his efforts," Egan wrote, and the old historiographer was never more correct. Rocky was thirty-one, not in the first flush of youth for a boxer, but Moore was only a few days short of thirty-nine, so age promised to be in the champion's favor if he kept pressing.

Moore's strategic problem, I reflected on the plane, offered more choices and, as a corollary, infinitely more chances for error. It was possible, but not probable, that jabbing and defensive skill would carry him through fifteen rounds, even on those old legs, but I knew that the mere notion of such a *gambade* would revolt Moore. He is not what Egan would have called a shy fighter. Besides, would Ahab have been content merely to go the distance with the White Whale? I felt sure that Archie planned to knock the champion out, so that he could sign his next batch of letters "The most appreciated and deeply opulent fighter in the world." I surmised that this project would prove a mistake, like Mr. Churchill's attempt to take Gallipoli in 1915, but it would be the kind of mistake that would look good in his memoirs.

The basis of what I rightly anticipated would prove a miscalculation went back to Archie's academic background. As a young fighter of conventional tutelage, he must have heard his preceptors say hundreds of times, "They will all go if you hit them right." If a fighter did not believe that, he would be in the position of a Euclidian without faith in the 180-degree triangle. Moore's strategy, therefore, would be based on working Marciano into a position where he could hit him right. He would not go in and slug with him, because that would be wasteful, distasteful, and injudicious, but he might try to cut him up, in an effort to slow him down so he could hit him right, or else try to hit him right and then cut him up. The puzzle he reserved for me—and Marciano—was the tactic by which he would attempt to attain his strategic objective. In the formation of his views, I believed, Moore would be handicapped, rather than aided, by his active, skeptical mind. One of the odd things about Marciano is that he isn't terribly big. It is hard for a man like Moore, just under six feet tall and weighing about 180 pounds, to imagine that a man approximately the same size can be immeasurably stronger than he is. This is particularly true when, like the light-heavyweight champion, he has spent his whole professional life contending with boxers—some of them considerably bigger—whose strength has proved so near his own that he could move their arms and bodies by cunning pressures. The old classicist would consequently refuse to believe what he was up against.

The light-heavyweight limit is 175 pounds, and Moore can get down to that when he must, in order to defend his title, but in a heavyweight match each Hero is allowed to weigh whatever he pleases. I was back in time to attend the weighing-in ceremonies, held in the lobby of Madison Square Garden at noon on the day set for the Encounter, and learned that Moore weighed 188 and Marciano 188¼—a lack of disparity that figured to encourage the rationalist's illusions. I also learned that, in contrast to Jack Solomons—the London promoter who held the Valdes-Cockell match in the rain—the I.B.C., which was promoting the Encounter, had decided to postpone it for twenty-four hours, although the weather was clear. The decision was based on apprehension of Hurricane Ione, which, although apparently veering away from New York, might come around again like a lazy left hook and drop in on the point of the Stadium's jaw late in the evening. Nothing like that happened, but the postponement brought the town's theaters and bars another evening of good business from the out-of-town fight trade, such as they always get on the eve of a memorable Encounter. ("Not a bed could be had at any of the villages at an early hour on the preceding evening; and Uxbridge was crowded beyond all former precedent," Egan wrote of the night before Neat beat Oliver.) There was no doubt that the fight had caught the public imagination, ever sensitive to a meeting between Hubris and Nemesis, as the boys on the quarterlies would say, and the bookies were laying eighteen to five on Nemesis, according to the boys on the dailies, who always seem to hear. (A friend of mine up from Maryland with a whim and a five-dollar bill couldn't get ten against it in ordinary barroom money anywhere, although he wanted Ahab.)

The enormous—by recent precedent—advance sale of tickets had so elated the I.B.C. that it had decided to replace the usual card of bad preliminary fights with some not worth watching at all, so there was less distraction than usual as we awaited the appearance of the Heroes on the fateful evening. The press seats had been so closely juxtaposed that I could fit in only sidewise between two colleagues—the extra compression having been caused by the injection of a prewar number of movie stars and politicos.

The tight quarters were an advantage, in a way, since they facilitated my conversation with Peter Wilson, an English prize-ring correspondent, who happened to be in the row behind me. I had last seen Mr. Wilson at White City the week before, at a time when the water level had already reached his shredded-Latakia mustache. I had feared that he had drowned at ringside, but when I saw him at the Stadium, he assured me that by buttoning the collar of his mackintosh tightly over his nostrils, he had been able to make the garment serve as a diving lung, and so survive. Like all British fight writers when they are relieved of the duty of watching British fighters, he was in a holiday mood, and we chatted happily.

There is something about the approach of a good fight that renders the spirit insensitive to annoyance; it is only when the amateur of the Sweet Science has some doubts as to how good the main bout will turn out to be that he is avid for the satisfaction to be had from the preliminaries. This is because after the evening is over, he may have only a good supporting fight to remember. There were no such doubts—even in the minds of the mugs who had paid for their seats—on the evening of September 21.

At about ten-thirty the champion and his faction entered the ring. It is not customary for the champion to come in first, but Marciano has never been a stickler for protocol. He is a humble, kindly fellow, who even now will approach an acquaintance on the street and say bashfully, "Remember

182

me? I'm Rocky Marciano." The champion doesn't mind waiting five or ten minutes to give anybody a punch in the nose. In any case, once launched from his dressing room under the grandstand, he could not have arrested his progress to the ring, because he had about forty policemen pushing behind him, and three more clearing a path in front of him. Marciano, tucked in behind the third cop like a football ball-carrier behind his interference, had to run or be trampled to death. Wrapped in a heavy blue bathrobe and with a blue monk's cowl pulled over his head, he climbed the steps to the ring with the cumbrous agility of a medieval executioner ascending the scaffold. Under the hood he seemed to be trying to look serious. He has an intellectual appreciation of the anxieties of a champion, but he has a hard time forgetting how strong he is; while he remembers that, he can't worry as much as he knows a champion should. His attendants—quick, battered little Goldman; Al Weill, the stout, excitable manager, always stricken just before the bell with the suspicion that he may have made a bad match; Al Columbo—are all as familiar to the crowd as he is.

Ahab's party arrived in the ring a minute or so later, and Charlie Johnston, his manager—a calm sparrow hawk of a man, as old and wise in the game as Weill—went over to watch Goldman put on the champion's gloves. Freddie Brown went to Moore's corner to watch *his* gloves being put on. Moore wore a splendid black silk robe with a gold lamé collar and belt. He sports a full mustache above an imperial, and his hair, sleeked down under pomade when he opens operations, invariably rises during the contest, as it gets water sloshed on it between rounds and the lacquer washes off, until it is standing up like the top of a shaving brush. Seated in his corner in the shadow of his personal trainer, a brown man called Cheerful Norman, who weighs 235 pounds, Moore looked like an old Japanese print I have of a "Shogun Engaged in Strategic Contemplation in the Midst of War." The third member of his group was Bertie Briscoe, a rough, chipper little trainer, whose more usual charge is Sandy Saddler, the featherweight champion—also a Johnston fighter. Mr. Moore's features in repose rather resemble those of Orson Welles, and he was reposing with intensity.

The procession of other fighters and former fighters to be introduced was longer than usual. The full galaxy was on hand, including Jack Dempsey, Gene Tunney, and Joe Louis, the *têtes de cuvée* of former-champion society; ordinary former heavyweight champions, like Max Baer and Jim Braddock, dock slipped through the ropes practically unnoticed. After all the celebrities had been in and out of the ring, an odd dwarf, advertising something or other—possibly himself—was lifted into the ring by an accomplice and ran across it before he could be shooed out. The referee, a large, craggy, oldish man named Harry Kessler, who, unlike some of his better-known colleagues, is not an ex-fighter, called the men to the center of the ring.

This was his moment; he had the microphone. "Now, Archie and Rocky, I want a nice, clean fight," he said, and I heard a peal of silvery laughter behind me from Mr. Wilson, who had seen both of them fight before. "Protect yourself at all times,"

Mr. Kessler cautioned them unnecessarily. When the principals shook hands, I could see Mr. Moore's eyebrows rising like storm clouds over the Sea of Azov. His whiskers bristled and his eyes glowed like dark coals as he scrunched his eyebrows down again and enveloped the Whale with the Look, which was intended to dominate his willpower. Mr. Wilson and I were sitting behind Marciano's corner, and as he came back to it, I observed his expression, to determine what effect the Look had had upon him. More than ever, he resembled a Great Dane who has heard the word "bone."

A moment later the bell rang, and the Heroes came out for the first round. Marciano, training in the sun for weeks, had tanned to a slightly deeper tint than Moore's old ivory, and Moore, at 188, looked, if anything, bigger and more muscular than Marciano; much of the champion's weight is in his legs, and his shoulders slope. Marciano advanced, but Moore didn't go far away. As usual, he stood up nicely, his arms close to his body and his feet not too far apart, ready to go anywhere but not without a reason—the picture of a powerful, decisive intellect unfettered by preconceptions. Marciano, pulling his left arm back from the shoulder, flung a left hook. He missed, but not by enough to discourage him, and then walked in and hooked again. All through the round he threw those hooks, and some of them grazed Moore's whiskers; one even hit him on the side of the head. Moore didn't try much offensively; he held a couple of times when Marciano worked in close.

Marciano came back to his corner as he always does, unimpassioned. He hadn't expected to catch

Moore with those left hooks anyway, I imagine; all he had wanted was to move him around. Moore went to his corner inscrutable. They came out for the second, and Marciano went after him in brisker fashion. In the first round he had been throwing the left hook, missing with it, and then throwing a right and missing with that, too. In the second he tried a variation—throwing a right and then pulling a shoulder back to throw the left. It appeared for a moment to have Moore confused, as a matador might be confused by a bull who walked in on his hind legs. Marciano landed a couple of those awkward hooks, but not squarely. He backed Moore over toward the side of the ring farthest from me, and then Moore knocked him down.

Some of the reporters, describing the blow in the morning papers, called it a "sneak punch," which is journalese for one the reporter didn't see but technically means a lead thrown before the other man has warmed up or while he is musing about the gate receipts. This had been no lead, and although I certainly hadn't seen Moore throw the punch, I knew that it had landed inside the arc of Marciano's left hook. ("Marciano missed with the right, trun the left, and Moore stepped inside it," my private eye, Whitey Bimstein, said next day, confirming my diagnosis, and the film of the fight bore both of us out.) So Ahab had his harpoon in the Whale. He had hit him right if ever I saw a boxer hit right, with a classic brevity and conciseness. Marciano stayed down for two seconds. I do not know what took place in Mr. Moore's breast when he saw him get up. He may have felt, for the moment, like Don Giovanni when the Commendatore's statue grabbed at him—startled because he thought he had killed the guy already—or like Ahab when he saw the Whale take down Fedallah, harpoons and all. Anyway, he hesitated a couple of seconds, and that was reasonable. A man who took nine to come up after a punch like that would be doing well, and the correct tactic would be to go straight in and finish him. But a fellow who came up on two was so strong he would bear investigation.

After that, Moore did go in, but not in a crazy way. He hit Marciano some good, hard, classic shots, and inevitably Marciano, a trader, hit him a few devastating swipes, which slowed him. When the round ended, the edge of Moore's speed was gone, and he knew that he would have to set a new and completely different trap, with diminished resources. After being knocked down, Marciano had stopped throwing that patterned right-and-left combination; he has a good nob. "He never trun it again in the fight," Whitey said next day, but I differ. He threw it in the fifth, and again Moore hit him a peach of a right inside it, but the steam was gone; this time Ahab couldn't even stagger him. Anyway, there was Moore at the end of the second, dragging his shattered faith in the unities and humanities back to his corner. He had hit a guy right, and the guy hadn't gone. But there is no geezer in Moore, any more than there was in the master of the Pequod.

Both came out for the third very gay, as Egan would have said. Marciano had been hit and cut, so he felt acclimated, and Moore was so mad at himself for not having knocked Marciano out that he almost displayed animosity toward him. He may have thought that perhaps he had not hit Marciano *just* right; the true artist is always prone to self-reproach. He would try again. A minute's attention from his squires had raised his spirits and slaked down his hair. At this point, Marciano set about him. He waddled in, hurling his fists with a sublime disregard of probabilities, content to hit an elbow, a biceps, a shoulder, the top of a head—the last supposed to be the least profitable target in the business, since, as every beginner learns, "the head is the hardest part of the human body," and a boxer will only break his hands on it. Many boxers make the systematic presentation of the cranium part of their defensive scheme. The crowd, basically anti-intellectual, screamed encouragement. There was Moore, riding punches, picking them off, slipping them, rolling with them, ducking them, coming gracefully out of his defensive efforts with sharp, patterned blows—and just about holding this parody even on points. His face, emerging at instants from under the storm of arms—his own and Rocky's—looked like that of a swimming walrus. When the round ended, I could see that he was thinking deeply. Marciano came back to his corner at a kind of suppressed dogtrot. He didn't have a worry in the world.

It was in the fourth, though, that I think Sisyphus began to get the idea he couldn't roll back the Rock. Marciano pushed him against the ropes and swung at him for what seemed a full minute without ever landing a punch that a boxer with Moore's background would consider a credit to his workmanship. He kept them coming so fast, though, that Moore tired just getting out of their way. One newspaper account I saw said that at this point Moore "swayed uncertainly," but his motions were about as uncertain as Margot Fonteyn's, or Artur Rubinstein's. He is the most premeditated and best-synchronized swayer in his profession. After the bell rang for the end of the round, the champion hit him a right for good measure—he usually manages to have something on the way all the time—and then pulled back to disclaim any uncouth intention. Moore, no man to be conned, hit him a corker of a punch in return, when he wasn't expecting it. It was a gesture of moral reprobation and also a punch that would give any normal man something to think about between rounds. It was a good thing Moore couldn't see Marciano's face as he came back to his corner, though, because the champion was laughing.

The fifth was a successful round for Moore, and I had him ahead on points that far in the fight. But it took no expert to know where the strength lay. There was even a moment in the round when Moore set himself against the ropes and encouraged Marciano to swing at him, in the hope the champion would swing himself tired. It was a confession that he himself was too tired to do much hitting.

In the sixth Marciano knocked Moore down twice—once, early in the round, for four seconds, and once, late in the round, for eight seconds, with Moore getting up just before the bell rang. In the seventh, after that near approach to obliteration, the embattled intellect put up its finest stand. Marciano piled out of his corner to finish Moore, and the stylist made him miss so often that it

189

looked, for a fleeting moment, as if the champion were indeed punching himself arm-weary. In fact, Moore began to beat him to the punch. It was Moore's round, certainly, but an old-timer I talked to later averred that one of the body blows Marciano landed in that round was the hardest of the fight.

It was the eighth that ended the competitive phase of the fight. They fought all the way, and in the last third of the round the champion simply overflowed Archie. He knocked him down with a right six seconds before the bell, and I don't think Moore could have got up by ten if the round had lasted that long. The fight by then reminded me of something that Sam Langford, one of the most profound thinkers—and, according to all accounts, one of the greatest doers—of the prize ring, once said to me: "Whatever that other man wants to do, don't let him do it." Merely by moving in all the time and punching continually, Marciano achieves the same strategic effect that Langford gained by finesse. It is impossible to think, or to impose your thought, if you have to keep on avoiding punches.

Moore's "game," as old Egan would have called his courage, was beyond reproach. He came out proudly for the ninth, and stood and fought back with all he had, but Marciano slugged him down, and he was counted out with his left arm hooked over the middle rope as he tried to rise. It was a crushing defeat for the higher faculties and a lesson in intellectual humility, but he had made a hell of a fight.

NORMAN MAILER
King of the Hill: Muhammad Ali

As writer Norman Mailer notes, in this expansive and entertaining essay on the rise and fall of an exceptional heavyweight, most of us learn to talk with our minds, but the fighter learns to speak with his body. Reviewing Muhammad Ali's meteoric career— the unforgettable fights against Liston, Patterson, and Frazier—Mailer analyzes the complex, elusive character who was at first the ebullient, unbeatable Cassius Clay but who later became the unfathomable, overconfident, and finally vulnerable Muhammad Ali.

Ali learned early on—when still brash Cassius Clay —how to put his opponents into psychological turmoil, even long before the fight began, by a pitiless stream of oratory always widely publicized by the press. And Mailer classifies Ali as the first "psychologist of the body," recalling how he would drop his hands during training and learn to absorb punishing body blows, as yet another strategy to confuse his opponent, so that he could suddenly jump back into the fight surprisingly fresh and strong.

Both adept at understanding the psychology of mind and body, essayist Mailer and fighter Ali were made for each other.

Okay. There are fighters who are men's men. Rocky Marciano was one of them. Oscar Bonavena and Jerry Quarry and George Chuvalo and Gene Fullmer and Carmen Basilio, to name a few, have faces which would give a Marine sergeant pause in a bar fight. They look like they could take you out with the knob of bone they have left for a nose. They are all, incidentally, white fighters. They have a code—it is to fight until they are licked, and if they have to take a punch for every punch they give, well, they figure they can win. Their ego and their body intelligence are both connected to the same source of juice—it is male pride. They are substances close to rock. They work on clumsy skills to hone them finer, knowing if they can obtain parity, blow for blow with any opponent, they will win. They have more guts. Up to a far-gone point, pain is their pleasure, for their character in combat is their strength to trade pain for pain, loss of faculty for loss of faculty.

One can cite black fighters like them. Henry Hank and Reuben Carter, Emile Griffith and Benny Paret. Joe Frazier would be the best of them. But black fighters tend to be complex. They have veins of unsuspected strength and streaks when they feel as spooked as wild horses. Any fight promoter in the world knew he had a good fight if Fullmer went against Basilio, it was a proposition as certain as the wages for the week. But black fighters were artists, they were relatively moody, they were full of the surprises of Patterson or Liston, the virtuosities of Archie Moore and Sugar Ray, the speed, savagery, and curious lack of substance in Jimmy Ellis, the vertiginous neuroses of giants like Buster Mathis. Even Joe Louis, recognized by a majority in the years of his own championship as the greatest heavyweight of all time, was surprisingly inconsistent with minor fighters like Buddy Baer. Part of the unpredictability of their performances was due to the fact that all but Moore and Robinson were heavyweights. Indeed, white champions in the top division were equally out of form from fight to fight. It can, in fact, be said that heavyweights are always the most lunatic of prizefighters. The closer a heavyweight comes to the championship, the more natural it is for him to be a little bit insane, secretly insane, for the heavyweight champion of the world is either the toughest man in the world or he is not, but there is a real possibility he is. It is like being the big toe of God. You have nothing to measure yourself by. Lightweights, welterweights, middleweights can all be exceptionally good, fantastically talented —they are still very much in their place. The best lightweight in the world knows that an unranked middleweight can defeat him on most nights, and the best middleweight in the world will kill him every night. He knows that the biggest strongman in a tough bar could handle him by sitting on him, since the power to punch seems to increase quickly with weight. A fighter who weighs two-forty will punch more than twice as hard as a fighter who weighs one-twenty. The figures have no real basis, of course, they are only there to indicate the law of the ring: a good big man beats a good little man. So the notion of prizefighters as hardworking craftsmen is most likely to be true in the light and middle divisions. Since they are fighters who know their limitations, they are likely to strive for excellence in their category. The better they get, the closer they have come to sanity, at least if we are ready to assume that the average fighter is a buried artist, which is to say a *body* artist with an extreme amount of violence in him. Obviously the better and more successful they get, the more they have been able to transmute violence into craft, discipline, even body art. That is human alchemy. We respect them and they deserve to be respected.

But the heavyweights never have such simple sanity. If they become champions they begin to have inner lives like Hemingway or Dostoyevsky, Tolstoy or Faulkner, Joyce or Melville or Conrad or Lawrence or Proust. Hemingway is the example above all. Because he wished to be the greatest writer in history of literature and still be a hero with all the body arts age would yet grant him, he was alone and he knew it. So are heavyweight champions alone. Dempsey was alone and Tunney could never explain himself and Sharkey could never believe himself nor Schmeling nor Braddock, and Carnera was sad and Baer an indecipherable clown; great heavyweights like Louis had the loneliness of the ages in their silence, and men like Marciano were mystified by a power which seemed to have been granted them. With the advent, however, of the great modern black heavyweights, Patterson, Liston, then Clay and Frazier, perhaps the loneliness gave way to what it had been protecting itself against—a surrealistic situation unstable beyond belief. Being a black heavyweight champion in the second half of the 20th Century (with black revolutions opening all over the world) was now not unlike being Jack Johnson, Malcolm X and Frank Costello all in one. Going down the aisle and into the ring in Chicago was conceivably more frightening for Sonny Liston than facing Patterson that night —he was raw as uncoated wire with his sense of retribution awaiting him for years of prison pleasures and underworld jobs. Pools of paranoia must have reached him like different washes of color from different sides of the area. He was a man who had barely learned to read and write—he had none of the impacted and mediocre misinformation of all the world of daily dull reading to clot the antenna of his senses—so he was keen to every hatred against him. He knew killers were waiting in that mob, they always were, he had been on speaking terms with just such subjects himself—now he dared to be king—any assassin could strike for his revenge upon acts Liston had long forgot; no wonder Liston was in fear going into the ring, and happier once within it.

And Patterson was exhausted before the fight began. Lonely as a monk for years, his daily gym work the stuff of his meditation, he was the first of the black fighters to be considered, then used, as a political force. He was one of the liberal elite, an Eleanor Roosevelt darling, he was political mileage for the NAACP. Violent, conceivably to the point of murder if he had not been a fighter, he was a gentleman in public, more, he was a man of the nicest, quietest, most private good manners. But monastic by inclination. Now, all but uneducated, he was appealed to by political blacks to win the Liston fight for the image of the Negro. Responsibility sat upon him like a comic cutback in a silent film where we return now and again to one poor man who has been left to hold a beam across his shoulders. There he stands, hardly able to move. At the end of the film he collapses. That was the weight put on Patterson. The responsibility to beat Liston was too great to bear. Patterson, a fighter of incorruptible honesty, was knocked out by punches hardly anybody saw. He fell in open air as if seized by a stroke. The age of surrealistic battles had begun. In the second fight with Liston, Patterson, obviously more afraid of a repetition of the first nightmare than anything else, simply charged his opponent with his hands low and was knocked down three times and out in the first round. The age of body psychology had begun and Clay was there to conceive it.

A kid as wild and dapper and jaybird as the president of a down-home college fraternity, bow-tie, brown-and-white shoes, sweet, happy-go-lucky, *raucous*, he descended on Vegas for the second Patterson-Liston fight. He was like a beautiful boy surrounded by doting aunts. The classiest-looking middle-aged Negro ladies were always flanking him in Vegas as if to set up a female field of repulsion against any evil black magnetic forces in the off-ing. And from the sanctuary of his ability to move around crap tables like a kitten on the frisk, he taunted black majestic king-size Liston before the fight and after the fight. "You're so ugly," he would jeer, crap table safely between them, "that I don't know how you can get any uglier."

"Why don't you sit on my knee and I'll feed you your orange juice," Liston would rumble back.

"Don't insult me, or you'll be sorry. 'Cause you're just an ugly slow bear."

They would pretend to rush at one another. Smaller men would hold them back without effort. They were building the gate for the next fight. And Liston was secretly fond of Clay. He would chuckle when he talked about him. It was years since Liston had failed to knock out his opponent in the first round. His charisma was majestic with menace. One held one's breath when near him. He looked forward with obvious amusement to the happy seconds when he would take Clay apart and see the expression on that silly face. In Miami he trained for a three-round fight. In the famous fifth round when Clay came out with caustic in his eyes and could not see, he waved his gloves at Liston, a look of abject horror on his face, as if to say, "Your younger brother is now an old blind beggar. Do not strike him." And did it with a peculiar authority. For Clay looked like a ghost with his eyes closed, tears streaming, his extended gloves waving in front of him like a widow's entreaties. Liston drew back in doubt, in bewilderment, conceivably in concern for his new great reputation as an ex-bully; yes, Liston reacted like a gentleman, and Clay was home free. His eyes watered out the caustic, his sight came back. He cut Liston up in the sixth. He left him beaten and exhausted. Liston did not stand up for the bell to the seventh. Maybe Clay had even defeated him earlier that day at the weigh-in when he had harangued and screamed and shouted and whistled and stuck his tongue out at Liston. The Champ had been bewildered. No one had been able ever to stare him in the eyes these last four years. Now a boy was screaming at him, a boy reported to belong to Black Muslims, no, stronger than that, a boy favored by Malcolm X who was braver by reputation than the brave, for he could stop a bullet any day. Liston, afraid only, as he put it, of crazy men, was afraid of the Muslims for he could not contend with their allegiance to one another in prison, their puritanism, their discipline, their martial ranks. The combination was too complex, too unfamiliar. Now, their boy, in a pain of terror or in a mania of courage, was screaming at him at the weigh-in. Liston sat down and shook his head, and looked at the Press, now become his friend, and wound his fingers in circles around his ear, as if saying, Whitey to Whitey, "That black boy is nuts." So Clay made Liston Tom it, and when Liston missed the first jab he threw in the fight by a foot and a half, one knew the night would not be ordinary in the offing.

For their return bout in Boston, Liston trained as he had never before. Clay got a hernia. Liston trained again. Hard training as a fighter grows older seems to speak of the dull deaths of the brightest cells in all the favorite organs; old fighters react to training like beautiful women to washing floors. But Liston did it twice, once for Clay's hernia, and again for their actual fight in Maine, and the second time he trained, he aged as a fighter, for he had a sparring partner, Amos Lincoln, who was one of the better heavyweights in the country. They had wars with one another every afternoon in the gym. By the day before the fight, Liston was as relaxed and sleepy and dopey as a man in a steambath. He had fought his heart out in training, had done it under constant pressure from Clay who kept telling the world that Liston was old and slow and could not possibly win. And their fight created a scandal, for Liston ran into a short punch in the first round and was counted out, unable to hear the count. The referee and timekeeper missed signals with one another while Clay stood over fallen Liston screaming, "Get up and fight!" It was no night for the fight game, and a tragedy for Clay since he had trained for a long and arduous fight. He had developed his technique for a major encounter with Liston and was left with a horde of unanswered questions including the one he could never admit—which was whether there had been the magic of a real knockout in his punch or if Liston had made—for what variety of reasons!—a conscious decision to stay on the floor. It did him no good.

He had taken all the lessons of his curious life and the outrageously deep comprehension he had of the motivations of his own people—indeed, one could even approach the beginnings of a Psychology of the Blacks by studying his encounters with fighters who were black—and had elaborated that into a technique for boxing which was almost without compare. A most cultivated technique. For he was no child of the slums. His mother was a gracious pale-skinned lady, his father a bitter wit pride-oriented on the family name of Clay—they were descendants of Henry Clay, the orator, on the white side of the family, nothing less, and Cassius began boxing at 12 in a police gym, and from the beginning was a phenomenon of style and the absence of pain, for he knew how to use his physical endowment. Tall, relatively light, with an exceptionally long reach even for his size, he developed defensive skills which made the best use of his body. Working apparently on the premise that there was something obscene about being hit, he boxed with his head back and drew it further back when attacked, like a kid who is shy of punches in a street fight, but because he had a waist which was more supple than the average fighter's neck, he was able to box with his arms low, surveying the fighter in front of him, avoiding punches by the speed of his feet, the reflexes of his waist, the long spoiling deployment of his arms which were always tipping other fighters off-balance. Added to this was his psychological comprehension of the vanity and confusion of other fighters. A man in the ring is a performer as well as a gladiator. Elaborating his technique from the age of 12, Clay knew how to work on the vanity of other performers, knew how to make them feel ridiculous and so force them into crucial mistakes, knew how to set such a tone from the first round—later he was to know how to begin it a year before he would even meet the man. Clay knew that a fighter who had been put in psychological knots before he got near the ring had already lost half, three quarters, no, all of the fight could be lost before the first punch. That was the psychology of the body.

Now, add his curious ability as a puncher. He knew that the heaviest punches, systematically delivered, meant little. There are club fighters who look like armadillos and alligators—you can bounce punches off them forever and they never go down. You can break them down only if they are in a profound state of confusion, and the bombardment of another fighter's fists is never their confusion but their expectation. So Clay punched with a greater variety of mixed intensities than anyone around, he played with punches, was tender with them, laid them on as delicately as you put a postage stamp on an envelope, then cracked them in like a riding crop across your face, stuck a cruel jab like a baseball bat held head on into your mouth, next waltzed you in a clinch with a tender arm around your neck, winged away out of reach on flying legs, dub a hook with the full swing of a baseball bat hard into your ribs, hard pokes of a jab into the face, a mocking soft flurry of pillows and gloves, a mean forearm cutting you off from coming up on him, a cruel wrestling of your neck in a clinch, then elusive again, gloves snake-licking your face like a whip. By the time Clay had defeated Liston once and was training for the second fight, by the time Clay, now champion and renamed Muhammad Ali, and bigger, grown up quickly and not so mysteriously (after the potent ego-soups and marrows of his trip through Muslim Africa) into a Black Prince, Potentate of his people, new Poombah of Polemic, yes, by this time, Clay—we will find it more natural to call him Ali from here on out (for the Prince will behave much like a young god)—yes, Muhammad Ali, Heavyweight Champion of the World, having come back with an amazing commitment to be leader of his people, proceeded to go into training for the second Liston fight with a commitment and then a genius of comprehension for the true intricacies of the Science of Sock. He alternated the best of sparring partners and the most ordinary, worked rounds of dazzling speed with Jimmy Ellis—later, of course, to be champion himself before Frazier knocked him out—rounds which displayed the high esthetic of boxing at its best, then lay against the ropes with other sparring partners, hands at his sides as if it were the 11th or 13th round of an excruciating and exhausting fight with Liston where Ali was now so tired he could not hold his hands up, could just manage to take punches to the stomach, rolling with them, smothering them with his stomach, absorbing them with backward moves, sliding along the ropes, steering his sparring partner with passive but off-setting moves of his limp arms. For a minute, for two minutes, the sparring partner—Shotgun Sheldon was his name—would bomb away on Ali's stomach much as if Liston were tearing him apart in later rounds, and Ali weaving languidly, sliding his neck for the occasional overhead punch to his face, bouncing from the rope into the punches, bouncing back away from punches, as if his torso had become one huge boxing glove to absorb punishment, had penetrated through into some further conception of pain, as if pain were not pain if you accepted it with a relaxed heart, yes, Ali let himself be bombarded on the ropes by the powerful bull-like swings of Shotgun Sheldon, the expression on his face as remote, and as searching for the last routes into the nerves of each punch going in as a man hanging on a subway strap will search into the meaning of the market quotations he has just read on the activities of a curious stock. So Ali relaxed on the ropes and took punches to the belly with a faint disdain, as if, curious punches, they did not go deep enough and after a minute of this, or two minutes, having offered his body like the hide of a drum for a mad drummer's solo, he would snap out of his communion with himself and flash a tattoo of light and slashing punches, mocking as the lights on water, he would dazzle his sparring partner, who, arm-weary and punched out, would look at him with eyes of love, complete was his admiration. And if people were ever going to cry watching a boxer in training, those were the moments, for Ali had the far-off concentration and disdain of an artist who simply cannot find anyone near enough or good enough to keep him and his art engaged, and all the while was perfecting the essence of his art which was to make the other fighter fall secretly, helpless, in love with him. Bundini, a special trainer, an alter ego with the same harsh, demoniac, witty, nonstop powers of oration as Ali himself—he even looked a little like Ali— used to weep openly as he watched the workouts.

Training session over, Ali would lecture the Press, instruct them—looking beyond his Liston defense to what he would do to Patterson, mocking Patterson, calling him a rabbit, a white man's rabbit, knowing he was putting a new beam on Patterson's shoulders, an outrageously helpless and heavy beam of rage, fear, hopeless anger and secret black admiration for the all-out force of Ali's effrontery. And in the next instant Ali would be charming as a movie star on the make speaking tenderly to a child. If he was Narcissus, so he was as well the play of mood in the water which served as mirror to Narcissus. It was as if he knew he had disposed of Patterson already, that the precise attack of calling him a rabbit would work on the weakest link—wherever it was—in Patterson's tense and tortured psyche and Patterson would crack, as indeed, unendurably for himself, he did, when their fight took place. Patterson's back gave way in the early rounds, and he fought twisted and in pain, half crippled like a man with a sacroiliac, for 11 brave and most miserable rounds before the referee would call it and Ali, breaking up with his first wife then, was unpleasant in the ring that night, his face ugly and contemptuous, himself well on the way to becoming America's most unpopular major American. That, too, was part of the art—to get a public to the point of hating him so much the burden on the other fighter approached the metaphysical—which is where Ali wanted it. White fighters with faces like rock embedded in cement would trade punch for punch, Ali liked to get the boxing where it belonged—he would trade metaphysic for metaphysic with anyone.

So he went on winning his fights and growing forever more unpopular. How he inflamed the temper of boxing's white establishment, for they were for most part a gaggle of avuncular drunks and hardbitten hacks who were ready to fight over every slime-slicked penny, and squared a few of their slippery crimes by getting fighters to show up semblance-of-sober at any available parish men's rally and charity church breakfast—"Everything I am I owe to boxing," the fighter would mumble through his dentures while elements of gin, garlic, and goddess-of-a-girlie from the night before came off in the bright morning fumes.

Ali had them psyched. He cut through moribund coruscated dirty business corridors, cut through cigar smoke and bushwah, hypocrisy and well-aimed kicks to the back of the neck, cut through crooked politicians and patriotic pus, cut like a laser, point of the point, light and impersonal, cut to the heart of the rottenest meat in boxing, and boxing was always the buried South Vietnam of America, buried for 50 years in our hide before we went there, yes, Ali cut through the flag-dragooned salutes of drunken dawns and said, "I got no fight with those Vietcongs," and they cut him down, thrust him into the three and a half years of his martyrdom. Where he grew. Grew to have a little fat around his middle and a little of the complacent muscle of the clam to his world-ego. And grew sharper in the mind as well, and deepened and broadened physically. Looked no longer like a boy, but a sullen man, almost heavy, with the beginnings of a huge expanse across his shoulders. And developed the patience to survive, the wisdom to contemplate future nights in jail, grew to cultivate the suspension of belief and the avoidance of disbelief—what a rack for a young man! As the years of hope for reinstatement, or avoidance of prison, came up and waned in him, Ali walked the tightrope between bitterness and apathy, and had enough left to beat Quarry and beat Bonavena, beat Quarry in the flurry of a missed hundred punches, ho! how his timing was off! beat him with a calculated whip, snake-lick whip, to the corrugated sponge of dead flesh over Quarry's Irish eyes—they stopped

205

it after the third on cuts—then knocked out Bonavena, the indestructible, never stopped before, by
working the art of crazy mixing in the punches he
threw at the rugged—some of the punches Ali
threw that night would not have hurt a little boy—
the punch he let go in the 15th came in like a wreck-
ing ball from outer space. Bonavena went sprawl-
ing across the ring. He was a house coming down.

Yet it may have been the blow which would defeat
him later. For Ali had been tired with Bonavena,
lackluster, winded, sluggish, far ahead on points
but in need of the most serious work if he were
to beat Frazier. The punch in the last round was
obliged, therefore, to inflame his belief that the
forces of magic were his, there to be called upon
when most in need, that the silent leagues of black
support for his cause—since their cause was as his
own—were like some cloak of midnight velvet, there
to protect him by black blood, by black sense of
tragedy, by the black consciousness that the guilt
of the world had become the hinge of a door that
they would open. So they would open the way to
Frazier's chin, the blacks would open the aisle for
his trip to the gods.

Therefore he did not train for Frazier as perhaps
he had to. He worked, he ran three miles a day
when he could have run five, he boxed some days
and let a day and perhaps another day go, he was
relaxed, he was confident, he basked in the un-
demanding winter sun of Miami, and skipped his
rope in a gym crowded with fighters, stuffed now
with working fighters looking to be seen, Ali comfortable and relaxed like the greatest of movie stars,

206

he played a young fighter working out in a corner on the heavy bag—for of course every eye was on him—and afterward doing sit-ups in the back room and having his stomach rubbed with liniment, he would talk to reporters. He was filled with confidence there was no black fighter he did not comprehend to the root of the valve in the hard-pumping heart, and yes, Frazier, he assured everybody, would be easier than they realized. Like a little boy who had grown up to take on a mountain of responsibility he spoke in the deep relaxation of the wise, and teased two of the reporters who were present and fat. "You want to drink a lot of water," he said, "good cold water instead of all that liquor rot-your-gut," and gave the smile of a man who had been able to intoxicate himself on water (although he was, by repute, a fiend for soft sweet drinks), "and fruit and good clean vegetables you want to eat and chicken and steak. You lose weight then," he advised out of kind secret smiling thoughts, and went on to talk of the impact of the fight upon the world. "Yes," he said, "you just think of a stadium with a million people, 10 million people, you could get them all in to watch they would all pay to see it live, but then you think of the hundreds of millions and the billions who are going to see this fight, and if you could sit them all down in one place, and fly a jet plane over them, why that plane would have to fly for an hour before it would reach the end of all the people who will see this fight. It's the greatest event in the history of the world, and you take a man like Frazier, a good fighter, but a simple hardworking fellow, he's not built for this kind of pressure, the eyes," Ali said softly, "of that many people upon him. There's an experience to pressure which I have had, fighting a man like Liston in Miami the first time, which he has not. He will cave in under the pressure. No, I do not see any way a man like Frazier can whup me, he can't reach me, my arms are too long, and if he does get in and knock me down I'll never make the mistake of Quarry and Foster or Ellis of rushing back at him, I'll stay away until my head clears, then I begin to pop him again, pop! pop!" a few jabs, "no there is no way this man can beat me, this fight will be easier than you think."

There was one way in which boxing was still like a street fight and that was in the need to be confident you would win. A man walking out of a bar to fight with another man is seeking to compose his head into the confidence that he will certainly triumph—it is the most mysterious faculty of the ego. For that confidence is a sedative against the pain of punches and yet is the sanction to punch your own best. The logic of the spirit would suggest that you win only if you deserve to win: the logic of the ego lays down the axiom that if you don't think you will win, you don't deserve to. And, in fact, usually don't; it is as if not believing you will win opens you to the guilt that perhaps you have not the right, you are too guilty.

So training camps are small factories for the production of one rare psychological item—an ego able to bear huge pain and administer drastic punishment. The flow of Ali's ego poured over the rock of every distraction, it was an ego like the flow of a river of constant energy fed by a hundred tributaries of black love and the love of the white left. The construction of the ego of Joe Frazier was of another variety. His manager, Yancey "Yank" Durham, a canny foxy light-skinned Negro with a dignified mien, a gray head of hair, gray mustache and a small but conservative worthy's paunch, plus the quick-witted look of eyes which could spot from a half-mile away any man coming toward him with a criminal thought, was indeed the face of a consummate jeweler who had worked for years upon a diamond in the rough until he was now and at last a diamond, hard as the transmutation of black carbon from the black earth into the brilliant sky-blue shadow of the rarest shining rock. What a fighter was Frazier, what a diamond of an ego had he, and what a manager was Durham. Let us look.

Sooner or later, fight metaphors, like fight managers, go sentimental. They go military. But there is no choice here. Frazier was the human equivalent of a war machine. He had tremendous firepower. He had a great left hook, a left hook frightening even to watch when it missed, for it seemed to whistle; he had a powerful right. He could knock a man out with either hand—not all fighters can, not even very good fighters. Usually, however, he clubbed opponents to death, took a punch, gave a punch, took three punches, gave two, took a punch, gave a punch, high speed all the way, always working, pushing his body and arms, short for a heavyweight, up through the middle, bombing through on force, reminiscent of Jimmy Brown knocking down tacklers, Frazier kept on coming, hard and fast, a hang-in, hang-on, go-and-get-him, got-him, got-him, slip and punch, take a punch, wing a punch, whap a punch, never was Frazier happier than with his heart up on the line against some other man's heart, let the bullets fly—his heart was there to stand up at the last. Sooner or later, the others almost all fell down. Undefeated like Ali, winner of 23 out of 26 fights by knockout, he was a human force, certainly the greatest heavyweight force to come along since Rocky Marciano. (If those two men had ever met, it would have been like two Mack trucks hitting each other head-on, then backing up to hit each other again—they would have kept it up until the wheels were off the axles and the engines off the chassis.) But this would be a different kind of fight. Ali would run, Ali would keep hitting Frazier with long jabs, quick hooks and rights while backing up, backing up, staying out of reach unless Frazier could take the punishment and get in. That was where the military problem began. For getting in against the punishment he would take was a question of morale, and there was a unique situation in this fight —Frazier had become the white man's fighter, Mr. Charley was rooting for Frazier, and that meant blacks were boycotting him in their heart. That could be poison to Frazier's morale, for he was twice as black as Clay and half as handsome, he had the rugged decent life-worked face of a man who had labored in the pits all his life, he looked like the deserving modest son of one of those Negro cleaning women of a bygone age who worked from 6 in the morning to midnight every day, raised a family, endured and occasionally elicited the exasperated admiration of white ladies who would kindly remark, "That woman deserves something better in her life." Frazier had the mien of the son, one of many, of such a woman, and he was the hardest-working fighter in training many a man had ever seen, he was conceivably the hardest-working man alive in the world, and as he went through his regimen, first boxing four rounds with a sparring partner, Kenny Norton, a talented heavyweight from the coast with an almost unbeaten record, then working on the heavy bag, then the light bag, then skipping rope, 10 to 12 rounds of sparring and exercise on a light day, Frazier went on with the doggedness, the concentration, and the pumped-up fury of a man who has had so little in his life that he can endure torments to get every-thing, he pushed the total of his energy and force into an absolute abstract exercise of will so it did not matter if he fought a sparring partner or the heavy bag, he lunged at each equally as if the exhaustions of his own heart and the clangor of his lungs were his only enemies, and the head of a fighter or the leather of the bag as it rolled against his own head was nothing but some ab-stract thunk of material, not a thing, not a man, but thunk! thunk! something of an obstacle, thunk! thunk! thunk! to beat into thunk! oblivion. And his breath came in rips and sobs as he smashed into the bag as if it were real, just that heavy big torso-sized bag hanging from its chain but he at-tacked it as if it were a bear, as if it were a great fighter and they were in the mortal embrace of a killing set of exchanges of punches in the middle of the eighth round, and rounds of exercise later, skipping rope to an inhumanly fast beat for this late round in the training day, sweat pouring like jets of blood from an artery, he kept swinging his rope, muttering, "Two-million-dollars-and-change, two-million-dollars-and-change," railroad train chugging into the terminals of exhaustion. And it was obvious that Durham, jeweler to his diamond, was working to make the fight as abstract as he could for Frazier, to keep Clay out of it—for they would not call him Ali in their camp—yes, Frazier was fortifying his ego by depersonalizing his opponent, Clay was, thunk! the heavy bag, thunk! and thunk!—Frazier was looking to get no messages from that cavern of velvet when black people sent their good wishes to Ali at midnight, no, Frazier would insulate himself with prodigies of work, hardest-working man in the hell hole of the world, and on and on he drove himself into the depressions each day of killing daily exhaustion.

That was one half of the strategy to isolate Frazier from Ali, hard work and thinking of thunking on inanimate Clay; the other half was up to Durham who was running front relations with the blacks of North Philly who wandered into the gym, paid their dollar, and were ready to heckle on Frazier. In the four rounds he boxed with Norton, Frazier did not look too good for a while. It was 10 days before the fight and he was in a bad mood when he came in, for the word was through the gym that they had discovered one of his favorite sparring partners, just fired that morning, was a Black Muslim and had been calling Ali every night with reports, that was the rumor, and Frazier, sullen and cold at the start, was bopped and tapped, then

walloped by Norton moving fast with the big training gloves in imitation of Ali, and Frazier looked
very easy to hit until the middle of the third round
when Norton, proud of his something like 20 wins
and one loss, beginning to get some ideas himself
about how to fight champions, came driving in to
mix it with Frazier, have it out man to man and
caught a right which dropped him, left him looking limp with that half-silly smile sparring partners
get when they have been hit too hard to justify any
experience or any money they are going to take
away. Up till then the crowd had been with Norton. There at one end of the Cloverlay gym, a
street-level store-front room which could have been
used originally by an automobile dealer, there on
that empty, immaculate Lysol-soaked floor, designed
when Frazier was there for only Frazier and his
partners to train (as opposed to Miami where Ali
would rub elbows with the people) here the people
were at one end, the end off the street, and they
jeered whenever Norton hit Frazier, they laughed
when Norton made him look silly, they called out,
"Drop the mother," until Durham held up a gentlemanly but admonishing finger in request for silence.
Afterward, however, training completed, Durham
approached them to answer questions, rolled with
their sallies, jived the people back, subtly enlisted
their sympathy for Frazier by saying, "When I
fight Clay, I'm going to get him somewhere in the
middle rounds," until the blacks quipping back
said angrily, "You ain't fighting him, Frazier is."

"Why you call him Clay?" another asked. "He
Ali."

"His name is Cassius Clay to me," said Durham.

"What you say against his religion?"

"I don't say nothing about his religion and he doesn't say anything about mine. I'm a Baptist."

"You going to make money on this?"

"Of course," said Durham, "I got to make money. You don't think I work up this sweat for nothing."

They loved him. He was happy with them. A short fat man in a purple suit wearing his revival of the wide-brim bebop hat said to Durham, "Why don't you get Norton to manage? He was beating up on *your* fighter," and the fat man cackled for he had scored and could elaborate the tale for his ladies later how he had put down Yank who was working the daily rite on the edge of the black street for his fighter, while upstairs, dressed, and sucking an orange, sweat still pouring, gloom of excessive fatigue upon him, Frazier was sitting through his two-hundredth or two-thousandth interview for this fight, reluctant indeed to give it at all. "Some get it, some don't," he had said for refusal, but relented when a white friend who had done roadwork with him interceded, so he sat there now against a leather sofa, dark blue suit, dark T-shirt, mopping his brow with a pink-red towel, and spoke dispiritedly of being ready too early for the fight. He was waking up an hour too early for roadwork each morning now. "I'd go back to sleep but it doesn't feel good when I do run."

"I guess the air is better that hour of the morning."

He nodded sadly. "There's a limit to how good the air in Philly can get."

214

"Where'd you begin to sing?" was a question asked.

"I sang in church first," he replied, but it was not the day to talk about singing. The loneliness of hitting the bag still seemed upon him as if in his exhaustion now, and in the thoughts of that small insomnia which woke him an hour too early every day was something of the loneliness of all blacks who work very hard and are isolated from fun and must wonder in the just-awakened night how large and pervasive was the curse of a people. "The countdown's begun," said Frazier, "I get impatient about now."

For the fight, Ali was wearing red velvet trunks, Frazier had green. Before they began, even before they were called together by the referee for instructions, Ali went dancing around the ring and glided past Frazier with a sweet little-boy smile, as if to say, "You're my new playmate. We're going to have fun." Ali was laughing. Frazier was having nothing of this and turned his neck to embargo him away. Ali, having alerted the crowd by this big first move, came prancing in again. When Frazier looked ready to block him, Ali went around, evading a contact, gave another sweet smile, shook his head at the lack of high spirit. "Poor Frazier," he seemed to say.

At the weigh-in early that afternoon Ali looked physically resplendent; the night before in Harlem, crowds had cheered him; he was coming to claim his victory on the confluence of two mighty tides —he was the mightiest victim of injustice in America and he was also—the 20th Century was nothing if not a tangle of opposition—he was also the mightiest narcissist in the land. Every beard, drop-out, homosexual, junkie, freak, swinger, and plain simple individualist adored him. Every pedantic liberal soul who had once loved Patterson now paid homage to Ali. The mightiest of the black psyches and the most filigreed of the white psyches were ready to roar him home, as well as every family-loving hard-working square American who genuinely hated the war in Vietnam. What a tangle of ribbons he carried on his lance, enough cross purposes to be the knight-resplendent of television, the fell hero of the medium, and he had a look of unique happiness on television when presenting his program for the course of the fight, and his inevitable victory. He would be as content then as an infant splashing the waters of the bathinette. If he was at once a saint and a monster to any mind which looked for category, any mind unwilling to encounter the thoroughly dread-filled fact that the 20th Century breed of man now in birth might be no longer half good and half evil—generous and greedy by turns—but a mutation with Cassius Muhammad for the first son—then that mind was not ready to think about 20th Century Man. (And indeed Muhammad Ali had twin poodles he called Angel and Demon.) So now the ambiguity of his presence filled the Garden before the fight was fairly begun, it was as if he had announced to that plural billion-footed crowd assembled under the shadow of the jet which would fly over them that the first enigma of the fight would be the way he would win it, that he would initiate his triumph by getting the crowd to laugh at Frazier, yes, first

216

premise tonight was that the poor black man in Frazier's soul would go berserk if made a figure of roll-off-your-seat amusement.

The referee gave his instructions. The bell rang. The first 15 seconds of a fight can be the fight. It is equivalent to the first kiss in a love affair. The fighters each missed the other. Ali blocked Frazier's first punches easily, but Ali then missed Frazier's head. That head was bobbing as fast as a third fist. Frazier would come rushing in, head moving like a fist, fists bobbing too, his head working above and below his forearm, he was trying to get through Ali's jab, get through fast and sear Ali early with the terror of a long fight and punches harder than he had ever taken to the stomach, and Ali in turn, backing up, and throwing fast punches, aimed just a trifle, and was therefore a trifle too slow, but it was obvious Ali was trying to shiver Frazier's synapses from the start, set waves of depression stirring which would reach his heart in later rounds and make him slow, deaden nerve, deaden nerve went Ali's jab flicking a snake tongue, whoo-eet! whoo-eet! but Frazier's head was bobbing too fast, he was moving faster than he had ever moved before in that bobbing nonstop never-a-backward step of his, slogging and bouncing forward, that huge left hook flaunting the air with the confidence it was enough of a club to split a tree, and Ali, having missed his jabs, stepped nimbly inside the hook and wrestled Frazier in the clinch. Ali looked stronger here. So by the first 45 seconds of the fight, they had each surprised the other profoundly. Frazier was fast enough to slip through Ali's punches, and Ali was strong enough

217

to handle him in the clinches. A pattern had begun. Because Ali was missing often, Frazier was in
under his shots like a police dog's muzzle on your
arm, Ali could not slide from side to side, he was
boxed in, then obliged to go backward, and would
end on the ropes again and again with Frazier be
laboring him. Yet Frazier could not reach him.
Like a prestidigitator Ali would tie the other's
punches into odd knots, not even blocking them
yet on his elbows or his arms, rather throwing his
own punches as defensive moves, for even as they
missed, he would brush Frazier to the side with
his forearm, or hold him off, or clinch and wrestle
a little of the will out of Frazier's neck. Once or
twice in the round a long left hook by Frazier just
touched the surface of Ali's chin, and Ali waved
his head in placid contempt to the billions watching as if to say, "This man has not been able to
hurt me at all."

The first round set a pattern for the fight. Ali
won it and would win the next. His jab was landing from time to time and rights and lefts of not
great consequence. Frazier was hardly reaching him
at all. Yet it looked like Frazier had established
that he was fast enough to get in on Ali and so
drive him to the ropes and to the corners, and that
spoke of a fight which would be determined by
the man in better condition, in better physical
condition rather than in better psychic condition,
the kind of fight Ali could hardly want for his
strength was in his pauses, his nature passed along
the curve of every dialectic, he liked, in short, to
fight in flurries, and then move out, move away,
assess, take his time, fight again. Frazier would

not let him. Frazier moved in with the snarl of a wolf, his teeth seemed to show through his mouthpiece, he made Ali work. Ali won the first two rounds but it was obvious he could not continue to win if he had to work all the way. And in the third round Frazier began to get to him, caught Ali with a powerful blow to the face at the bell. That was the first moment where it was clear to all that Frazier had won a round. Then he won the next. Ali looked tired and a little depressed. He was moving less and less and calling upon a skill not seen since the fight with Chuvalo when he had showed his old ability, worked on all those years ago with Shotgun Sheldon, to lie on the ropes and take a beating to the stomach. He had exhausted Chuvalo by welcoming attacks on the stomach but Frazier was too incommensurable a force to allow such total attack. So Ali lay on the ropes and wrestled him off, and moved his arms and waist, blocking punches, slipping punches, countering with punches—it began to look as if the fight would be written on the ropes, but Ali was getting very tired. At the beginning of the fifth round, he got up slowly from his stool, very slowly. Frazier was beginning to feel that the fight was his. He moved in on Ali jeering, his hands at his side in mimicry of Ali, a street fighter mocking his opponent, and Ali tapped him with long light jabs to which Frazier stuck out his mouthpiece, a jeer of derision as if to suggest that the mouthpiece was all Ali would reach all night.

There is an extortion of the will beyond any of our measure in the exhaustion which comes upon a fighter in early rounds when he is already too tired to lift his arms or take advantage of openings there before him, yet the fight is not a third over, there are all those rounds to go, contractions of torture, the lungs screaming into the dungeons of the soul, washing the throat with a hot bile that once belonged to the liver, the legs are going dead, the arms move but their motion is limp, one is straining into another will, breathing into the breath of another will as agonized as one's own. As the fight moved through the fifth, the sixth and the seventh, then into the eighth, it was obvious that Ali was into the longest night of his career, and yet with that skill, that research into the pits of every miserable contingency in boxing, he came up with odd somnambulistic variations, holding Frazier off, riding around Frazier with his arm about his neck, almost entreating Frazier with his arms extended, and Frazier leaning on him, each of them slowed to a pit-a-pat of light punches back and forth until one of them was goaded up from exhaustion to whip and stick, then hook and hammer and into the belly and out, and out of the clinch and both looking exhausted, and then Frazier, mouth bared again like a wolf, going in and Ali waltzing him, tying him, tapping him lightly as if he were a speed bag, just little flicks, until Frazier, like an exhausted horse finally feeling the crop, would push up into a trot and try to run up the hill. It was indeed as if they were both running up a hill. As if Frazier's offensive was so great and so great was Ali's defense that the fight could only be decided by who could take the steepest pitch of the hill. So Frazier, driving, driving,

220

trying to drive the heart out of Ali, put the pitch of that hill up and up until they were ascending an unendurable slope. And moved like somnambulists slowly working and rubbing one another, almost embracing, next to locked in the slow moves of lovers after the act until, reaching into the stores of energy reaching them from cells never before so used, one man or the other would work up a contractive spasm of skills and throw punches at the other in the straining slow-motion hypnosis of a deepening act. And so the first eight rounds went by. The two judges scored six for Frazier, two for Ali. The referee had it even. Some of the Press had Ali ahead—it was not easy to score. For if it were an alley fight, Frazier would win. Clay was by now hardly more than the heavy bag to Frazier. Frazier was dealing with a man, not a demon. He was not respectful of that man. But still! It was Ali who was landing the majority of punches. They were light, they were usually weary, but some had snap, some were quick, he was landing two punches to Frazier's one. Yet Frazier's were hardest. And Ali often looked as tender as if he were making love. It was as if he could now feel the whole absence of that real second fight with Liston, that fight for which he had trained so long and so hard, the fight which might have rolled over his laurels from the greatest artist of pugilism to the greatest brawler of them all—maybe he had been prepared on that night to beat Liston at his own, be more of a slugger, more of a man crude to crude than Liston. Yes, Ali had never been a street fighter and never a whorehouse knock-it-down stud, no, it was more as if a man with the exquisite reflexes of Nureyev had learned to throw a knock-out punch with either hand and so had become champion of the world without knowing if he was the man of all men or the most delicate of the delicate with special privilege endowed by God. Now with Frazier, he was in a sweat bath (a mudpile, a knee, elbow, and death-thumping chute of a pit) having in this late year the fight he had sorely needed for his true greatness as a fighter six and seven years ago, and so whether ahead, behind or even, terror sat in the rooting instinct of all those who were for Ali for it was obviously Frazier's fight to win, and what if Ali, weaknesses of character now flickering to the surface in a hundred little moves, should enter the vale of prizefighting's deepest humiliation, should fall out half conscious on the floor and not want to get up. What a death to his followers.

The ninth began. Frazier mounted his largest body attack of the night. It was preparations-for-Liston-with-Shotgun-Sheldon, it was the virtuosity of the gym all over again, and Ali, like a catcher handling a fast-ball pitcher, took Frazier's punches, one steamer, another steamer, wing! went a screamer, a steamer, warded them, blocked them, slithered them, winced from them, absorbed them, took them in and blew them out and came off the ropes and was Ali the Magnificent for the next minute and thirty seconds. The fight turned. The troops of Ali's second corps of energy had arrived, the energy for which he had been waiting long agonizing heart-sore vomit-mean rounds. Now he jabbed Frazier, he snake-licked his face with jabs faster than he had thrown before, he anticipated each attempt of Frazier at counterattack and threw it back, he danced on his toes for the first time in rounds, he popped in rights, he hurt him with hooks, it was his biggest round of the night, it was the best round yet of the fight, and Frazier full of energy and hordes of sudden punishment was beginning to move into that odd petulant concentration on other rituals besides the punches, tappings of the gloves, stares of the eye, that species of mouth-piece-chewing which is the prelude to fun-strut in the knees, then Queer Street, then waggle on out, drop like a steer.

It looked like Ali had turned the fight, looked more like the same in the 10th, now reporters were writing another story in their mind where Ali was not the magical untried Prince who had come apart under the first real pressure of his life but was rather the greatest Heavyweight Champion of all time for he had weathered the purgatory of Joe Frazier.

But in the 11th, that story also broke. Frazier caught him, caught him again and again, and Ali was near to knocked out and swayed and slid on Queer Street himself, then spent the rest of the 11th and the longest round of the 12th working another bottom of Hell, holding off Frazier who came on and on, sobbing, wild, a wild honor of a beast, man of will reduced to the common denominator of the will of all of us back in that land of the animal where the idea of man as a tool-wielding beast was first conceived. Frazier looked to get Ali forever in the 11th and the 12th, and Ali, his legs slapped and slashed on the thighs between each round by Angelo Dundee, came out for the

13th and incredibly was dancing. Everybody's story switched again. For if Ali won this round, the 14th and the 15th, who could know if he could not win the fight? . . . He won the first half of the 13th, then spent the second half on the ropes with Frazier. They were now like crazy death-march-maddened mateys coming up the hill and on to home, and yet Ali won the 14th, Ali looked good, he came out dancing for the 15th, while Frazier, his own armies of energy finally caught up, his courage ready to spit into the eye of any devil black or white who would steal the work of his life, had equal madness to steal the bolt from Ali. So Frazier reached out to snatch the magic punch from the air, the punch with which Ali topped Bonavena, and found it and thunked Ali a hell and hit Ali a heaven of a shot which dumped Muhammad into 50,000 newspaper photographs—Ali on the floor! Great Ali on the floor was out there flat singing to the sirens of the mistiest fogs of Queer Street (same look of death and widowhood on his far-gone face as one had seen in the fifth blind round with Liston) yet Ali got up, Ali came sliding through the last two minutes and thirty-five seconds of this heathen holocaust in some last exercise of the will, some iron fundament of the ego not to be knocked out, and it was then as if the spirit of Harlem finally spoke and came to rescue and the ghosts of the dead in Vietnam, something held him up before arm-weary triumphant near-crazy Frazier who had just hit him the hardest punch ever thrown in his life and they went down to the last few seconds of a great fight, Ali still standing and Frazier had won.

224

The world was talking instantly of a rematch. For Ali had shown America what we all had hoped was secretly true. He was a man. He could bear moral and physical torture and he could stand. And if he could beat Frazier in the rematch we would have at last a national hero who was hero of the world as well, and who could bear to wait for the next fight? Joe Frazier, still the champion, and a great champion, said to the press, "Fellows, have a heart—I got to live a little. I've been working for 10 long years." And Ali, through the agency of alter-ego Bundini, said—for Ali was now in the hospital to check on the possible fracture of a jaw —Ali was reported to have said, "Get the gun ready—we're going to set traps." Oh, wow. Could America wait for something so great as the Second Ali-Frazier?

FISHING

NORMAN MACLEAN
A River Runs through It

An excerpt from Norman Maclean's memorable tale of a minister and his two sons, and their long-standing relationship to fishing. The father's detailed instructions to his sons on the correct way to cast with a fly rod are an unforgettable description of the art, as practiced by a devotee. The younger brother inherits a true gift for the sport despite his other noticeable failings. The older brother acknowledges both his brother's greater gift and his greater frailties.

In our family, there was no clear line between religion and fly fishing. We lived at the junction of great trout rivers in western Montana, and our father was a Presbyterian minister and a fly fisherman who tied his own flies and taught others. He told us about Christ's disciples being fishermen, and we were left to assume, as my brother and I did, that all first-class fishermen on the Sea of Galilee were fly fishermen and that John, the favorite, was a dry-fly fisherman.

It is true that one day a week was given over wholly to religion. On Sunday mornings my brother, Paul, and I went to Sunday school and then to "morning services" to hear our father preach and in the evenings to Christian Endeavor and afterwards to "evening services" to hear our father preach again. In between on Sunday afternoons we had to study *The Westminster Shorter Catechism* for an hour and then recite before we could walk the hills with him while he unwound between services. But he never asked us more than the first question in the catechism, "What is the chief end of man?" And we answered together so one of us could carry on if the other forgot, "Man's chief end is to glorify God, and to enjoy Him forever." This always seemed to satisfy him, as indeed such a beautiful answer should have, and besides he was anxious to be on the hills where he could restore his soul and be filled again to overflowing for the evening sermon. His chief way of recharging himself was to recite to us from the sermon that was coming, enriched here and there with selections from the most successful passages of his morning sermon.

Even so, in a typical week of our childhood Paul and I probably received as many hours of instruction in fly fishing as we did in all other spiritual matters.

After my brother and I became good fishermen, we realized that our father was not a great fly caster, but he was accurate and stylish and wore a glove on his casting hand. As he buttoned his glove in preparation to giving us a lesson, he would say, "It is an art that is performed on a four-count rhythm between ten and two o'clock."

As a Scot and a Presbyterian, my father believed that man by nature was a mess and had fallen from an original state of grace. Somehow, I early developed the notion that he had done this by falling from a tree. As for my father, I never knew whether he believed God was a mathematician but he certainly believed that God could count and that only by picking up God's rhythms were we able to regain power and beauty. Unlike many Presbyterians, he often used the word "beautiful."

After he buttoned his glove, he would hold his rod straight out in front of him, where it trembled with the beating of his heart. Although it was eight and a half feet long, it weighed only four and a half ounces. It was made of split bamboo cane from the far-off Bay of Tonkin. It was wrapped with red and blue silk thread, and the wrappings were carefully spaced to make the delicate rod powerful but not so stiff it could not tremble.

Always it was to be called a rod. If someone called it a pole, my father looked at him as a sergeant in the United States Marines would look at a recruit who had just called a rifle a gun.

My brother and I would have preferred to start learning how to fish by going out and catching a few, omitting entirely anything difficult or technical in the way of preparation that would take away from the fun. But it wasn't by way of fun that we were introduced to our father's art. If our father had had his say, nobody who did not know how to fish would be allowed to disgrace a fish by catching him. So you too will have to approach the art Marine- and Presbyterian-style, and, if you have never picked up a fly rod before, you will soon find it factually and theologically true that man by nature is a damn mess. The four-and-a-half-ounce thing in silk wrappings that trembles with the underskin motions of the flesh becomes a stick without brains, refusing anything simple that is wanted of it. All that a rod has to do is lift the line, the leader, and the fly off the water, give them a good toss over the head, and then shoot them forward so they will land in the water without a splash in the following order: fly, transparent leader, and then the line—otherwise the fish will see the fly is a fake and be gone. Of course, there are special casts that anyone could predict would be difficult, and they require artistry—casts where the line can't go over the fisherman's head because cliffs or trees are immediately behind, sideways casts to get the fly under overhanging willows, and so on. But what's remarkable about just a straight cast—just picking up a rod with line on it and tossing the line across the river?

Well, until man is redeemed he will always take a fly rod too far back, just as natural man always overswings with an ax or golf club and loses all his power somewhere in the air; only with a rod it's worse, because the fly often comes so far back it gets caught behind in a bush or rock. When my father said it was an art that ended at two o'clock, he often added, "closer to twelve than to two," meaning that the rod should be taken back only slightly farther than overhead (straight overhead being twelve o'clock).

Then, since it is natural for man to try to attain power without recovering grace, he whips the line back and forth making it whistle each way, and sometimes even snapping off the fly from the leader, but the power that was going to transport the little fly across the river somehow gets diverted into building a bird's nest of line, leader, and fly that

232

falls out of the air into the water about ten feet in front of the fisherman. If, though, he pictures the round trip of the line, transparent leader, and fly from the time they leave the water until their return, they are easier to cast. They naturally come off the water heavy line first and in front, and light transparent leader and fly trailing behind. But, as they pass overhead, they have to have a little beat of time so the light, transparent leader and fly can catch up to the heavy line now starting forward and again fall behind it; otherwise, the line starting on its return trip will collide with the leader and fly still on their way up, and the mess will be the bird's nest that splashes into the water ten feet in front of the fisherman.

Almost the moment, however, that the forward order of line, leader, and fly is reestablished, it has to be reversed, because the fly and transparent leader must be ahead of the heavy line when they settle on the water. If what the fish sees is highly visible line, what the fisherman will see are departing black darts, and he might as well start for the next hole. High overhead, then, on the forward cast (at about ten o'clock) the fisherman checks again.

The four-count rhythm, of course, is functional. The one count takes the line, leader, and fly off the water; the two count tosses them seemingly straight into the sky; the three count was my father's way of saying that at the top the leader and fly have to be given a little beat of time to get behind the line as it is starting forward; the four count means put on the power and throw the line into the rod until you reach ten o'clock—then check-cast, let the fly and leader get ahead of the

233

line, and coast to a soft and perfect landing. Power comes not from power everywhere, but from knowing where to put it on. "Remember," as my father kept saying, "it is an art that is performed on a four-count rhythm between ten and two o'clock."

My father was very sure about certain matters pertaining to the universe. To him, all good things —trout as well as eternal salvation—come by grace and grace comes by art and art does not come easy.

So my brother and I learned to cast Presbyterian-style, on a metronome. It was mother's metronome, which father had taken from the top of the piano in town. She would occasionally peer down to the dock from the front porch of the cabin, wondering nervously whether her metronome could float if it had to. When she became so overwrought that she thumped down the dock to reclaim it, my father would clap out the four-count rhythm with his cupped hands.

Eventually, he introduced us to literature on the subject. He tried always to say something stylish as he buttoned the glove on his casting hand. "Izaak Walton," he told us when my brother was thirteen or fourteen, "is not a respectable writer. He was an Episcopalian and a bait fisherman." Although Paul was three years younger than I was, he was already far ahead of me in anything relating to fishing and it was he who first found a copy of *The Compleat Angler* and reported back to me, "The bastard doesn't even know how to spell 'complete.' Besides, he has songs to sing to dairy-maids." I borrowed his copy, and reported back to him, "Some of those songs are pretty good."

He said, "Whoever saw a dairymaid on the Big Blackfoot River?

"I would like," he said, "to get him for a day's fishing on the Big Blackfoot—with a bet on the side."

The boy was very angry, and there has never been a doubt in my mind that the boy would have taken the Episcopalian money.

When you are in your teens—maybe throughout your life—being three years older than your brother often makes you feel he is a boy. However, I knew already that he was going to be a master with a rod. He had those extra things besides fine training—genius, luck, and plenty of self-confidence. Even at this age he liked to bet on himself against anybody who would fish with him, including me, his older brother. It was sometimes funny and sometimes not so funny, to see a boy always wanting to bet on himself and almost sure to win. Although I was three years older, I did not yet feel old enough to bet. Betting, I assumed, was for men who wore straw hats on the backs of their heads. So I was confused and embarrassed the first couple of times he asked me if I didn't want "a small bet on the side just to make things interesting." The third time he asked me must have made me angry because he never again spoke to me about money, not even about borrowing a few dollars when he was having real money problems.

We had to be very careful in dealing with each other. I often thought of him as a boy, but I never could treat him that way. He was never "my kid brother." He was a master of an art. He did not want any big brother advice or money or help, and, in the end, I could not help him.

Since one of the earliest things brothers try to find out is how they differ from each other, one of the things I remember longest about Paul is this business about his liking to bet. He would go to county fairs to pretend that he was betting on the horses, like the men, except that no betting booths would take his bets because they were too small and he was too young. When his bets were refused, he would say, as he said of Izaak Walton and any other he took as a rival, "I'd like to get that bastard on the Blackfoot for a day, with a bet on the side."

By the time he was in his early twenties he was in the big stud poker games.

Circumstances, too, helped to widen our differences. The draft of World War I immediately left the woods short of men, so at fifteen I started working for the United States Forest Service, and for many summers afterwards I worked in the woods, either with the Forest Service or in logging camps. I liked the woods and I liked work, but for a good many summers I didn't do much fishing. Paul was too young to swing an ax or pull a saw all day, and besides he had decided this early he had two major purposes in life: to fish and not to work, at least not allow work to interfere with fishing. In his teens, then, he got a summer job as a lifeguard at the municipal swimming pool, so in the early evenings he could go fishing and during the days he could look over girls in bathing suits and date them up for the late evenings.

When it came to choosing a profession, he

236

became a reporter. On a Montana paper. Early, then, he had come close to realizing life's purposes, which did not conflict in his mind from those given in answer to the first question in *The Westminster Catechism*.

Undoubtedly, our differences would not have seemed so great if we had not been such a close family. Painted on one side of our Sunday school wall were the words, God Is Love. We always assumed that these three words were spoken directly to the four of us in our family and had no reference to the world outside, which my brother and I soon discovered was full of bastards, the number increasing rapidly the farther one gets from Missoula, Montana.

HERBERT HOOVER

The Reasons Why
They Get That Way

*Fishing is essentially a participatory sport, and some of
those who participate get wholly caught up in their
love for this particular activity. President Herbert
Hoover was one of those who fully appreciated its
rewards—enough to set down his opinions on why
those who passionately love to fish get that way. If
you never thought about it before, Hoover explains
why "fishing is much more than fish."*

Fishing is a chance to wash one's soul with pure
air, with the rush of the brook, or with the shim-
mer of the sun on the blue water.

It brings meekness and inspiration from the
scenery of nature, charity toward tackle makers,
patience toward fish, a mockery of profits and egos,
a quieting of hate, a rejoicing that you do not have
to decide a darned thing until next week.

And it is discipline in the equality of man—for
all men are equal before fish.

The reason for it all is that fishing is fun and good
for the soul of man.

The human animal originally came from out-of-
doors. When spring begins to move in his bones,

238

he just must get out again. Moreover, as civilization, cement pavements, office buildings, and radios have overwhelmed us, the need for regeneration has increased, and the impulses are even stronger. When all the routines and details and the human bores get on our nerves, we just yearn to go away from here to somewhere else.

When you get full up of telephone bells, church bells, office boys, columnists, pieces of paper and the household chores—you get that urge to go away from here. Going fishing is the only explanation in the world that even skeptics will accept.

Nor is it the fish we get that count. We could buy them in the market for mere silver at one percent of the cost. Fishing is much more than fish; it is the vitalizing lure to outdoor life. It is the great occasion when we may return to the fine simplicity of our forefathers.

And there is the chance to associate with fishermen. You have the opportunity to renew old and long-time friendships. All fishermen and fisherladies are by nature friendly and righteous persons. No one of them ever went to jail while fishing—unless they forgot to buy a license.

I need not extol to you the joys of outdoor life, its values in relaxation, its contribution to real and successful work. The spiritual uplift of the good will, cheerfulness and optimism that accompanies every fishing expedition is the particular spirit that our people need in these troublous times of suspicion and doubt.

Life is not comprised entirely of making a living or of arguing about the future or defaming the past. It is the break of the waves in the sun, the contemplation of the eternal flow of the stream, the stretch of forest and mountain in their manifestation of the Maker—it is all these that soothe our troubles, shame our wickedness, and inspire us to esteem our fellow men—especially other fishermen.

Strong primary instincts—and they are useful instincts—get rejuvenation by a thrust into the simpler life. For instance, we do not catch fish in the presence of, or by the methods of, our vast complex of industrialism, nor in the luxury of summer hotels, nor through higher thought, for that matter. In our outdoor life we get repose from the troubles of soul that this vast complex of civilization imposes upon us in our working hours and our restless nights. Association with the placid ripples of the waves and the quiet chortle of the streams is soothing to our "het-up" anxieties.

I am for fishing for fun as a contribution to constructive joy because it gives an excuse and an impulse to take to the woods and to the water. Moreover, fishing has democratic values because the same privilege of joy is open to the country boy as to the city lad. (And equally to his properly brought-up city or farmer dad.)

Lots of people committed crimes during the year who would not have done so if they had been fishing. The increase of crime is among those de-

deprived of the regenerations that impregnate the mind and character of fishermen.

Our standards of material progress include the notion and the hope that we shall lessen the daily hours of labor on the farm, at the bench, and in the office. We also dream of longer annual holidays and more of them, as scientific discovery and mass production do our production job faster and faster. But they dull the souls of men. Even now, the great majority of us really work no more than eight hours a day. And if we sleep eight hours we have eight hours in which to ruminate and make merry or stir the caldron of evil. This civilization is not going to depend upon what we do when we work so much as what we do in our time off.

The moral and spiritual forces of our country do not lose ground in the hours we are busy on our jobs; their battle is the leisure time. We associate joy with leisure. We have great machinery for joy, some of it destructive, some of it synthetic, some of it mass production. We go to chain theaters and movies; we watch somebody else knock a ball over the fence or kick it over the goal post. I do that too and I believe in it. I do, however, insist that no organized joy has values comparable to the outdoors. . . . We gain none of the rejuvenating cheer that comes from return to the solemnity, the calm and inspiration of primitive nature.

Contemplation of the eternal flow of the stream, the stretch of forest and mountain, all reduce our egotism, soothe our troubles, and shame our wickedness. And in it we make a physical effort that no

241

sitting on cushions, benches, or side lines provides. To induce people to take this joy they need some stimulant from the hunt, the fish or the climb. I am for fish.

NICK LYONS
Gray Streets, Bright Rivers

Well-known as an editor and publisher of books devoted to sports, Nick Lyons here contrasts the constrictions of the workaday world with the freedom and peace of clear free-running rivers. The differences between oppressive New York City street life and the rich and mysterious natural world, particularly the trout in its natural environment, provide Lyons' subject. In coming to terms with his attraction to rivers and fishing, he locates "those parts of myself that have been lost in cities."

Every object rightly seen unlocks a quality of the soul.

RALPH WALDO EMERSON

In the evening on upper Broadway, two blocks from my apartment, lynx-eyed women stand near the bus stop as the buses go by, waiting. They wait patiently. Their impassive rouged faces show only the slightest touch of expectation; their gold high-heeled shoes glitter. Their dresses are exceedingly short. One of them hums, and the sound is like a low cacophonous motor, in perpetual motion.

A man asks, with startling politeness, "Would

243

you be kind enough to spare me fifty cents, sir, for a cup of coffee?" Later I see him caterwauling, along with a young tough, eyes wild, waving a pint bottle of Seagram's. Nothing here is quite as it seems.

Four blocks away, only last month, an ex-cop "looking for action" found himself dismembered by a pimp and then deposited, piecemeal, in several ash cans in front of a Chinese laundry I once used.

On a given evening you can see:

The diminutive Arab who every night paces rapidly back and forth in front of the old church, talking incessantly to no one in particular; men rigged up to look like women, with bandanas and false breasts, arm in arm, leering; more lynx-eyed women, one of whom, quite tall and extraordinarily thin, reminds me of a Doberman pinscher; a few tired old men closing up their fruit stalls after working sixteen hours; some fashionable people in front of Zabar's or one of the new restaurants, who look like they've been imported, to dress up the place, from Central Casting; the bald, immie-eyed Baptist—his eyes like those little marbles we used to call steelies—his face bass-belly white, with placards and leaflets, proclaiming to all who will listen that the end of all things is surely at hand. Perhaps. Or perhaps not.

Everyone is an apparition, connected to me by eye only. Why am I always looking over my shoulder, around corners, then, to see who's tracking me or what will be? Hunted by ghosts. I want to become part of them, any one of them, to feel their pulse and know their heart, but I fail; some part of me is locked. Bill Humphrey says these people are only ahead of their time: we'll all be there soon.

And sometimes I see, in the early evening, a glimpse of sunset through the rows of stone, catch the faintest smell of salt, and even see the Hudson itself, sullied but flowing water.

I know no more than ten people among the thousands who live within two blocks of my apartment. . . .

Downtown, where the game for the big green is played, I go to a meeting that lasts eight hours. After the first ten minutes, I feel the tightening in my chest. I begin to doodle; I scribble out a meaningless note and pass it to someone I know across the table, because I've seen executives in the movies do that. I look for the windows, but they're hidden behind heavy, brocaded draperies so that the air conditioning will take—anyway, we're in the back of the hotel so even if the windows were open, I'd only see the backs of other buildings. Everyone is talking with pomp and edge; I jot down Evelyn Waugh's observation, "that neurosis people mistake for energy." I drink two glasses of ice water. I speak like a good boy, when spoken to.

Suddenly I begin to sweat. I've been in this windowless room for fifteen years. I have been a juggler, flinging my several lives high and carelessly into the air, never catching them, barely feeling one as it touches my hand. Nine to five I am here; then a salt stick on the subway and five hours in the classroom; then I am the fastest ghostwriter in the East, becoming a lawyer one week, an expert on Greece the next, then an adopted girl searching for the blood link. When there is time, after midnight, I write high-toned scholarship—on Chrétien de Troyes and Thomas Nashe and William Ellery Channing and Saint Augustine—and shaggy-fish stories; or I prepare a lecture on "The Generosity of Whitman." A smorgasbord, my life. Five hours of sleep and back at 'em again, the ghost who is not what he seems, back at meetings like this one, dreaming.

I say my piece in front of all these important men as enthusiastically as I can. These are the rules of the game. Part of what I say—a few words —has to do with rivers. From my words I catch their briefest warbling sound, like the faint rush of wind among the leaves, or a rushing faucet, and when I sit down, there in the back of the hotel, with the windows covered by heavy drapes and the smoke from cigars (mine among them) thick around our heads, as strategies unfold and campaigns thicken, I see a glimpse of them, inside. Deep within me they uncoil.

Rivers.

Bright green live rivers.

The coil and swoop of them, their bright dancing riffles and their flat dimpled pools at dusk. Their changes and undulations, each different flowing inch of them. Their physics and morphology and entomology and soul. The willows and alders along their banks. A particular rock the size of an igloo. Layers of serrated slate from which rhododendron plumes like an Inca headdress, against which the current rushes, eddies. The quick turn of a yellow-bellied trout in the lip of the current. Five trout, in loose formation, in

246

a pellucid backwater where I cannot get at them. A world. Many worlds.

> . . . oft, in lonely rooms, and 'mid the din
> Of towns and cities . . .

as Wordsworth said in "Tintern Abbey," about a nature he felt but never really saw,

> . . . I have owed to them
> In hours of weariness, sensations sweet,
> Felt in the blood, and felt along the heart. . . .

Yes, I owe rivers that. And more. They are something wild, untamed—like that Montana eagle riding a thermal on extended wings, high above the Absaroka mountain pasture flecked with purple lupine. And like the creatures in them: quick trout with laws we can learn, sometimes, somewhat.

I do not want the qualities of my soul unlocked only by this tense, cold, gray, noisy, gaudy, grabby place—full of energy and neurosis and art and anti-art and getting and spending—in which that business part of my life, at this time in my life, must of necessity be lived. I have other needs as well. I have other parts of my soul.

Nothing in this world so enlivens my spirit and emotions as the rivers I know. They are necessities. In their clear, swift or slow, generous or coy waters, I regain my powers; I find again those parts of myself that have been lost in cities. Stillness. Patience. Green thoughts. Open eyes. Attachment. High drama. Earthiness. Wit. The Huck

247

Finn I once was. Gentleness. "The life of things." They are my perne within the whirling gyre.

Just knowing they are there, and that their hatches will come again and again according to the great natural laws, is some consolation to carry with me on the subways and into the gray offices and out onto upper Broadway at night.

Rivers have been brought to me by my somewhat unintelligible love of fishing. From the little Catskill creek in which I gigged my first trout to the majestic rivers of the West—the Madison, the Yellowstone, the Big Hole, the Snake—fishing has been the hook. And in the pursuit of trout I have found much larger fish.

"Must you actually *fish* to enjoy rivers?" my friend the Scholar asks.

It is difficult to explain but, yes, the fish make every bit of difference. They anchor and focus my eye, rivet my ear.

And could this not be done by a trained patient lover of nature who did not carry a rod?

Perhaps it could. But fishing is *my* hinge, the "oiléd ward" that opens a few of the mysteries for me. It is so for all kinds of fishermen, I suspect, but especially so for fly-fishermen, who live closest to the seamless web of life in rivers. That shadow I am pursuing beneath the amber water is a hieroglyphic: I read its position, watch its relationship to a thousand other shadows, observe its steadiness and purpose. That shadow is a great glyph, connected to the darting swallow overhead; to that dancing cream caddis fly near the patch of alders; to the little cased caddis larva on the streambed; to the shell of the hatched stone fly on the rock; to the contours of the river, the velocity of the flow, the chemical composition and temperature of the water; to certain vegetable life called plankton that I cannot see; to the mill nine miles upstream and the reservoir into which the river flows—and, oh, a thousand other factors, fleeting and solid and telling as that shadow. Fishing makes me a student of all this—and a hunter.

Which couldn't be appreciated unless you fish?

Which mean more to me because I do. Fishing makes rivers my corrective lens; I see differently. Not only does the bird taking the mayfly signify a hatch, not only does the flash of color at the break of the riffle signify a fish feeding, but my powers uncoil inside me and I must determine which insect is hatching and what feeding pattern the trout has established. Then I must properly equip myself and properly approach the fish and properly present my imitation. I am engaged in a hunt that is more than a hunt, for the objects of the hunt are mostly to be found within myself, in the nature of my response and action. I am on a Parsifalian quest. I must be scientist, technician, athlete, perhaps even a queer sort of poet.

The Scholar smiles wanly and says, "It all sounds like rank hedonism. And some cultism. With some mumbo jumbo thrown in."

Yes, I am out to pleasure myself, though sometimes after I've been chewed by no-see-ums until I'm pocked like a leper you wouldn't think that. There is a physical testing: the long hours at early morning, in bright sun, or at dusk; casting until your arm is like lead and your legs, from wading against the stiff current, are numb. That is part of the quest: to cleanse through exertion.

And the cultism and mumbo jumbo?

Some of trout fishing has become that, perhaps always was that. It is a separate little world, cunningly contrived, with certain codes and rules and icons. It is not a religion, though some believers make it such, and it is less than an art. But it has qualities of each. It touches heart and head; it demands and builds flexibility and imagination; it is not easy. I come to rivers like an initiate to holy springs. If I cannot draw from them an enduring catechism or from their impulses even very much about "moral evil and of good," they still confer upon me the beneficence of the only deity I have been able to find. And when the little world becomes *too* cunningly contrived? Wit helps.

My friend the Scholar says he is not a puritan or a moralist but that it seems to him it would be more satisfying to make something that would last —a book, a poem, a cabinet, a wooden bowl—than merely to fish well. He quotes Cézanne, from a letter, after a day of fishing: "All this is easier than painting but it does not lead far."

Not hardly. Not very far at all. Except that this may be precisely where I want it to lead. Let the world lead far—as one should frame it to do; let art last long and lead far and to form. Let a few other human activities lead far, though most of them lead us up a tree or up the asshole of the world. Let fly-fishing be temporary and fleeting and inconsequential. I do not mind.

Enough. Enough.

Too much theory and this pleasant respite from

the north Broadway renaissance and gray offices will become an extravagant end that leads too far. Fishing is nothing if not a pastime; it would be hell if I did it all the time.

Beyond the dreams and the theories, there are the days when a close friend will pick me up at dawn on my deserted city block and we will make the long drive together, talking, connected, uncoiling, until we reach our river for the day. It is a simple adventure we are undertaking; it is a break from the beetle-dull routine, a new start, an awakening of the senses, a pilgrimage.

Flooded with memories and expectations, we take out our rods, suit up in waders and vest, special fish hats and nets, arrange flies and leaders, and take to the woods. Each article of equipment, each bit of gear in our ritualistic uniform, is part of the act. The skunk cabbage is thrusting up, lush and green-purple out of the moist brown mulch of last year's leaves; we flush a white-tailed deer that bounds off boldly; we see the pale-green buds pressing out of the birch branches. "Spring has come again," said Rilke. "The earth is like a little child who knows poems by heart—many, so many." We wonder whether the Hendricksons will or will not hatch at midday. We have our hopes.

With rivers as with good friends, you always feel better for a few hours in their presence; you always want to review your dialogue, years later, with a particular pool or riffle or bend, and to live back through layers of experience. We have been to this river before and together. We have much to relive.

Then we are on the river. It is still there. So

much is perishable, impermanent, dispensable today, so much is gobbled up by industry and housing and the wanton surge of people, we half thought it might be gone, like that river we used to fish in Dutchess County, now bludgeoned by tract homes and industrial plants and trailers, now littered and warm and dead. Trout are yardsticks; they are an early warning system like the canary in the mine—when they go, what will happen to the rest of the planet, to the quality of life?

Yes, this river is still there, still alive, still pregnant with possibility.

"There's a swirl," I say, pointing.

"I saw one upstream, too."

"A few flies are coming off, see?"

"Yes, we're going to make a day of it."

My pulse quickens, the long gray city winter vanishes. In a moment we separate and belong to the river and to its mysteries, to its smooth glides and pinched bends, to the myriad sweet problems that call forth total concentration, that obviate philosophy.

Yes, these are Hendricksons, *Ephemerella subvaria*, and the hatch, on schedule, is just beginning. I am by profession neither an angler nor a scientist but there's always more pleasure in knowing than in not knowing. I take the lower pool and spot four good trout, poised high in the clear, flat water, waiting for the duns to hatch in the riffles and float down. By tilting my head close to the surface, I can see them, like little sailboats, drifting down. Two, three, there's another. Not many yet. A couple of birds are working, dipping and darting; against the light sky above the treeline I

252

pick out one mayfly, watch it flutter, watch a swallow swoop, hesitate, and take it. What looks so pastoral is violent; it is, only on a smaller, more civilized scale, a horde of bluefish slashing a bunker school to bits, leaving blood and fin and head everywhere, to be picked up by the ravenous sea birds. The bites are cleaner here: the birds and trout take a whole creature in one mouthful.

Then back to the river. There are circles below me; the fish are feeding steadily. Shall I fish above or below them? They are so still, so firmly established in an irregular row across the channel in that clear flat water, that I elect the road less traveled and decide to fish down to them on a slack line—this way I won't have to cast over their backs.

It is delicate work, but I know that this year I have an excellent imitation of the natural fly, that my 5X leader is light enough, and that I've done just enough slack-line downstream casting to manage. Fishing is cumulative, though you don't learn all of it, ever.

I position myself carefully on the bank—it would be fatal to wade above such fish—strip about forty feet of line from my reel, and false cast twice.

My rod jerks backward. I've hung my fly in that low brush.

The interruption of the music, like the needle hitting a scratch on a recording of the Brandenburg Concerto, irritates madly but is not final.

When I return, the fish are still feeding, more steadily now, even rhythmically.

My cast lands well above the fish, and my fly floats without drag a few feet short of their feeding station before the line tightens; a little V forms behind the fly and it goes under.

I retrieve the fly slowly, unwilling to ruffle the surface until there are no more than ten feet of line still in the water, then cast again. The fly floats freely and I hold my breath. This time it will go far enough. It's two feet upstream of the first fish; I'm still holding my breath; the snake in the line unwinds and begins to straighten, slowly, then faster; I lean forward to give it another foot, another few inches; I watch the fish move slightly, turn toward the fly, inspect it, nose up to it, and then the fly drags and the fish turns away.

A deep breath.

Two more casts: one that quarters the river too amply and causes the fly to drag within two feet; another that floats properly but gets there a second after the trout has taken a natural. Then a good cast, a good float, and the fish pivots and takes, feels the hook, jumps twice, and burrows across and upstream. It's thirteen inches and not strong enough to cause much mischief; anyway, after the strike, after I have successfully gulled this creature from another element, linked my brain to its brain, I am less interested. After a few minutes I have the fish near my bank, lean down and twitch the hook free, and it is gone, vigorously—sleek and spotted and still quick.

When I've taken the slime off the fly and air-dried it, I notice that most of the fish have left their stations; only one fish is working in the pool now, across the main current, in a little backwater. It will require a different approach, a different strategy. I take fully five minutes to work my way downstream along the bank, into the water, and across to the other side, moving slowly so as not to disturb the life of the river. I am only its guest. The fish is still working when I get there.

I am directly below the trout now and can see only the periodic circles about forty feet above me. I don't want to put the fly line over it, and I know its actual feeding position in the water will be at least several feet above the mark of the rise form, which is floating downstream and is the final mark of his deliberate inspection ritual. I elect to cast into the edge of the main current above the fish and hope the fly will catch an eddying current and come down into the trout's position. The cast is good. Squinting, I watch the fly float down, then free of, the fast center current and my fly line hug the nearly dead water. There is an electric moment when the circle forms. My arm shoots up. The fish has taken the fly solidly and feels like a good one. It does not jump but bores into its little pool, then into the current; then it gets below me. I slip, recover, and begin to edge downstream, the fish stripping line from the reel now, boiling at the surface twice, then coming upstream quickly while I raise the rod high and haul in line to keep the fish from slipping the hook.

A little later I release the fish from the net, turning it out—a beautiful seventeen-inch brown.

I take two more fish, smaller ones, in the riffle below the pool, then head upstream again to where the first fish were feeding, approaching the spot from below. The hatch has peaked and is tapering now; the late-afternoon chill of late April has set in and I feel it for the first time. One fish is still feeding but I cannot, in six or seven casts, raise it, and finally it stops.

I breathe deeply and take out a pipe. There may be a spinner fall in another hour but I am exhausted. The river is placid, calm now. No fish are rising. The drama is over; the actors have retired to the wings. I have been caught for two hours in an intensely sensual music, and I want to stop, perhaps for the day—to smoke the pipe now, watch that squirrel in the oak, look for deer tracks and chipmunk holes. The city has become a bad dream, a B movie I once saw that violates my imagination by returning at odd moments. Most of the world would be bored by these past two hours. Most of the world? Most of the world is polluting the rivers making the worse appear the better cause, peaing, grating on each other's ears, gouging, putting their fingers on others' souls or their hands in the wrong pockets, scheming, honking, pretending, politicking, small-talking, criticizing.

"Is that *all* you find?" I hear the Scholar ask me.

"Nope. But there's a damned lot of it."

"You're a misanthrope, a hater of cities," he says. "You claim to love gentleness but . . ."

I don't especially want to answer his questions now so I look back at the river. We invented the non sequitur for just such moments.

Yes, we have made a day of it. Two, three hours sandwiched in. Little enough. But deep. And durable. And more than a day's worth. We've earned memories—full and textured—that live now in our very marrowbones, that make us more alive. Our thoughts will be greener, our judgments perhaps

256

sharper, our eyes a bit brighter. We live day to day with little change in our perceptions, but I never go to a river that I do not see newly and freshly, that I do not learn, that I do not find a story.

On the way home I still feel the tug of the river against my thighs, and in my mind's eye I can see that largest rising trout, the neat circle when it took a natural, the quick dramatic spurt— electric through my whole body—when it took my fly and I felt its force. And I wondered why I had not raised that last fish.

It was not the ultimate river, the ultimate afternoon; it was not so exquisite as a Keatsian moment frozen and anguished because it would not last. There will be others—never equal, always discretely, sharply different. A thousand such moments. Days when, against all expectation, the river is dead; days when it is generous beyond dreams.

A luxury? A mere vacation?

No, those rivers are more. They are my Pilgrim Creek and Walden Pond, however briefly. Those rivers and their bounty—bright and wild—touch me and through me touch every person whom I meet. They are a metaphor for life. In their movement, in their varied glides, runs, and pools, in their inevitable progress toward the sea, they contain many of the secrets we seek to understand about ourselves, our purposes. The late Roderick Haig-Brown said, "Were it not for the strong, quick life of rivers, for their sparkle in the sunshine, for the cold grayness of them under rain and the feel of them about my legs as I set my feet hard down on rocks or sand or gravel, I should fish less often." Amen. When such rivers die, as so many have, so

257

too dies an irretrievable part of the soul of each of the thousands of anglers who in their waters find deep, enduring life.

Visit a few of them with me. We won't linger long. I know how fearfully busy and hurried you are. But perhaps a few moments will be of some profit. Perhaps you will meet some old friends, smile (with-out seeking to gull someone thereby), and make a new friend or two as we travel: first near, then far.

ED ZERN

To Hell with Fishing

Although many writers on fishing approach the sport with a reverence some devote to religion and art, Zern takes a more down-to-earth approach. In these four vignettes, he pokes fun at those who take their fishing too seriously. The one-liners are choice: "If you ask a wet-fly fisherman why a natural insect would be swimming around like crazy under water, he gets huffy and walks away." Everything sacred to the fishing crowd is play for Zern's wit.

HOW TO DISPOSE OF DEAD FISH

A recent survey showed that roughly two-thirds of all fishermen never eat fish. This should surprise nobody. Fish is brain food. People who eat fish have large, well-developed brains. People with large, well-developed brains don't fish. It's that simple.

The question a fisherman faces, then, is how to get rid of the fish he has caught. There are several schools of thought on this problem.

The Pilgrim Fathers buried a dead fish in each hill of corn to make it grow. Unfortunately, few fishermen have access to cornfields. Most farmers would sooner have a cyclone.

Some fishermen try to palm off their catch on kindhearted friends and neighbors. Naturally, it doesn't take *those* folks long to learn that when a trout has been lugged around all day in a hot creel, it is poor competition for a pork chop.

Other methods of fish disposal are (1) stuffing them in a corner mailbox when nobody is looking, (2) hiding them under potted palms, (3) checking them at the Union Depot and throwing away the check, (4) hurling them from fast-moving cars on lonely roads late at night, (5) mailing them to the Curator of the Museum of Natural History, requesting an identification of the species and giving a phoney name and return address, and (6) baiting walrus-traps with them.

None of these methods is satisfactory. (1) Is probably illegal, (2), (3), (4), and (5) are in lousy taste, and (6) brings up the problem of walrus-disposal. Walrus-disposal makes fish-disposal seem like child's play.

My friend Walt Dette throws back all the trout he catches in the Beaverkill, and keeps only chubs to feed to his seven Siamese cats. This is dandy for people who have (a) sense enough to put back trout for future sport and who also have (b) seven Siamese cats. Few fishermen have both.

Both, hell. *Either*.

AIN'T IT THE TRUTH? NO

Fishermen are born honest, but they get over it.

When a fisherman is going to tell you about the

big musky he caught, he knows you will subtract ten pounds to allow for his untruthfulness.

So he adds ten pounds to allow for your subtraction.

The other ten pounds he adds on account of being such a liar.

Then he adds five pounds for good measure because what is five pounds more or less on such a big fish?

As a matter of fact, he didn't even catch that musky. He found it floating belly-up.

It died laughing at a Hokum's DeLuxe Weedless Streamlined Hollow-ground Galvanized Non-skid Semi-automatic Husky-Musky Lure with Centerboard Optional, $1.50 at all sporting-goods stores.

Lizzie Greig, the Gal Fly-tier of the Angler's Roost, was born in Scotland on the River Tweed. It was too late at night to borrow the greengrocer's scales, so they used the one her father used for salmon.

She weighed 34 lbs., 5 ozs.

HOW TO CATCH FISH WITH FLIES

Some wiseguy once defined a fishing line as a piece of string with a worm on one end and a damn fool on the other.

This is a silly definition, of course—for many fishermen use flies instead of worms. They think it is more hoity-toity. If worms cost two bits apiece, and you could dig Royal Coachmen and Parmacheene Belles out of the manure pile, they would think differently. This is called human nature.

Fly fishermen spend hours tying little clumps of fur and feathers on hooks, trying to make a trout fly that looks like a real fly. But nobody has ever seen a natural insect trying to mate with a Fanwing Ginger Quill.

Of course, every once in a while a fly fisherman catches a trout on a trout fly, and he thinks this proves something. It doesn't. Trout eat mayflies, burnt matches, small pieces of inner tube, each other, caddis worms, Dewey buttons, crickets, lima beans, Colorado spinners, and almost anything else they can get in their fool mouths. It is probable they think the trout fly is some feathers tied to a hook. Hell, they're not blind. They just want to see how it tastes.

Trout flies are either wet flies or dry flies, depending on whether they are supposed to sink or float. If you ask a wet-fly fisherman why a natural insect would be swimming around like crazy under water, he gets huffy and walks away.

Many fishermen think trout are color-blind, but that is nothing to what trout think of fishermen.

HOW TO TELL FISH FROM FISHERMEN

Hardly a day goes by at my office but that some damn fool wakes me out of a sound sleep to complain he has difficulty telling fish from fishermen. Actually, it is a simple matter, once you get the hang of it.

There are several methods of telling the difference. One way is to observe the subject while it is reading a newspaper. If its lips do not move, it is a fish.

The most dependable way is to carry a copy of *American Food and Game Fishes*, by Jordan and Everman. Anything not listed in the index is a fisherman.

A much tougher problem is how to tell small-mouth bass from large-mouth bass. Here are a few simple rules to remember:

Small-mouth bass like the cold, clear water of spring-fed ponds and swift streams. Large-mouth bass figure water is water.

Large-mouth bass think wobbling plugs look like crippled minnows. This just goes to show you.

Small-mouth bass adore spinner-and-fly combinations. Gollup Kuhn, the Champeen Liar of Lackbaen, caught a small-mouth bass by trolling a privy-door hinge in the Delaware River. It is this sort of thing that makes the Anglers Club of New York blow its top.

Large-mouth bass hang around stumps and lily pads, passing the time of day. Small-mouth bass prefer rocky ledges. Ask them why and they hem and haw. Paradoxically, small-mouth bass fishermen tell bigger lies than large-mouth bass fishermen.

Incidentally, the flavor of a large-mouth bass is vastly improved by popping it into the garbage can and going out for dinner.

During severe droughts, the catfish buries itself in the mud. On him, it looks good.

FOOTBALL

PAUL GALLICO
Knute Rockne of Notre Dame

When college football first moved into national news in the twenties, Notre Dame and coach Knute Rockne became the center of popular attention and the favorites of the press, inducing each fall "a six-week emotional binge." Rockne, as a player on the Notre Dame team, had helped popularize the forward pass as a standard offensive play—not a desperation move. The forward pass brought breath-taking excitement and more varied plays for spectators than the running game ever had.

Among those Rockne coached was a boy, always in trouble, named George Gipp, who was supposed to have said on his deathbed, "Go win this one for the Gipper"—but this, like most myths, has been amplified in the telling, according to Paul Gallico's investigation of it.

Notre Dame under Rockne compiled a solid winning record and fans nationwide, even those who had no direct associations with the college, adopted the team as their own; even subway-riding New Yorkers of many different ethnic backgrounds identified themselves with the "Fighting Irish" when Notre Dame came east to take on Army at Yankee Stadium.

If you are interested in the passage of time and the changes it brings about, you have only to glance at the photographs of the football teams of the 1900s and those of today and, if nothing else, note the difference in attire and armor plating.

Our forefather, his hair neatly parted in the middle, wore short pants known as "moleskins," either quilted or with some sort of ribbed stiffening in them, a woolen jersey, and over it a kind of leather jerkin. Underneath was a device of leather called schimmels, that laced across the shoulders, to protect the collarbone from breakage. The helmet, if and when worn, was of soft leather and covered the ears. Some players used a rubber noseguard.

Compare this mild sort of padding with the almost rigid armor worn today and in particular the solid, rock-hard, plastic helmet with its steel projections.

The uniforms have altered, as have the size and shape of the ball, and the rules of the game itself have been changed incessantly, to the point where a veteran of the year 1900 might not understand the play of 1965 unless an interpreter were at hand to explain it to him.

It was during that famous decade of 1920 to 1930 that football underwent possibly its greatest transition from old-fashioned to modern.

But it was also during that period that a brand-new phenomenon appeared in American football and one which has all but disappeared today. It developed a nationwide emotion that before the decade was out had become almost religious in its nature, and Knute Rockne was its high priest.

At this extraordinary time in the history of American sports as well as that of the people of the United States, Knute Kenneth Rockne, football coach of Notre Dame, was himself a most prodigious, phenomenal, and singular person and more than any other, directly responsible for the extent and violence of the spirit that infected the game and spread to the farthest corners of the country. For ten years this bald, round-faced man with the squashed-in nose and his sensational teams, each fall, initiated a six-week emotional binge among fans, but particularly involving heretofore non-fans of the game of football, that amounted almost to the hysteria of evangelism.

Prior to this, football player Joe College was something of a comic figure with his turtle-necked sweater, Buster Brown haircut, flying wedge, and determination, if need be, to "Die for dear old Rutgers," to the accompaniment of a chant of "Rah-Rah-Rah, Sis Boom Ah" from the crowd on the sidelines, to stimulate him to the sacrifice. Mass cheering has survived in modern football, but it is today nothing but a spectator catharsis and is considered a nuisance by the player who has business to get on with and signals of logarithmic complication to remember and transmit in the pre-play huddles.

Early interest centered around the Big Three, the Universities of Yale, Princeton, and Harvard, but the crowds attending their annual titanic clashes were composed of alumni and their families. Considering the enrollment of these universities, graduating hundreds of nubile young men every year, it did not take long for them to breed pennant-waving partisan and vociferous audiences for these contests. There might be a few outsiders, ambitious youngsters of the ever-increasing middle class, who hoped someday to attain university status, who were "for" Yale, or "for" Harvard, but by and large the rivalries between these great seats of learning were family affairs.

Newspapers in the East were beginning to give publicity to the annual games involving the three, since many of their readers were connected in one way or another as partisans of the universities. Socially the Big Game was a wonderfully gay and youthful affair, featuring the prettiest girls in the world decked out in chrysanthemums and bright ribbons, accompanied by handsome, coonskin-coated young men, bearing pennants showing the names and colors of the universities and with flasks on their hips since Prohibition was with us. These clashes often coincided with the Thanksgiving festival; November winds brought carmine to fresh, young faces; young hearts, particularly feminine ones, beat high, and on the field below, twenty-two heroes patriotically and chivalrously battled for the glory of alma mater and the admiring glances of the little beauties in the stands.

The man in the street, however, largely ignored it. The hullabaloo struck him as juvenile, the game of football itself as faintly ridiculous, with its pushing and shoving and piling up, and there was still largely the situation of town and gown; the self-made man versus the college smartie. It was Knute Rockne, in the main, who brought about a drastic change in the situation.

Neither a born American nor an Irishman, nor a Catholic, until toward the end of his life he became a convert, he was the coach of the University of Notre Dame, located at South Bend, Indiana; a Catholic university and a stronghold of Irish

Catholicism in the Middle West. It was the semi-religious background of this school which lent just that touch of mysticism and emotionalism as a starter. But all the rest of the extraordinary spirit and hysteria which marked so many of the games played by Notre Dame during that decade were supplied by Rockne.

The sentimental jag reached its high point in the month of October before, during, and after the annual contest between Notre Dame and the cadets of the United States Military Academy at West Point, played in New York City; an affair which took on almost the quality of a pagan autumnal rite, and engaged the passionate observation of millions of people.

You will see if you look at photographs of the early Notre Dame teams which first came to New York, that their costumes and headgear are old-fashioned, somewhat between the earliest uniforms and the modern. But there is something equally old-fashioned belonging to that era of the twenties that doesn't show up in pictures. It is the aura of dedication that was quite different from anything one seems to feel or experience about football and its participants now, except perhaps, curiously enough, in the ranks of the professionals and their adherents. It is the pros and their fans who, by and large, have taken over the fervency that used to attend the college games.

That difference, I am convinced, was supplied by one man, this same Knute Rockne, himself a football star of Notre Dame from 1911 through 1913 and head coach at the university from 1919 until his tragic death in an airplane crash in the West in 1931.

He was a hired hand, engaged like so many others to teach the sport to university students, train and advise them, prepare them physically as well as spiritually and strategically and turn out winning teams if possible. But more than any other in his profession he captured the hearts and imaginations of the Americans of his time.

He was responsible for many strategic innovations in football play, such as the shift and dramatic use of the forward pass that opened up the attack and made it more visual. But it was for quite a different contribution that he made his major impact upon both his day and the game.

He brought an extra dimension to football and in particular to the teams he coached, which enabled the spectators to share in the emotions engendered by the struggle on the field far more than they had ever done before.

American college football was a battle which very often transcended not only itself but those participating in it as well, to the point where suddenly the onlooker saw it no longer as a spectacle provided by two sets of young men, but rather as a giant and abstract manifestation of two contending wills. It offered a phase of the classic physics paradox of what happens when an unstoppable force encounters an immovable object.

Further, unlike other sports, there were no villains in these college clashes. The teams were too ephemeral, here one year, graduated the next. Partisanship was a matter of adherence to a university rather than individual members of its football squads. Outstanding stars achieved tremendous followings, but whoever heard of hating a halfback or an end?

And finally, there was another kind of sharing for which Knute Rockne was responsible, since it was his teams that sent the renown and name of Notre Dame soaring. It took the form of the famous assistant Irish and Subway Alumni of the South Bend institution, whose headquarters were in New York, but whose members were scattered to the four corners of the land wherever there was anyone named Ryan or Rafferty, Clancy or O'Houlahan; or Kraus or Cohen or Tony Bacigalupo.

This was quite one of the most amazing phenomena and transitions of the times. Suddenly everybody wanted to get into the act and belong. Hundreds of thousands of people prior to this time who had looked down upon the game as "Rah-Rah" stuff now wanted to identify themselves with it, an identification, incidentally, far more rabid and partisan even than that exhibited by the alumni, or family members of universities.

Dates and facts here become a matter of some importance. The initial Army-Notre Dame meeting took place at West Point in the fall of 1913. Up to that time few had ever known Notre Dame in the East. The Westerners won 35 to 13 and from then on one heard plenty about the Catholic school.

One of the players on the Notre Dame team of that year was an end by the name of Rockne, another was a young back, Gus Dorais. The Notre Dame coach was Jesse Harper. For the first time experts in the East saw the forward pass—mostly Dorais to Rockne, used as a part of sustained of-

fensive football rather than a last-minute desperation. Overnight it seemed that the game had been
opened up, revolutionized, and turned into a thrilling and dramatic spectacle, no longer dependent
upon partisan loyalties for thrills. It had become
something to watch. But the Subway Alumni were
not yet.

In 1919, the year when Knute Rockne was
appointed head coach at Notre Dame, and subsequently in 1920 and 1921, his teams were Western
champions and national champions winning a total
of twenty-eight games and losing one.

From 1920 through 1930, Notre Dame won
ninety-six, lost twelve, and was tied three times.

The man behind this fantastic string of victories was this same Rockne, and West Point and
Notre Dame acquired the greatest rooting sections
in the history of the game. Only seventy thousand
at a time could crowd into Yankee Stadium in
New York actually to see them play, but millions
became fanatical adherents via the radio and the
newspapers. The game of football—at least this particular one involving Army and Notre Dame—had
broken through every class barrier that still existed
in the United States.

World War I had supplied a new and ready-
made cheering section for the two service teams. If
during our brief embroilment in that catastrophe
you had worn khaki, you were for Army; if bell-
bottomed trousers, Navy was your team from then
on. The annual clash between Army and Navy
took on an importance it never had before, far
transcending even the game between Yale and
Harvard, for now we had alumni, if not actually

of West Point or the Naval Academy, at least of the two services. But until the advent of Notre Dame there was no school which extended a mass appeal to ordinary civilians.

With the sky-rocketing of this university out of the West, their brand of exciting, razzle-dazzle, wide-open football, the wonderful sobriquet of "Fighting Irish" pinned on them by the sportswriters (in spite of the fact that the majority of the names of the team members were not Irish—of the thirty letter-winners in 1927, for instance, only seven could be said to have monickers stemming from the Ould Sod), everything changed. The warm affection and the curious kind of sports love engendered by the unique personality of Rockne led literally millions of people who had never been to college or seen a campus to adopt Notre Dame as their very own and thereafter identify themselves with the school.

Beginning with 1923, New Yorkers had the opportunity of seeing this team in action, provided they could buy their way into the baseball parks. That year the Army-Notre Dame tussle was played at Ebbets Field in Brooklyn. In 1924 and 1925, fifty-five thousand souls jammed the Polo Grounds beneath Coogan's Bluff. From then on it was seventy thousand persons packing every nook and cranny of Yankee Stadium.

New York was never before, or since, so sweetly gay and electric as it was when Rock brought his boys to town; the city was wild with excitement and filled with pretty girls and gray-clad cadets who thronged the hotel ballrooms when it was over, while the civilian fans argued or battled it out in the Third Avenue speakeasies.

275

These Interborough Rapid Transit Notre Damers came from every walk of life; Gentile and Jew, Broadway show-biz and nightclub dolls, bartenders, prize fighters, cab drivers, bookmakers, delicatessen store owners, denizens of the half as well as the whole underworld, rich man, poor man, beggarman, thief—and, of course, the Irish.

For a nickel train ride, a scalper's price of admission, and two bits more for a feather, or a banner, they became faithful and fervent rooters. They felt that they belonged, and that the wonderful bizarre and romantic mantle of Irishness was spread over them. A large portion of them were no more genuine Hibernians than were those members of the Notre Dame squads whose names ended in "ski," "berger," "isch," or "vitch," but it made no difference to the self-appointed alumni. Once they had decked themselves out in the Notre Dame colors, predominantly green, naturally, their identities were merged with those extraordinary football wizards from the West.

The very fact that this squad came from that part of the country and the never-before-heard-of town of South Bend, lent added mystery and fascination. There were some pretty good football players and teams around the East at that time too: Syracuse, Colgate, Cornell, Pennsylvania, not to mention the Big Three, Princeton, Harvard, and Yale, as the game developed. But when the brilliant and winning "Irish" arrived, the masses ignored the local squads, allied themselves with the strangers, and took them to its collective heart. In the mongrel mixture of the melting pot, all became Irish and "Fighting Irish" as well.

When the November sun had set behind the Polo Grounds or Yankee Stadium, and the Notre Dame eleven had quit the gridiron with the football and the winning score, it would be these same bartenders, bookmakers, shopkeepers, nightclub doormen, and Broadway bums who would flood onto the field and begin rocking the goalposts to bring them down, cart them off, and carve them up into souvenir splinters to be carried thereafter as talismans of the luck of the Irish.

One famous backfield of those days was most felicitously named "The Four Horsemen" by star sportswriter and poet the late Grantland Rice. He took the name from the Ibanez novel and moving picture: the Four Horsemen of biblical lore, Famine, Pestilence, Destruction, and Death, and this kind of publicity and dramatic buildup was on a par with that which was greeting heroes and billionaires in other big-league sports. Cash began to flow into the coffers of university athletic associations as never before.

But if, as noted, players were somewhat ephemeral—three years saw them graduated and replaced by others—one gigantic figure remained, the high priest of those football days and the idol of not only small boys, but adults as well, and that was Rockne himself. He had magnetism to burn and that indefinable champion's touch, that intangible something that inspired not only his players, but reached beyond them to the lowliest self-appointed Subway Alumnus who loved and rooted for "Kanute Rockne of Noter Dame's Fightin' Irish." Dempsey had it, Tunney had it; so had Johnny Weissmuller, Tommy Hitchcock, Earl Sande, Bobby Jones, the

Babe, Red Grange, champions all. When they came into a room, you knew they were there. Wherever and whenever Rockne appeared there was no doubt as to who was the star of the show.

Since this is not a biography of Rockne but only an estimate of his influence on his times, it will suffice to remind you that he came to the United States as a boy of five in 1893 with his immigrant Norwegian family which made its home on Chicago's northwest side in the Logan Square area, populated mainly by Irish and Swedes, and here his Americanization commenced. It progressed via the American love of sports through sandlot football, baseball, and track; grammar school and high school, to the halls of Notre Dame—then an unpretentious Catholic school where young Rockne opted to go instead of to the University of Illinois, because he would be able to work his way through, and the one thousand dollars he had saved at odd jobs to pay his way would go farther.

There were many other great football teachers in that era, contemporary with him: Pop Warner, Hurry-Up Yost, Amos Alonzo Stagg, and Percy Haughton, but none of them had that extra, star quality that Knute possessed and the ability so to fuse eleven men into a unit representative of his own peculiar and often impish spirit. His teams sometimes played football that had a definite tinge of humor, because Rockne was a gay, witty man, and made his practice sessions light-hearted and enjoyable. And this, too, managed to communicate itself to us.

Coaches are often overrated. After all, it is the boys who get out onto the field, take the knocks, and carry the ball. But every so often a genuine colossus appears whose influence and teaching cannot be underestimated, and Rockne towered head and shoulders over the best of his profession. He took four of the worst freshman bumblers ever seen falling over their own feet, or running into one another —Miller, Layden, Stuhldreher, and Crowley—a quartet of totally different characters and temperament, and within a year welded them into the greatest backfield combination ever seen on a football gridiron up to that time. These were Grantland Rice's famous "Four Horsemen" who flourished in 1922, 1923, and 1924 to tie Army once and beat it twice, winning the national championship in their final year, and concluding with a 27–10 win over Stanford in the Rose Bowl, a record of ten won, none lost, none tied, against such opposition as Army, Princeton, Georgia Tech, Wisconsin, Nebraska, Northwestern, and Carnegie Tech.

The Four Horsemen passed on. Notre Dame continued to win. Others, too, could play the Rockne brand of football and react to that irresistible fascination. It was not until after 1931, when this great coach died, that his accomplishment became apparent in the university's won-and-lost column. Rockne's over-all record as Notre Dame coach, starting in 1918 and continuing through 1930, was: 105 won, 12 lost, and 5 tied. He fielded five undefeated and untied teams. Two decades later another Irish coach, Frank Leahy, ran up a string of thirty-nine consecutive victories. But that was later —much later. It was Rockne who broke the ground and taught his boys the best and brainiest football that had been seen up to his day, and then fired them up to play it beyond anything that had ever been experienced before.

How was this accomplished?

It was again the combination of the times, the psychological climate, but above all the man. For over and beyond the personality of Rockne, pumped up by the publicity flacks of Notre Dame, and believe me there was some pumping, there was a genuinely unique individual. In the games played by Notre Dame under Rockne, and in particular those classics against Army, there were some brand-new elements introduced: humor, affection, and a curious kind of sports love that manifested itself in odd ways.

Notre Dame played hard, rough, out-to-win football, but many of their players were witty and great kidders and often put their opponents out of stride with their sallies. The team spirit of these boys was tremendous. They sacrificed and blocked for one another, fought for one another, but in a strange way they loved their enemies too, and could be chivalrous because their coach was a chivalrous man.

Earlier, when Army was playing Notre Dame at West Point, Rockne's version of the shift was throwing the soldiers badly off balance, instigating complaints that it was an illegal maneuver.

It was not actually so, for Rockne never played illegal football, but after the first half Referee Tom Thorpe said to Rockne, "I just don't know what to do about that shift of yours, Rock. The Army is on my neck that it's illegal. I know it isn't, but it's so close that it's difficult for anyone but an official to judge."

Rockne said, "All right, Tom, I'll tell you what we'll do. We'll play the second half without the shift."

They did and scored the same number of touchdowns as in the first half.

This was the kind of story which appealed so strongly to the people we were then.

Rockne was a very moral man and we were just emerging from a period when morality was still adjudged a virtue. An ebullient substitute scored a touchdown, and as he raced across the goal line, he raised five fingers to his nose and cocked a snook at the pursuit. Rockne yanked him and took his suit away.

He was moral in the sexual sense, another characteristic of an era which once denied entrance to a European countess on the grounds of "moral turpitude" because she'd had a boy friend. He closed down a *maison de joie* known as "Sally's," above a feed store on La Salle Street in South Bend, as having a deteriorating effect on the neighborhood. The police dragged their feet when requested to cooperate, since apparently some kind of profit-sharing plan was in operation. When repeated appeals failed, Rockne made another suggestion. Either Sally's closed, or he would bring his football team down and take the place apart. The threat of this kind of publicity shook the city fathers to the soles of their shoes, and Madam Sally's establishment took over premises in another town.

Rockne was known for his psychological warfare and the sentimentality of his dressing room pep talks, two of the most famous of which are revealing. In one, after his team had taken a first-half

281

shellacking and sat waiting for the blast, Rockne merely poked his head in the door of the dressing room and remarked quietly, "Oh, excuse me, ladies! I thought this was the Notre Dame team." He was a master at reducing swelled heads, and when his Four Horsemen had an off day, he would suggest that they carry their press clippings onto the field with them and read them aloud to the enemy.

Another famous dressing room oration concerned the plea from the dead—"Go out and win this one for the Gipper, boys!"

According to the legend, George Gipp, probably the most celebrated football player ever developed at Notre Dame and coached by Rockne, lay on his deathbed from pneumonia brought on by overindulgence in all manner of things, and dying, is supposed to have said to Rockne, "If you ever need to win one badly, ask the team to go out and do it for me," etc. etc. The whole thing sounds apocryphal, but quite classical for our times and the kind of treacle we loved to swallow. Actually, the real deathbed story was quite different. Rockne, holding the boy's hand, said, "It must be tough to go, George," to which Gipp replied unequivocally, "What's tough about it?"

At any rate, it was currently acknowledged that Rockne had used the "Win this one for Gipp" plea and the boys had come through.

What was not common currency was that George Gipp, in addition to being a brilliant football player, was a very bad little boy. He was everything that a Notre Dame college boy ought not to be, a womanizer, a pool shark, a card player, a gambler, and a drunk, and Rockne was attached to him. And with this love for a sinner who could deliver the goods on the football field, any phonyness in Rockne's morality falls away and he stands exposed to us as a genuine human being.

How the great Gipp regarded these dressing room orations was told to me privately by a contemporary of those days when, in 1920, Rockne found himself ten points behind Indiana at the half, after an undefeated season in 1919.

The coach went into his locker room oration and was in full swing when he noticed that Gipp was not anywhere around. He finally located him standing in a doorway, leaning against the sill, looking bored as he flicked cigarette ashes outside.

Rock was speechless but the Gipper said, "Aw, these pep talks are O.K., Rock, I guess, but I got two hundred bucks bet on this game and if you think I'm lying down out there, you're crazy!"

It was one of the few times when Knute Rockne was struck dumb. In the second half Gipper went out, scored two touchdowns, and drop-kicked the points. His two hundred dollars were safe.

But the story of how Gipp was able to place a wager, an act which today would have gotten him disqualified not only from amateur but from professional football as well, is even better. He had "agents" who did his betting for him, and they reported that for the Indiana game at Bloomington, the gamblers wanted no part of Notre Dame or brother Gipp. The "agents" were planted in the local betting emporium where, the night before the game, a tall, muffled figure with his overcoat collar turned up, marched in and shakingly demanded a Bromo Seltzer, in those days a popular cure-all for hangover. He shivered, and with trembling fingers raised the glass to his lips, swallowed, coughed, gagged, and finally after downing it, staggered out of the door. Someone asked, "Who the hell was that wreck?"

Here, an "agent" volunteered the reply, "Why, don't you know? That's George Gipp. He's been like that just about all week. I doubt if he'll get into the game at all tomorrow. It won't even be a contest without him."

The whole thing, of course, was an act. Gipp hadn't had a drop, got his bet down, and collected the money.

The Gipper could make a living out of pool room hustling and did. He bet heavy sums of money on the games in which he played and spent more time carousing in off-limit South Bend hangouts and saloons, and card-playing, and eventually he was expelled from Notre Dame. But upon Rockne's plea and the passing of a stiff oral examination, he was readmitted.

The friendship between the nineteenth-century-type tough-guy Americano and the soft-spoken, twentieth-century Rockne was the stuff of which our stories were made.

Rockne had the ability to associate names and faces and remembered hundreds upon hundreds of boys. One of his old students recalls the day when nearly six hundred boys went out for freshman football. Rockne divided them into eleven sections, in accordance with the positions they said they played. When these formed groups, Rock asked each one his name. The following day, when they assembled,

Rockne had them form a huge circle, and without notes called out every one of them by name and assigned him to the proper assistant coach.

Five days a week between twelve-thirty and one o'clock in the afternoon, in the basement of the old library building, Rockne conducted skull practice in a football clinic. He and Hunk Anderson would pose hypothetical problems of rules and situations and ask for solutions, and it was through these sessions that Notre Dame players acquired such a knowledge of every aspect of the game that they were able to take advantage of any situation which might develop on the field.

Small boys hanging about Cartier Field got into the second half free, until the empty seats were filled. But there were some who passionately wanted to see the first half as well. In those days members of the team ran from the locker rooms onto the field swathed in blankets, and it was not unusual to spot two big cleated feet under one of those coverings surrounded by four, or six, smaller feet, trying to keep in step. Rockne would never see this. Some of these stowaways later became Notre Dame stars themselves.

He was a brilliant raconteur and was in tremendous demand at Rotary luncheons, Lions Club dinners, or any large stag function where men got together to feed and listen to after-dinner speeches.

Added to all of this was the fact that the public at large believed him to be something of a wizard, for there certainly seemed to be magic connected with his successes. Everything he touched turned to gold. He wove his spell over his own players and produced strange miracles, such as the time Tom

Walsh, his All-America center, once played the entire last half of a game with two broken hands. But what were crippled digits compared to love of Rockne and the determination not to let him down? Not a single bad pass was charged against him through this whole agonizing half.

Knute's influence extended not only to his own squad, but during his all-too-short career as a coach, many hundreds of thousands of other young men warmed their own competitive spirits at the bright fire of this man who stood for everything that was right, good, and successful in American sports of his era.

All this, of course, led to the cult of Rockne. Just as the melting pot of Assistant Noter Damers and hoi polloi alumni attached themselves to the Notre Dame team, so Rockne became their Shaman and High Priest, and was worshiped, back-slapped, and adulated wherever he went. The phenomenon was unique. Much of the fame of Notre Dame of today rests upon his shoulders, because of what he did and was.

And withal, just like with the other great champions who populate this volume, even though you collected and enumerated their extraordinary qualities, skills, and abilities, there was still that mysterious intangible that made them into these special people.

The record of Frank Leahy in the decade 1940 through 1949 was hardly less than that of Rockne. But there was no Leahy cult that I can remember. He was simply a popular, successful coach of a famous university. It was Rock the pioneer who had that extra-added, super champion quality which was unforgettable. I can see him still today, with his squashed-in nose (from baseball, incidentally), jug-handle ears, and humorous mouth, striding the Notre Dame sidelines during a game, or deep in conversation with his second-in-command on strategy as the pattern of victory, or the threat of defeat, began to emerge upon the gridiron. His presence made itself felt. Eleven young men on the field running, kicking, passing, and carrying the ball, but behind them was Rockne.

For all that, the man was no paragon or goody-goody, nor was he faultless. He made mistakes but he never lacked the courage to face up to them and admit his errors. He could apologize to the world or to the most humble freshman candidate. But his faults fade into insignificance today beside the memories of his towering character and ability.

At forty-three his life came to an end, far too young, when on a flight to the Coast from Kansas City, his plane crashed into the Flint Hills in a fog. Perhaps a character so unique and adulated was fortunate to quit the scene at his peak. Certainly his passing marked the end of that particular football era with its newborn excitement. It is all different now. The great school at South Bend is continuing to score successes. What it does or doesn't do is still newspaper copy. But that vital spark, the electric force and the personality that was Rockne is no longer there, and somehow not even the Subway Alumni and all of the Assistant Noter Damers seem to care quite so much any more.

JOHN ED BRADLEY

The Private Wars of an Old Soldier

Ohio State coach Woody Hayes was interviewed after his retirement by John Ed Bradley, sports writer and novelist, in this article originally written for the Washington Post. *The violent flare-up that ended Hayes's football career is poignantly referred to and put to rest by Hayes himself. The reader will ponder the mysterious connection between the violence of the game and the occasional sudden violence that eventually destroyed Hayes, in sharp contrast to Hayes's otherwise gentlemanly demeanor.*

Woody Hayes once said, "Without winners there wouldn't even be any goddamned civilization."

Now he was saying, *"What?* What on earth do you mean?" to a parking garage attendant, a huge specimen of authority in tight blue coveralls, here at the Hyatt Regency.

Hayes had just taken a little pink ticket from a woman in a glass booth, asked where to park and, upon hearing that he could park his El Camino anywhere, had turned into the first queue available. But now this giant, built like the company store, had come off his bar stool and was shouting, "You can't leave your machine there, Chief! That ain't

288

no place!" and sending an echo across the continent like an ugly mule song.

"But this is a place," Hayes protested, pointing at the two yellow lines that created the parking space, and ignoring the day-glo bright cones with little signs hanging by chains that read, "Reserved."

"No, it ain't, Chief. That ain't no place. Get back in your car and move on down the road."

"It looks like a place to me," Hayes said finally, and the attendant cocked his head back the way hardtimers do when prepared to deliver the Word, and gave the former Ohio State University football coach a pair of eyes that said, "Don't get sassy with me, old man."

Hayes grabbed the door handle and shook his head in plain disgust while I waited for him to thrust a toe of his snow boots into the whitewall of the front tire. He mumbled something under his breath, the voice of suppressed rage, of a hard heart clanking against a busy pair of lungs. But I knew that when he got back behind the wheel and headed up the ramp, passing a dozen open spaces without the least bit of outcry, climbing higher and higher until there was enough room to parallel park a caravan of 18-wheelers, that this was what hot-tempered fools considered the stuff of "minor victories."

Woody Hayes, 71 and dead-set in his ways, had not allowed stubbornness to defeat his goodwill. He had come to tell members of the Ohio Agro Expo what it meant, exactly, to be good and decent and rightly American. And maybe that was why he said, *"Aaaahhh,"* when he finally parked his El Camino and stepped outside. We were standing in an open concrete forest of parking queues, all alone on the sixth floor. Ohio was a storm around us, a white nightmare of snow falling in hard, horizontal sheets, as if on its way south to West Virginia. And still, the old coach found cause to run his hands over his belly and suck in new life. "Damn man called me Chief," he said and pocketed his keys, while I led the way to civilization.

On a cold day early this month, I met him before noon at his office in the Military Science Building, Room 201, on the OSU campus, where he is a professor emeritus in the Department of Health, Physical Education and Recreation. Outside his door and a short walk down the hall, there was a bulletin board with pictures of soldiers dressed in combat gear and of tanks and all the mighty machines of war, and these words in stencil type: "Do You Have What It Takes?"

His secretary was typing up notes of preliminary chapter sketches on a book he's writing called, "Football, History and Woody Hayes." The blackboard on the wall directly across from his desk listed each chapter—*The Starting Eleven, Specialty Teams*, etc.—and it was so messy it looked as though a yard bird had stepped in a mess of chalk and walked right across it. There was an old-time phonograph on the table next to him and a stack of albums by folks like Tony Bennett and Glenn Miller. The one on top was an oldie, "Nice 'n Easy," by Frank Sinatra.

And there was his vast collection of history

books, most of them pertaining to war and the great leaders of war. They crowded his desk and the bookshelves behind him. Two entire shelves contained books on Gen. George S. Patton.

"The thing about Patton," he would say on the drive to the Ohio Center, "is that his casualties amounted to about one-third of those of the other generals. You had to fight for him, but you didn't have to die."

Woody Hayes wears eyeglasses with frames the color of his hair, the kind punk rockers wear nowadays to look mad with things. And he still has a particular look of dignity about him, a certain stillness that belongs only to those removed of the vicious, old grind. He may well be, as his secretary suggested, the most recognized man in Ohio, for he looks no different now than he did the last time you saw him—the last time everybody saw him—either live and in a rage on the sidelines of the Gator Bowl, slugging a Clemson player for intercepting a pass and killing a last-chance Buckeye drive, or on the 5 o'clock news doing the same.

That all came down on December 30, 1978, the year of injury and ignominy and insult. Now, as folks passed him on their way out of the Ohio Center and offered a word of greeting, he never failed to say, "Men," to the men, tapping the brim of his fancy suede hat, and "Ladies," to the ladies.

Inside the giant convention center, a group of agribusiness sponsors gave him a tour of the tractors and trucks and fertilizer spreaders that crowded the showroom floor, and he had a way of saying, "*Izzat-so?*" in such a way as to make them believe they were showing a retired military leader the

291

awesome machines of the Third World War. He stopped before a mammoth Field Gymmy truck and asked, "How much does one of those big tires cost?"

A guide replied with pride, "These babies go for $3,100 a pair, Coach." And Woody Hayes stood incredulous, scratching his scalp in disbelief. "Thirty-one, you say?" he asked.

"Yes, sir," the man said. "Thirty-one for these babies."

"Well, I'll be doggone," he said and muffed up his lips. "I'll just be doggone."

Then the man said, "Now you wanta talk combines, I'll talk combines with you, Coach. You talkin' combines, you talkin' big money."

Hayes said, "Combines, huh?"

Banquet food will give you heartburn, Woody Hayes learned long ago. But he eats it anyway. Sometimes that and the price of gas is all a gathering of two or more needs to offer to get him to talk about right and wrong in America and about the game he sorely misses. On occasion he has drawn as much as $3,000 for a speaking engagement, but the run over the past two weeks has been to small Catholic schools and groups of fraternity and sorority kids and most anybody who'd lend him an ear. He doesn't do it for money. "You can't pay the people back for being good to you," he says. "But you can always pay forward."

After the Agro Expo speech, which drew a standing ovation and a chorus of bird whistles, he said we would take turns driving the three-hour haul to South Point, which was off Highway 52, just below Ironton. At first it was so cold in the cab of the El Camino that you could bite your arm and feel nothing. Then Coach Hayes turned on the heater and it got so hot so quickly that I was struck suddenly with a rust of vertigo and thought I might faint. Coach Hayes said, "Too warm for ya?" and I lied. I said no, it wasn't. He was smiling and squinting into the spinning white face of the road, as George Washington had in the famous painting, "Crossing the Delaware."

His teeth were bared and his brow buckled, and there was an obvious sense of mission in the way he gripped the wheel. He looked perfectly at war with the elements, but perfectly at peace. I tapped him on the knee and said, "I feel fine, Coach. Just fine."

Visibility was poor, but if you squinted and looked hard enough, you could see the open box-cars in the train yards and the simple white farm-houses in the hills, smoke rising from chimney stacks and cows and sheep huddled under dilapi-dated tin sheds, and all the cars that were stranded in the ditches and in the median. A grader had scraped the road half-clean, and boulder-like chunks of snow and ice were pushed onto the shoulder of the road. Everybody drove with their lights and windshield wipers on, everybody except Hayes, of course, who was well aware of the difference be-tween day and night and would be hardpressed to compromise at 3 in the afternoon.

"I've noticed something about cars," he said. "Your real big cars and your real little cars are the ones that get stuck in the snow. Your medium-sized cars always keep moseying along."

He had owned two Cadillacs for a day back in 1979, gifts from friends of the university in appreciation of 28 years as the head football coach. He refused one entirely and cashed the other in and set up a scholarship fund with the money. The fanciest car he ever drove was a Buick Riviera and it was so fancy it was assuming, pretentious. It wasn't Woody. He had been driving the El Camino pickup for about 29,000 miles and liked it except for the matter of its light rear end.

"I got stuck trying to get up a hill the other day," he said. "I had to get out and walk for it. It was hard. I don't walk so well anymore, not like I used to."

He hated to think or talk about it, but his eyes weren't what they used to be, either. His great love of books had been stifled of late by his inability to call the words from the pages and to hold them in his mind. Even his level of comprehension was not what it had once been. A lady in England had mailed him a book on world history she considered well worth his study time, but he was having the damndest struggle getting through it.

Former President Richard Nixon, whom Hayes has considered a "close, personal friend" ever since their meeting in 1958, when Nixon was vice president and in attendance at a game in Ohio Stadium, had sent him a copy of his work-in-progress, "Real Peace," and Hayes had read it through but with no small degree of difficulty. He memorized entire passages from the book, lines about the future of "this wonderful land," and he could deliver them in such a way as to make you want to stop whatever it was you're doing and run down to your local recruiting office and enlist in the United States Marine Corps.

"Sometimes now," Hayes said in a broken voice, "I get a little bored with myself. I might watch a game on TV, and I worry about it a little. I worry about the game getting out of hand. I do. I really do. The money involved. The overcommercialization of it. Even average football players are making as much as $700,000 a year, *Seven hundred thousand dollars a year to play football!* Do we even know what is happening? Do we really?"

Outside of Circleville, we passed a graveyard on a hill, with its white expanse of stone tablets and angels and obelisks barely visible in the deep white cover of snow. "Why are so many of the men I loved dead now?" he wondered aloud. "Doggone, I miss 'em." And he named a score of them, told stories about them that had somehow remained as bright and burning in his mind as the vision of the road in front of him. He called them all "great Americans."

He talked about the living, too. About his wife Anne, who was once informed by an irate fan that she was married to a fathead. "Of course he is," she had replied quite agreeably. "All husbands are."

And he talked about his sister Mary, who, in 1929, was the headliner in a Broadway play and shared the backside of a marquee with another Hayes of enormous fame, Helen Hayes. Mary had won the part mainly because she could play the piano with the skill of a virtuoso. Hayes remembered that Thomas Wolfe was her favorite writer, and there was a line he knew: "Oh, lost and by the wind grieved, ghost, come back again," from *Look Homeward, Angel*. But Hayes had never read him. "Mary says he's dandy, just dandy," he said. "He died young, you know. He wasn't yet 40. And he's gone from us. A young man, Thomas Wolfe."

Mary lived in New Jersey now. She was 78. He said he regretted having never seen her play the piano on Broadway. And he regretted the matter of Wolfe's early passing.

We reached the River Cities Inn almost two hours before the banquet was scheduled to begin and the management said there was a room waiting, in case we might want to wash up. I gave the key to Coach Hayes, but he suggested we go in the bar for a while, to wind down over a glass of juice. "Don't be afraid of drinking the hard stuff," he said. I ordered a Coke.

We sat at the bar with our backs to the crowd of eyes that fell powerfully upon him and before long a skinny, rawboned woman in high heels tapped Coach Hayes on the shoulder and asked him to please sign a couple of pictures for "little babies back home." The photographs were both black-and-white 8x10s, and depicted Hayes wearing an OSU baseball cap and the same suit he wore this day, a navy coat and slacks and a striped tie that reached way short of his belt buckle. "Make one out to Terry," the woman said, and Hayes wrote best wishes to Terry, then his name. He added a flare to his last name, whipping out a couple of loops that extended across the bottom of the picture. "How old is little Terry?" he asked. And the woman said, without shame, "He's 47."

Hayes put the cap back on his pen, and before he could turn to thank the woman, she had reached for a napkin on the bar and was wiping a greasy run of mascara from her cheek. "The day you dotted the i," she said, referring to an Ohio State tradition in which a celebrated alumnus stands in with the band during the pregame performance, "I never cried so much in my life. Ohio is not Ohio with you gone, Coach. And football isn't football either."

There were women of property crying in the audience—here at the banquet for the Boys' and Girls' Club of Ironton-Lawrence County—women with diamonds on their ears and fancy designs stitched onto their black lace stockings. And their husbands, good-looking farm boys in three-piece suits and store-bought neckties, coughed into clinched fists as if trying to unclog all the pain and thunder the old man had just shoved down their throats. They had come in their Sunday best to pick clean a buffet of sliced turkey and pork, roast beef and spaghetti salad, and to hear a voice they worshipped shout in defense of truth, beauty, love and honor, democracy and above all else, the American Way.

And they had come simply to gaze upon the man the master of ceremonies had called "one of the greatest leaders in the history of Ohio." But when he was done, they followed him out to the car and stood in the breezeway and waved goodby, as if they were certain never to see him again. I started the car and made way to the highway, trying to beat the storm of traffic on the trip north to Ironton. He started to hum when we were just five miles out of town, then he sang a verse or two. The snow had stopped, and it was so dark outside that it seemed as though this journey held no real destination. "What's that you're singing," I asked, and he shrugged his shoulders. "Just a song," he said. "But a pretty song."

I was getting sleepy long before he suggested we pull over and get some gas. He got out and stood with his hands in his pockets and his legs wide apart, facing the cold night. He was still standing that way—his eyes blurred by the distance, his tie pushed over his shoulder and flapping in the wind —when I noticed the station attendant staring at him in both awe and wonder, as if gazing into the face of an apparition. "You who I think you are?" the man asked.

Hayes, unmoving except to raise big eyebrows, said, "I have no idea who you think I am, young man."

"Are you Woody Hayes?" the man asked. "Are you *Coach* Woody Hayes?"

Hayes let the sound of his name sink in, and by the sour expression that gripped his countenance I wondered how pleased he was with what he heard. "I might be," he said. "I might be him."

"You like football?" I asked the man.

"I used to," he said. "I hate to say this, but the last football game I ever saw was in Jacksonville, at the Gator Bowl. I was there when you hit that feller, Coach."

Five years ago, when Woody Hayes slammed his clenched fist into the neck of Clemson nose guard Charlie Bauman, he proved that some generals do lead by rolling up their sleeves and charging into battle. But he took on more than an army that day. He took on the world. I know now that his fury was not directed at Bauman so much as it was a day of defeated dreams and of a failure to grasp the final victory that would forever elude him. His war was hopeless and probably stupid, but damn if he didn't fight. He had offered no half-cocked explanations of the matter later and thus spared himself the impossible task of explaining how it feels to be a man at war with something like time.

We were coming on Columbus when I asked him why, why he had ever hit Charlie Bauman, and he said he didn't know why. "But you know what (Michigan Coach) Bo Schembechler said about all that? He asked me if I had any intention of hurting that young man and I said no, I didn't. I didn't hit him to hurt him. It hurt only me. You see, it hurt only *me*. But you can't always explain everything. Some things are beyond you."

We pushed on through the snow, and he said he wanted to show me a "place I know of" before I turned in for the night at my hotel. He gave me directions, saying only "left here," and "quick right here," but soon we came upon an intersection with a great white sign burning in the blaze of our headlights. The sign said: *Woody Hayes Road.*

It was almost 1 in the morning and the snow began to fall harder and harder. I waited out the red light, then turned left and worked through the Ohio State campus until we crossed the mushy snow that covered the road between the assembly center and the great gray ghost of Ohio Stadium, *his* stadium. I stopped the car for a moment, and he

299

started to sing again, a song I didn't know. A pretty song. Then he told me to move on. "You must be proud," I said, "to have a road named after you."

He looked out the window and up into the heavens. Then he looked at me. "It's only a road," he said. "But it's a good road."

VINCE LOMBARDI WITH W. C. HEINZ
Run to Daylight

A day in the football-filled life of Coach Vincent Lombardi as he prepares for a game of the 1962 pro football season. An hour-by-hour narrative of all the daily tasks, meetings, thoughts, and responsibilities of a driving and driven coach. Lombardi's perfectionist coaching style embodied a new professional rigor and single-mindedness applied to the game of football. The many successful seasons of the Green Bay Packers brought credibility to his simple approach—of nothing less than winning. As Lombardi succinctly phrased it, "success demands singleness of purpose." In this non-stop monologue, we are inside the mind of Lombardi, as he frankly assesses his players, his ideas on discipline, his strategic plays, and describes his personal philosophy of "mental toughness."

MONDAY

3:15 A.M.

I have been asleep for three hours and, suddenly, I am awake. I am wide awake, and that's the trouble with this game. Just twelve hours ago I walked off that field, and we had beaten the Bears 49 to 0. Now I should be sleeping the satisfied sleep of the contented but I am lying here awake, wide

301

awake, seeing myself walking across that field, seeing myself searching in the crowd for George Halas but really hoping that I would not find him.

All week long there builds up inside of you a competitive animosity toward that other man, that counterpart across the field. All week long he is the symbol, the epitome, of what you must defeat and then, when it is over, when you have looked up to that man for as long as I have looked up to George Halas, you cannot help but be disturbed by a score like this. You know he brought a team in here hurt by key injuries and that this was just one of those days, but you can't apologize. You can't apologize for a score. It is up there on that board and nothing can change it now. I can just hope, lying here awake in the middle of the night, that after all those years he has had in this league—and he has had forty-two of them—these things no longer affect him as they still affect me. I can just hope that I am making more of this than he is, and now I see myself, unable to find him in the crowd and walking up that ramp and into our dressing room, now searching instead for something that will bring my own team back to earth.

"All right!" I said. "Let me have your attention. That was a good effort, a fine effort. That's the way to play this game, but remember this. You beat the Bears, but you know as well as I do that they weren't ready. They had key personnel hurt and they weren't up for this game. Those people who are coming in here next week will be up. They won again today, so they're just as undefeated as we are. They'll be coming in here to knock your teeth down your throats, so remember that.

Have your fun tonight and tomorrow, but remember that."

"Right, coach!" someone behind me, maybe Fuzzy Thurston or Jerry Kramer or Ray Nitschke, shouted. "Way to talk, coach!"

Am I right and is that the way to talk, or has this become a game for madmen and am I one of them? Any day that you score seven touchdowns in this league and turn in a shutout should be a day of celebration. Even when the Bears are without Bill George, who is the key to their defense, and Willie Galimore, who is their speed, this is a major accomplishment. But where is the elation?

Once there was elation. In 1959, in the first game I ever coached here, that I ever head-coached anywhere in pro ball, we beat these Bears 9 to 6 and I can remember it clearly. I can remember them leading us into the last period and then Jimmy Taylor going in from the 5 on our 28-Weak, and Paul Hornung kicking the point, and then Hank Jordan breaking through on the blitz and nailing Ed Brown in the end zone for the safety. The year before, this team had won only one game and tied one out of twelve, so now they were carrying me off the field because a single league victory was once cause enough for celebration.

What success does to you. It is like a habit-forming drug that, in victory, saps your elation and, in defeat, deepens your despair. Once you have sampled it you are hooked, and now I lie in bed, not sleeping the sleep of the victor but wide awake, seeing the other people who are coming in next Sunday with the best defensive line in the league, with that great middle linebacker, that left defensive halfback who is as quick and agile as a cat and a quarterback who, although he is not as daring as Johnny Unitas or Y. A. Tittle or Bobby Layne, can kill you with his consistency.

I don't see them as I do from the sideline, but as I have seen them over and over in the films. I see them beating us 17–13 in our opener in Milwaukee in 1961. I see them beating us 23–10 in their own park the year before, and that's what I mean about success. My mind does not dwell on the two games we beat them in 1959 or the single games we took from them in 1960 and again in 1961. For the most part you remember only your losses, and it reminds me again of Earl Blaik and West Point after Navy beat our undefeated Army team 14–2 in 1950.

"All right," the Colonel would say whenever there was a lull. "Let's get out that Navy film."

You could see the other coaches sneak looks at one another, and although you couldn't hear the groans you could feel them in the room. Then we'd all file out and into the projection room once more.

"Look at that," the Colonel would say. "The fullback missed the block on that end."

How many times we had seen that fullback miss that block on that end I do not know. I do know that every time we saw that film Navy beat Army again, 14–2, and that was one of the ways Earl Blaik, the greatest coach I have ever known, paid for what he was.

So what I see now is that opener in '61, the last time they beat us. I see them stopping us twice inside their 5-yard line. I see us running their quarterback out of his pocket, the rhythm of that pass play broken, and both their split end and Jesse Whittenton relax. I see that end start up and Whittenton slip and that end catch it and run it to the 1, and on the next play their fullback takes it in. Then I see them on our 13-yard line and their fullback misses his block and falls. As he gets up, their quarterback, in desperation, flips the ball to him and he walks the 13 yards for the score.

Lying there like this, in the stillness of my house and conscious of any sound and every sensation, I am aware now of the soreness of my gums. It is this way every Monday, because for those two hours on the sideline every Sunday I have been grinding my teeth, and when I get up at eight o'clock and put in my bridge I'll be aware of it again. That, come to think of it, is only fitting and proper, because that bridge had its beginnings in the St. Mary's game my junior year at Fordham. Early in that game I must have caught an elbow or forearm or fist, because I remember sitting in that Polo Grounds dressing room during halftime and it felt like every tooth in my head was loose.

8:40 A.M.

"So I judge you won't be home for dinner," Marie says, while I am having my second cup of coffee.

"No," I said, and that is another part of the price that you and your family must pay. Maybe I'm wrong, but the only way I know how to coach this game is all the way, and what it costs, Marie once explained.

"From Monday until Wednesday night," she said, "we don't talk to him. On Wednesday he has to go out there and convince himself and five other coaches and thirty-six football players."

8:50 A.M.

I drive down our street to the corner, and I have to wait there because at this hour the traffic is heavy going into town. It is heavy with men who must convince other men that they need more insurance or new storm windows or a new car or who must solve a heat-conduction problem or an efficiency lag, and there is not much difference between us. Some of us will do our jobs well and some will not, but we will all be judged by only one thing—the result.

"That's where I can't see that it means much," Vincent, Jr., said one evening last summer just before we went into training camp. Marie and our Susan were at the Fond Du Lac horse show, where Susan was showing her mahogany mare, and Vincent and I were eating out.

"I don't know what you're talking about," I said.

"You're always saying," Vincent said, "that the only way to play the game or do the job is the way you're convinced is right for you."

"That's correct," I said. "The rest will follow, or it won't."

"Then I can't see where there's much difference between winning or losing," Vincent said, "as long as you've done your job."

"There isn't much difference," I said, "except economic. You know that scoreboard doesn't begin to tell the story, but what goes up there controls your economic future and your prestige."

306

"They can keep the prestige," Vincent said.

He was twenty years old last summer, and I know what he meant. He was seventeen when we moved here from the East and he had no vote in our move, nor had Susan. He was 5 feet 10 and weighed 180 and had been an all-conference full-back in New Jersey, but one of the Wisconsin papers listed him at 6 feet 2, 210 and all-state, and another carried that ridiculous story that he was being offered cars to pick between the four high schools.

"I'll never forget that first day out here," he has said since. "There are a thousand kids in that school, and the first time I walked into that cafeteria a thousand heads turned and a thousand kids looked at me."

One afternoon Marie drove out to watch Vincent practice. While she was sitting in her car another car drove up and one of the kids in it shouted to someone on the sidelines.

"Which one is Lombardi?" he shouted, and Marie said she thought: Oh, please. Please leave him alone! He's just a seventeen-year-old boy. Please get off his back.

It must have been just about then that Marie came off the phone one evening. Someone had wanted her to do something and she had turned it down.

"Sometimes they claw at you," she said. "Just because your husband knows how to coach football they claw at you."

And Vincent looked up from that book he was reading and said, "Join the crowd, Mom."

8:52 A.M.

I'm in the line of traffic now, and I guess what it comes down to is that success demands singleness of purpose. In this game we're always looking for catch-phrases, especially with a connotation of masculinity, so I call it mental toughness. They have written about the mental toughness with which I supposedly have instilled this team and, when they ask me what it is, I have difficulty explaining it. I think it is singleness of purpose and, once you have agreed upon the price that you and your family must pay for success, it enables you to forget that price. It enables you to ignore the minor hurts, the opponent's pressure and the temporary failures, and I remember my first year here. I remember that first day of full practice in training camp, and when I walked back to the dressing room I wanted to cry. The lackadaisical ineptitude, almost passive resistance, was like an insidious disease that had infected almost a whole squad. The next morning, when I walked into the trainer's room, there must have been fifteen or twenty of them waiting for the whirlpool bath or the diathermy or for rubdowns.

"What is this?" I said. "An emergency casualty ward? Now get this straight. When you're hurt you have every right to be in here. When you're hurt you'll get the best medical attention we can provide. We've got too much money invested in you to think otherwise, but this has got to stop. This is disgraceful. I have no patience with the small hurts that are bothering most of you. You're going to have to learn to live with small hurts and

308

play with small hurts if you're going to play for me. Now I don't want to see anything like this again."

Then I walked out. The next day when I walked into that room there weren't fifteen or twenty in there. There were two, so maybe that's how you do it.

8:56 A.M.

There is a traffic light at the corner of Monroe and Mason and I stop behind a line of cars in the left lane. When that left-turn arrow turns green, and if everyone moves promptly, six cars can make that turn. Six days a week this traffic light is the one thing that invades my consciousness as I drive to work, that consistently interrupts that single purpose of winning next Sunday's game.

I tried to plant that seed of single purpose in the first squad letter I wrote before training camp that first year. I must have rewritten it ten or twelve times, trying to tell them what I hoped to do and how I hoped to do it without making it sound like I was setting up a slave-labor camp.

That summer, as every summer, the first-year men, which is what I call the rookies because I think it implies more respect, came into camp at St. Norbert College, just up the Fox River from here. They arrived three days before the veterans were due, but a half dozen of the veterans came with them. Then two of these veterans, two of my stars, took off on a frolic and I didn't see them again until I collared them in the hall on the third day.

"What do you think we're running here?" I hollered at them. "Just a home base where you can pick up your mail between social engagements? When you came into this camp, no matter how early, it was expected that you came here to work. . . ."

I've got all the emotions in excess and a hair-trigger controls them. I anger and I laugh and I cry quickly, and so I couldn't have told you five minutes later what else I said or just what I did. I have heard it told that I had one of them by his lapels and that it looked like I was going to bang his head against the wall. They say you could hear it all over Sensenbrenner Hall, and that after it was over the two of them walked into somebody's room and one of them said, "I'm not gonna play for this——. He's a madman."

An hour later I was leaving the dormitory to walk across the campus to the science building for the first full-squad meeting. They say I caught up with one of the two and slapped him on the back and said, "C'mon, let's go to that meeting." It's possible, because as fast as I heat up I cool off.

"And there's nothing personal about any of this," I was telling them all a few minutes later. "Any criticism I make of anyone, I make only be cause he's a ballplayer not playing up to his potential. Any fine I levy on anyone, I levy because he's hurting not only himself but thirty-five other men."

They were big men wedged into those varnished oak classroom chairs with the writing arms on the right. They were wearing shorts and slacks and short-sleeved sports shirts, and I went into the regulations, and my system of fines because big as they are, sports-page heroes though they may be, there is an almost adolescent impulsiveness in many of them.

This is something that the abandon with which football must be played encourages. Beyond that, and for as long as most of them can remember, which would be back to their first days in grade school, they have been subject to regulation. As their athletic ability turned them into privileged high school and college celebrities, many of them became masters at the art of circumvention.

I remember the two at the Giant camp at Winooski, Vermont, who climbed the fire escape after curfew but picked the wrong window and became entangled in the venetian blinds in the room of Doc Sweeny, the Giant trainer. I remember the defensive end who was tiptoeing down the hall one night, his shoes in his hand, when Jim Lee Howell, who was coaching the Giants then, surprised him.

"You going somewhere?" Jim said.

"Why, yes," the end said, and you had to grade him high on his speed of reaction. "I lost my wallet, so I thought I'd go out and try to find it."

"I see," Jim said, looking at the shoes. "You planning to sneak up on it?"

So in that first meeting I gave them the camp curfew: in bed and lights out by eleven o'clock, midnight on Saturdays. Any breaking of that curfew would cost the player $500. Any player late for a meeting or practice would be fined $10 a minute, and any of them caught standing at a bar would be knicked for $150. Then I took a little off it by telling them to appoint an Executive Committee, empowered to discuss any fines or any grievances with me, and I said that all money collected would go into a team fund. With it the team could throw a party, at a proper time, or put it to any other use

311

that they preferred, with the restriction that none of it was to be returned to any fined player.

"Now I've already told you," I said, "the names of the places that are off-limits in town. When we travel you'll be given the names of all off-limits spots in every city. If you're found in one of those places you won't be fined. You'll be off the ball club."

I was reaching them where I knew I could hurt them—in their pocketbooks—but a week later I caught the first one. I hit him for $500, and when the Executive Committee came to me, protesting that it was too stiff, I told them that if we didn't set an example none of our regulations would be worth anything, and I told them to talk it over again.

"We've talked it over," they said when they came back, "and we agree the fine should stand."

But the game goes on. I would be naive to believe that we can keep every one of thirty-six healthy, adventuresome males confined for eight weeks with only an hour and a half off six days a week and five hours off on Saturdays. Every year there are three or four who try me, and every year there are three or four who get knicked, and I can tell you beforehand who they'll be and just about when they'll make their tries.

So our five coaches and our personnel director pair off and stand the watches. The first week of camp the heroes are muscle sore and body weary, but a half hour after curfew on the second Saturday one of them walks down the hall from his room and stands in the open doorway of the office. He is wearing undershorts and shower clogs and he waits, like a small boy, for the coaches to look up.

"You want something?" one of them says.

"Yes," he says. "May I get a drink of water?"

"Why not?" the coach says.

"Thank you," he says.

They listen to the sound of the shower clogs on the hard floor of the hall. They hear the clink of the coin in the pay phone.

"He just dropped a dime in the water fountain," one of them says. "He's going tonight."

"And I know who's going with him," the other coach says.

They hear the shower clogs coming back and they watch him pass the door. They go to bed and one of them gets up at 2 A.M. and checks the room, and our parched hero, who stood there like that small boy and asked for that drink of water, and his roommate are both gone.

"I've got to go tonight," another finally announces to his associates every year. "I've just got to try him."

So he tries me, some of his clothes and some towels rolled up to bulk his body under the covers of his bed, and I knick him. . . .

9:15 A.M.

I have looked through the sports pages and I see that Paul Dudley, who was a fourth draft pick for us and one of our first-year men this year, scored his first touchdown for the Giants. He couldn't break into our backfield but he's got good speed and fine moves and he's rugged enough and he's a good one, and every time you trade off

313

one of those, because you happen to be deep at the moment, you wonder if you're not making a mistake, if he might be even better than you think and you'll be haunted by him for years. This year they're haunting Paul Brown for having traded Bobby Mitchell, but it could happen to me.

In the stories about our game with the Bears the papers all say the same thing, each in their own words. We're "power-packed" and "precision-timed" or "all-powerful" or "indestructible." They don't overlook that the Bears were hurt coming in, but that 49–0 score in the big black numbers in the headlines makes us look better than we are and I wish we had a couple of those touchdowns in the bank for this week.

9:20 A.M.

Bud Lea of the *Milwaukee Sentinel* and Gene Hintz of United Press International come in, and I have been told that any time a sportswriter asks me a question I almost visibly flinch. I haven't been hurt yet and I've had the best press anyone can expect, but the off-the-cuff statement is not one of my big plays. I have seen too many seemingly sound statements blow up in the faces of too many sound coaches and I'm not at my best when I'm walking off the practice field, honestly feeling that my whole future will depend upon my discovery of some way to rearrange our blocking on our 49-Sweep to take care of some particular beast of a linebacker, and a sportswriter comes up to me and says, "Well, coach, what do you think today?"

The problem with the press this week, after that 49 to 0, will be to convince them I mean it when I say that if we don't play our best game of the season on Sunday, these other people will knock us on our tails. Bud Lea and Gene Hintz start out asking me about injuries.

"Tom Moore has a muscle pull in his shoulder," I say, "and Hornung pulled a groin muscle. I think they'll be in shape, but I don't know."

It's an odd thing about that Moore. He was the first ballplayer I ever drafted for the Packers. He was our number one draft choice in 1960 and I've never regretted it. He's got good size and speed and power, and in his first year scored five touchdowns and caught five passes and led the league in kickoff returns. I have had to play him behind Jim Taylor at fullback, or Hornung at halfback, and the odd thing is that, when one or the other is hurt and I send in Moore, he gets banged up, too. He is an upright runner, and I wouldn't change that for a minute because it's his way of going, but I've got to get him to button up as he gets hit, which is something that Taylor does instinctively and Hornung has mastered. You can't go in there upright in this league without getting racked.

"If I know Paul Hornung," Bud Lea says, "he'll be ready, if it's possible."

If I, too, know Paul Hornung he'll be ready because this is one of those great money ballplayers, but he was in the army for nine months, seven of them after the season ended. From June into the third week in July the newspapers were carrying rumors of when he would get out and, finally, one evening of our second week in camp he showed up and I saw him getting out of his car in front of Sensenbrenner Hall.

It was dark by then and he walked over into the light from the doorway. You have to know what Paul Hornung means to this team to read all the meaning into the searching inspection I was giving him. I have heard and read that Paul Hornung is not a great runner or a great passer or a great field-goal kicker, although no one can fault him as a great blocker, but he led the league in scoring for three seasons; in 1960 he broke Don Hutson's all-time league seasonal scoring record with 176 points and he was twice voted the league's outstanding player. What it comes down to is that in the middle of the field he may be only slightly better than an average ballplayer, but inside that 20-yard line he is one of the greatest I've ever seen. He smells that goal line. Henry Jordan, our defensive right tackle, expressed what Hornung means to our team when he said, "Before our 1961 championship game I was under the impression that Moore could run as well as Hornung and that Ben Agajanian could kick as well or better, but the week before the game, when Paul got that leave from the army and walked into that locker room, you could just feel the confidence grow in that room."

We were shaking hands now in the light from that doorway, and he had on dark gray slacks and a T-shirt. He is not a Spartan liver and there were those months in the army and I was looking for fat.

"What do you weigh?" I said.

"Oh, about 222," he said. "I'm only about seven pounds over."

"Good," I said, and that's what I thought. He checked in then and for four or five days on that practice field I watched him building himself back in shape. Late in practice on the fifth or sixth day just before sending them in, we lined up our kickoff team against our receiving team. They were all in shorts and T-shirts, just to run through it and to reacquaint them with their assignments after seven months, and Paul, in a sweatsuit, was the deep man to the right in the end zone.

"Watch this," someone on the sideline said. "Aggie will kick it to Hornung to make him run."

Agajanian was in camp to work with our kickers, and he booted it to Paul, who took it about 5 yards deep in the end zone. He tucked it in and started out and was great for the first 15 yards. At the 20-yard line he was absolutely coming apart. He was trying to get his knees up and the effort was almost bending him over backward and he looked like he was a participant in a potato race at an Elks picnic.

"All the way!" I was shouting at him. "Run it all the way to that goal line!"

On the sideline now some of the other players were cat-calling and whistling at Paul Hornung. Watching him, barely able to run, all I could think was: Can this be the famous "Golden Boy"? Can this be the most valuable player in the National Football League, the most publicized ballplayer in pro football, that runner, blocker, kicker and great competitor on whom so much depends if we are going to hold on to that title? And I closed practice.

"Well," I said to him, walking off the field, "I guess you got the news."

"I got it," he said, trying to get his breath, the sweat running off his face.

"That was ludicrous," I said. "That was absurd. What the blast have you been doing with yourself?"

"I don't know," he said. "I don't know."

This is a man with great pride, I knew, and he loves this game, and that would have to be the saver. When the Packers drafted him in 1957 he was All-America at Notre Dame for two years and the Heisman Trophy winner his last year and he came here preceded by all that publicity. They tried him at quarterback and then fullback, and like many a great college star who does not make it big with the pros he fell into that what's-it-to-you attitude that they erect as a defensive perimeter around their egos.

When I joined this club in 1959 Paul Hornung was more celebrated for his reputed exploits off the field than on, but after the months I had spent studying the movies of Packer games I knew that one of the ballplayers I needed was Paul Hornung. With those I could take into my confidence I investigated meticulously that reputation and I found that, although Paul Hornung had given the gossip cause, their malicious imaginations had taken it the rest of the way, and the first talk I ever had with him was right here in this office and it was about that reputation.

"If that's the way they want to think," he said, "that's the way they'll think."

I liked the way he looked me right smack in the eye and I found that, while you have to whip him a little, he is no malingerer. This is a good-looking, intelligent and charming celebrity whom I can't expect to lead a life of a monk, but he is also a dedicated ballplayer who, pre-season, will run up and down those steep steps of City Stadium to get his legs in shape—and we'll need him this Sunday.

10:12 A.M.

I drive one block out South Washington Street and turn right over the Mason Street Bridge. The weather is still good, but there is a slight haze over everything now. Yesterday it was so clear that the sky was like a blue bowl over the stadium. It will not surprise me if we get rain for this next one, and I doubt that anyone in this league ever wants rain. We all draw our plays on dry paper and we count on the ability of our backs and our receivers to make their cuts on a dry field. I don't think that there is a mud-thinker among us, because we all have to conceive of this game as it should be played.

As I turn onto Oneida Avenue, the two practice fields, the camera tower between them, are on the left, the low green bleachers, empty now, along the avenue, and the stadium are on the right atop the rise of the vacant parking fields. For every hour of game play that we put in at that stadium and at the others around the league, we put in fourteen on those fields. That is pre-season and during the season, and then there are those equal hours spent in those meetings, and all of this does not include the time we coaches spend in preparation for those practice sessions and those meetings, and that time seems to me to be almost incalculable.

I see my coaches' cars and maybe a half dozen others parked outside now, and I walk through the empty dressing room and into the trainer's room.

319

Tom Moore is sitting on one of the rubbing tables, stripped to the waist, and Bud Jorgensen, our trainer, is using the diathermy on Moore's shoulder.

"How does it feel?" I say.

"Not so good," Moore says. "It's pretty sore right now."

"Will he be all right?" I say to Jorgensen.

"I think so," he says.

"How about Hornung?" I say. "Is he in yet?"

"No," Jorgensen says. "He'll be in later. The pull isn't in the groin, it's inside the thigh."

Every week there are the injuries. It is foolish to think that, the way this game is played, you can escape them, but every week I feel that same annoyance, and I need Hornung and I need Moore if we are going to beat these people.

"Gentlemen," I say, when I walk into the coaches' room, "that was a good game yesterday."

They are all there—Bill Austin and Norb Hecker and Phil Bengston and Tom Fears and Red Cochran. Phil coaches the defensive line and linebackers, Norb the defensive backs, Bill the offensive line, Red the offensive backfield and Tom handles those receivers.

"It wasn't a bad one, at that," Phil says. He was an All-America tackle at Minnesota in 1933–34, and coached college ball under Don Faurot at Missouri and Clark Shaughnessy at Stanford. For eight years, before I got him, he coached the line for the Forty-Niners, and he is not given to exaggeration. "I thought we looked pretty good out there."

"You really think that was pretty good?" Red Cochran says. "Pretty good?"

He is out of the Carolinas and was a back at

Wake Forest and, from 1947 through 1950, with the Chicago Cardinals. He coached the backfield for five years at Wake Forest and for three with the Lions. Putting this staff together in 1959, I met him for the first time between planes in that remodeled hangar at the old Willow Run airport in Detroit. We were to have an hour between planes, but ours was fifty minutes late and, as we were coming in, I asked Marie to take care of the tickets for the flight out for Green Bay so that I could have at least five minutes with Red Cochran.

"I don't know this Red Cochran," she said, "but I know you. All I can hope for him is that he's not sitting in the bar but that he's waiting at the gate."

He was waiting at the gate.

"Well," I say to Bill Austin, "let's look at them, and I hope we're not disappointed."

Once a game is won and in the bank I would rather not look at the movies. No matter how good we look on the field I can find so many things wrong in the pictures.

"If we're not disappointed," Bill Austin says, "it'll be the first time."

Bill Austin played four years at tackle for Oregon State and in 1949, although he was only 20, he was first-string with the Giants. He put in three years in service and was All-Pro offensive guard with the Giants when I coached their offense. I got him from Wichita, where he was coaching the line, and he is our resident authority on the significance of approaching weather fronts and our first-string motion-picture projectionist.

"Look at this!" I'm saying now, watching Ronnie Bull of the Bears take Willie Wood's kickoff and bring it back to the Bears' 37. "We are absolutely the world's worst team on covering kicks. What have we got those two men sitting on the outside for?"

The kickoff is always a scary play, but there is equal nervousness on both sides. You try to get all the speed you can into your kickoff team, because it's a sprint for everyone, but you cannot sacrifice size. You need that size, particularly in the middle to meet their wedge, and you put your two real speed burners as the third men in from either sideline. They are the ones who have to force the action, who must make the other people show their play, and your two outside men have to be strong enough and active enough to keep that play to the inside. Those outside men have got to stay upright and protect those sidelines, but they can't be so sideline-conscious that they just stand around out there like a couple of program venders.

I throw the switch and reverse the projector. They are all running backward now and the ball is leaving Bull's hands and returning to Willie Wood's toe, and I run it again.

"Look at this," I say again, a half dozen plays later. "You can see Hornung pull up with that muscle."

Bart Starr fakes a handoff to Hornung, and Paul actually executes his own fake into the line with so much sincerity that you can see he has pulled that muscle and is in pain. The play is a swing pass to Jimmy Taylor to the left but the pass doesn't lead Jimmy enough and he tries to turn for it and drops the ball.

That's a problem with Taylor, and sincerity costs us twice on that one play. He's not big for a fullback—6 feet and 212 pounds—but he is so sincere in that all-year muscle-building program of his that when you bump against him it's like bumping into a cast-iron statue. Nothing gives, and he has developed those neck muscles to the point where, when he wants to turn his head, he has to turn his whole upper body.

"What's the matter with you?" I said to him on the practice field the other day when he couldn't turn for the ball on that very play. "Can't you twist your head?"

"You just can't make a greyhound out of a bull-dog, coach," he said.

And he is a bulldog. Your fullback must be big enough to make the tough yardage, have enough speed to go the distance when you break him into the clear and he should, as should all backs, have that real quick start. He should be a great blocker, because he is that remaining back on passes, when the center and the fullback pick up the red-doggers. He must have good enough hands to go out on pass routes, too, because if he hasn't it won't be long before the other defenses learn to ignore him as they do some fullbacks.

In an open field our James is something else again. I think that when he sees a clear field ahead he hunts down somebody to run into, and while you have to enjoy body contact to play this game, Jimmy exults in it. After one of our 1960 games with the Bears I made him watch himself on the film going out of the way to run over Charlie Sumner, who was then their weak-side safety.

"What were you trying to do out there?" I said.

"You gotta sting 'em a little, coach," Jimmy said. "You know you've gotta make those tacklers respect you."

They respect him. In fact, every time he carries a ball there are eleven of them, all of whom want to pay their respects to him personally, and in our game with the Rams in 1961 in Los Angeles I remember four of them nailing him right in front of the Rams' bench.

"How to go, you guys!" they tell me Jimmy said when he jumped up. "That's the way to play this game!"

Now, if I could just get him to block with the same abandon, he might be the best in the business. He is not a bad blocker, but he would be a great one with his ruggedness, his quickness and his agility, if they would just change the rules to let him carry a football while he's blocking.

On the screen now Bart Starr is faking to Tom Moore, who went in for Hornung, and then he drops back and throws toward Max McGee, our split left end, who had run a Zig-In pass route. Max has a step on Dave Whitsell, but Starr's pass is behind him and Whitsell intercepts.

Bart's too tense, I'm thinking. I noticed it last week and the week before, and I can understand it because there is no one on this team who is more conscientious and dedicated than Bart Starr. By the nature of his position your quarterback is your number one man, and we are the champions and I know that Bart feels that he has the whole burden of our offense on his shoulders and I will have to try to relax him.

When I joined this team the opinion around here and in the league was that Starr would never make it. They said he couldn't throw well enough and wasn't tough enough, that he had no confidence in himself and that no one had confidence in him. He was a top student at Alabama so they said he was smart enough, and after looking at the movies that first pre-season I came to the conclusion that he did have the ability—the arm, the ball-handling techniques and the intelligence—but what he needed was confidence.

He is the son of a regular army master sergeant and he grew up on army posts and air force bases and he still calls me "sir." When I first met him he struck me as so polite and so self-effacing that I wondered if maybe he wasn't too nice a boy to be the authoritarian leader that your quarterback must be.

He impressed me getting ready for our first pre-season game in 1959. At our quarterback meetings, even though he was not first-string, he could repeat almost verbatim everything we had discussed the previous three days, and that meant he had a great memory, dedication and desire. He is also a great student of the game, always borrowing movies from our film library during the season and between seasons, to take them home and study them over and over, and with our success and his own success I have seen his confidence grow.

"A couple of years ago," he said to me the day last summer when he brought his contract into the office, "I'd have signed anything you gave me, but now you've taught me to be more aggressive and self-assertive and you've given me more confidence, and this is what I want."

"So that's it," I said. "Like Frankenstein, I've created a monster."

He's tough enough on that field, too. In 1961 he played the first half of the season with a torn stomach muscle, and for three games he kept it from me. He was throwing so poorly to one side that I was trying to change his feet and do anything else I could think of until the trainer told me. He has licked himself and he has licked public opinion. It's just that when you combine sincerity with sensitivity and intelligence the individual tends to be tense, and I'll have to find the right time this week to try somehow to relax him.

"Look at Willie Davis come across on this one," I say, "and Quinlan plays this good, too."

Willie Davis on our left, and Bill Quinlan, on our right, are our defensive ends. Willie has pursued the play across the whole line and, as Quinlan rolls off the block to the outside and hits Ronnie Bull from the front, Willie grabs him from the back.

From morning until night and week after week in those first months here in 1959, we ran and re-ran the films of the eighteen previous Packer games. We graded every player, and then each coach sat down and wrote a report on each and we compared these and came to our conclusions. Our primary need was for defensive help, because there is nothing more demoralizing to a whole squad than to see the opposition run roughshod over you. We needed an offensive guard and more running strength, and got Fuzzy Thurston from Baltimore and Lew Car-

326

penter from Cleveland. But your defense can make believers of your offense, too, and so we made those trades with the Giants for Emlen Tunnell, their great but aging defensive back, and with the Browns for Quinlan and Hank Jordan that first year and Willie Davis the next.

Your defensive end in pro football today must have size and strength because, with those corner linebackers either in the line with him or back off his outside shoulder, he becomes basically a tackle in play. He must have mobility, too, and if you took a look at Quinlan faking those calisthenics on that practice field every day you'd say how can he ever play football?

"I'll tell you one thing," Quinlan said one day. "When I give up this game and start to miss it I'll have it solved. I've got some film on this grass drill, and I'll run that and sit back and say: 'The hell with it!' "

He had a reputation as a bad actor, but there are ballplayers who won't play their best for me but will play for others, and that can work both ways. The Michigan State coaches who had him in college said they thought he could be handled, and I know he's a celebrater, but I also know that in a game he is a 6-foot-3 250-pound hard-nose tough guy who doesn't think anyone can beat the Packers. He's a ballplayer.

"What?" Quinlan said, when he heard we wanted to trade for him, and at that time the Packers had the worst record in the league. "Me go to Siberia? I'll quit first."

So I called him at his home in Lawrence, Massachusetts. I told him what I hoped to do with the Packers, and that I needed him to make it go.

"You know," Quinlan said later, telling about the call, "he's pretty smart. He tells me I'm a good player. He acts like a Quinlan fan, as if that's why he traded for me. He gets me with this kind of talk, because I'm a Quinlan fan, too. So I sign." . . .

"See this?" I'm saying now, watching that screen as the Bears kick and Willie Wood takes it on our 23 and starts upfield. "If Gremminger throws his block, Willie would know which way to go."

Willie Wood and Hank Gremminger are in our defensive backfield with Jesse Whittenton and Herb Adderley, and John Symank in reserve. Willie, at 5-10, is the shortest man on our squad, and he weighs only 185. When he was a quarterback and defensive back at Southern California, our scouts said he was too small and that he didn't have enough speed. No one drafted Willie but he wrote letters to all the clubs and, because we were so desperate for defensive backs in 1960, we invited him to camp. They were right about his size and his lack of top speed, but what they didn't know is that he can jump like a gazelle. He can touch the crossbar on the goalposts with his wrist and he has great timing and that sixth sense for being in the right place at the right time. He is the most natural defensive back we have, and Mike Ditka of the Bears has said that no one has ever tackled him harder than our little Willie.

The first time we ever used Willie Wood, though, was against the Colts in Baltimore, and Willie said later he thought that was the end for him. In this league when you put in a first-year man, especially at defensive back and particularly a corner man, they love to go to work on him. They hit for four touchdowns right over Willie, but the one I remember was a draw fake and Willie came up and tackled the fullback and Johnny Unitas hit Ray Berry 30 yards behind Willie, and that just about took us out of it.

They have to learn by experience, though, and Willie is a smart one. After the season he teaches science and math in junior high school in Washington, and the way we lucked into him is enough to make you wonder. It costs us well over $50,000 a year to scout the colleges and we got Willie through a letter he wrote and mailed with a 4-cent stamp.

If Willie Wood is a natural, I would say that no one has worked harder at making himself a fine defensive back than Hank Gremminger. Hank just won't take your word for anything. You have to prove it to him and, unlike some of them, he's mature enough to take criticism. He was an offensive end at Baylor, so he's got the agility and the hands and the timing you need, and he's a great student of his opponent. The odd thing about him is that he's high-strung and nervous and tends to brood when he gets beat by a receiver. That's unusual among defensive backs, because when you get beat back there you have to forget it and concentrate on the next play. . . .

So we eat our hamburgers and Tom Fears has his dill pickle and then we watch the second half. I see us score five more touchdowns, but I see Bart Starr is ignoring our quick man, the tight end, on our Flood pass and that quick man will always be open before the deep man is. I see that our guards aren't always pulling out of there as they should and that on our sweep right our blocking back has got to stop cutting off our lead guard. I mean he has to get to his man quicker. That's why, even when we win by seven touchdowns, my instincts are to resist looking at those movies. When you walk off the field after a game like that you think they looked great and you can only be disappointed. The satisfactions are few, I guess, for perfectionists, but I have never known a good coach who wasn't one.

"All right," I say. "It's almost one o'clock, so let's get on with the real business."

It is the same every week. You spend six days building for one opponent, and on Monday you have to forget it. Win or lose, if you don't put it behind you, you'll be wading around all week, knee deep in confusion. So now we will look at the other people who are coming in here Sunday, and Bill Austin puts on the first reel of their game of eight days ago against the San Francisco Forty-Niners.

It is just Bill Austin, Red Cochran, Tom Fears and me now, and the film has been edited so that we see our opponent only on defense. In the visitors' dressing room Phil Bengtson and Norb Hecker have the other portions, so that while we are putting in our offense they can be working out our defenses against our opponent's offensive plays.

"Right end, 89," Bill Austin says. "Right tackle, 76."

"Left end, 78," Tom Fears says. "Left tackle, 71. Middle linebacker, 56."

330

While they watch the first Forty-Niner play, Austin and Fears call off the jersey numbers and positions of the other people and Red Cochran lists them on the first of the many sheets of lined, yellow, legal-pad paper we will fill this week.

"Forty-Niners in Red Right," Austin says.

I do not believe this game is as complex as many people think it is and as some try to make it. At the same time I don't think it is as simple as it was twenty years ago. We try to make it as uncomplicated as we can, because I believe that if you block and tackle better than the other team and the breaks are even you're going to win, but we can't make it quite as simple as playground tag, and what Bill Austin has called off is the first Forty-Niner formation.

We have four basic offensive formations and they are standard in this league. In Red Right the fullback takes his position not in a line with the quarterback and the center, as he does in Black, Brown and Blue formations, but almost directly behind our right tackle. Any play may be run from any one of these formations, the halfback positions varying in the others. Bill Austin has called off the formation because it is not the play but rather the formation that dictates the defense.

"4-3," Tom Fears says, calling off the defensive alignment.

We record the position of the ball on the field, the down and yardage, as well as the formation and the defense, on each play. In this way we build up our whole picture of their defensive preferences, what defenses they use under what situations, so that on Wednesday we will be able to sit down

331

with our offensive team and say that, in a certain situation, the other people can be expected to be in a certain defense 85 or 90 or 95 percent of the time.

"That 56 is just as fast as ever," I say, "and they get a lot of pursuit out of that 71."

They are the two best the defense has up front, and that 56 is disarming. He is rather round-faced and soft looking and he does not impress you off the field, but on it he is as good a middle linebacker as there is in the business. That 71 is just a great tackle, and those are the two who will plague me most of all.

"The right end should be open for something," Tom Fears says, meaning the Forty-Niner right end, but thinking of our Ron Kramer. "The middle and right linebackers pull off to the left."

"But there's no use flying him," I say, meaning there is no point in just sending him straight downfield at full speed and without a fake. "That left safety will just pick him up."

We have twenty-five pass routes for our ends and our wingback, or flanker. We have fifteen for our remaining backs, our halfback and our fullback. Then there are our combination patterns, but there are some that you know right away are dead against certain secondaries and others that you can forget on a certain Sunday because of specific characteristics of the individuals in that secondary. There are some defensive halfbacks or safety men whom you may beat short but never long, or long but never short, or outside but never inside or inside short but never outside short. And that is another reason why I say this has become a game for madmen.

"I don't know whether that 81 thinks he's slowing up," I say, meaning their left defensive halfback, "but he's giving a lot more room than he used to."

"He's 10 yards off that flanker," Red Cochran says.

"He may be slowing up," Bill Austin says, "but not much."

"He's still quick as a cat," I say. "Let's think."

Bill Austin stops the projector and Tom Fears turns on the ceiling light. We have a multiple number of plays, but you don't begin to give them all to the team. Regardless of what you do put in, every game boils down to doing the things you do best and doing them over and over again. We have seven plays to get us around end and there are two or three ways of blocking each. One of the plays is our 29, our pitch-out to Jimmy Taylor, and I want us to stop right here and think a little about any adjustments we might make in blocking against the defenses we have seen the defense deploy up to now on the screen.

"Maybe if we release that end," I say, meaning our tight end, Ron Kramer, "that safety man won't come up as fast."

"Let Dowler crack back on that left linebacker," Bill Austin says.

I diagram it and we talk it over. I would like to free Ron Kramer from that blocking assignment and release him downfield to give the pitchout the appearance of a pass, and after we rearrange the blocking Bill Austin starts the projector again.

333

"We shouldn't have any trouble with our pass blocking," I say. "They're not doing anything of consequence that I can see."

The most difficult thing we have to teach our offensive linemen is pass protection. When they come to us their experience is limited by the fact that 75 percent of the passes thrown in college evolve out of their running game and they use aggressive-type blocks up front. We use drop-back protection, either man-to-man or area, to form that pocket, and it is not easy to teach that upright, ground-giving but still tenacious block that we demand. To the aggressive types who play this game the concept of retreat is strange and unnatural, but we want aggressive retreat, and I tell them all the same thing: "This is a personal battle between you and your opponent."

"All right," I say. "It's four-fifteen. Let's knock off for now."

JIM KLOBUCHAR

Fran Tarkenton's Double Loss

Fran Tarkenton's background was unusual for a pro player: his father, the Reverend Dallas Tarkenton, was a preacher in the Pentecostal Church. And on the sports pages, Fran Tarkenton was known for his religiosity as well as for his unorthodox technique of scrambling when a play fell apart.

As quarterback for the Minnesota Vikings, Tarkenton struggled through an important playoff game on December 28, 1975, to disprove what was said about him, that he never won the Big One. This playoff game, one with a Super Bowl riding on it, would prove unforgettable to Tarkenton on a deeply personal level.

December 28, 1975

Cliff Harris of the Dallas Cowboys stared into the Minnesota backfield. The vibrations he transmitted were intended to convey menace. Among the safety-men in professional football, he had more than the normal allocations of shrewdness, range, and ego. What set Harris apart from most of his peers at that position was the maniacal zeal with which he collided with people. These urges were almost to-tally impartial. He crashed into enemies and friends (if they happened to be in the target zone) with equal enthusiasm.

His belligerence was both heartfelt and calculated. He understood that there are certain types in football, particularly the thoroughbred wide receivers, who are capable of being terrorized. That he had a bald head and weighed only 195 pounds in no way discouraged Harris in the pursuit of this mission. Although he was one of the most skilled craftsmen of all National Football League defensive backs, he was much more touched by his reputation as the thinking man's sadist.

Walking to the line on the Vikings' first offensive series, Francis Tarkenton glanced at Cliff Harris. It was a subtle movement in no way recognizable to the crowd, which was zestfully burrowing in for 2½ hours of December football in suburban Minneapolis' Met Stadium. Out of the grandstands wafted the usual light mist created by more than 46,000 frosted breaths. The communal exhalings had more intensity today. This was playoff football, the Vikings against Dallas, December 28, 1975. Whatever the emotional status of their football team, the Viking crowds were always keyed up psychologically for December football. They came in bizarre antifreeze dress that gave the occasion the tone of a polar Mardi Gras. They also had commitment, because playoff football meant their team once more was within two games of the Super Bowl. And today, as they almost always were when icicles formed on the goalpost crossbars, the Vikings were favored.

Yet it was a relatively congenial day by Minnesota's nostril-numbing standards for winter, and

Cliff Harris was grateful for that. Tarkenton saw him standing there poised, mustache and all. He would be a man to contend with. Tarkenton's brain spun a few cogs. What Harris valued above most of the treasures of life was to knock somebody's jock off. The owner of the most endangered member that day, Tarkenton determined, was Jimmy Lash. Lash was one of the Vikings' regular outside receivers, a young man who was tall and capable but largely anonymous in the eyes of the nation's television audiences. The main-eventer on the outside for Minnesota was John Gilliam. Yet in the past two years Lash was almost as productive as Gilliam and possibly more reliable, although never the same deep touchdown threat as his faster and more dramatic partner.

Tarkenton had important schemes involving Jimmy Lash, Cliff Harris, and John Gilliam.

All right, Cliff, he was going to say, come with all of your *machismo*. Lash would run some slants and curls and Zs that waved the red flag at Harris, challenging Cliff to make a commitment. Gilliam, in the meantime, would run foot races with young Mark Washington on the Dallas corner. If Harris committed prematurely to Lash, believing the ball was going into an intermediate zone, the swirl of all the bodies downfield would leave Gilliam one-on-one against Washington. For quarterbacks and flankers it was the big banana split in the sky. It never happened quite that simply in the era of the zone and oddball defenses, but it was a situation that a quarterback with fifteen years' experience could connive for and create. It demanded patience, art, and a memory bank with miles of invisibly filed printouts that Francis Tarkenton brought to the ball park every Sunday afternoon.

So this was another Sunday afternoon at the ball park. It was burdened by the orthodox pressures of a divisional playoff game. Tarkenton felt no grimness, no sense of being measured for excellence or immortality. It was his seventh playoff game, his how many hundredth day at the ball park?

The arena had no more mysteries for him. The phantoms were gone, the genii and the visions. The juices always flowed faster when it was a day of occasion, and in his own private critiques he was gratified to feel that he usually played better on these days. Yet even to this variable he had made his adjustment.

If you played badly, it didn't mean you choked. And if you lost, it didn't mean you played badly. Or if you won, you had a lock on the next reservation in Valhalla. The slogans of the grandstand absorbed a lot of earthy derision in the locker rooms of the pros. But they fascinated Tarkenton because the whole canvas of football was his milieu. He was paid better than two hundred thousand dollars a year to play the game. But to him the psychology of the fan was just as provocative—if not quite as rewarding—as the evolution of the blitz.

At the age of thirty-five, with most of his personal ogres buried, with most of his personal goals achieved, he was simply comfortable to be back in the arena each week on Sunday afternoon. The record book now said bluntly that Francis A. Tarkenton was the No. 1 passer in pro football history. It didn't say that he had the most powerful arm or the biggest harem or the loudest mouth. It certified that somewhere in the snowstorm at Buffalo the week before, he had thrown his 290th touchdown pass to tie John Unitas' record, and then a few minutes later threw his 291st. The record book might not explain that Chuck Foreman had dragged half of the Buffalo defense into the end zone to pull Tarkenton even with Unitas. But it was equally silent on the kind of defenses Unitas was throwing against fifteen years ago. And if statistics are reality, or at least an unbiased measure of it, Tarkenton in his fifteenth year of pro football stood on a special kind of mountaintop that no other quarterback had reached.

Although he didn't plaster it on a billboard, it mattered. Nobody who had exercised any control over his early career—from Wally Butts, his coach at the University of Georgia, to Norm Van Brocklin, his first coach in the pros—believed him capable of enduring in pro football, much less outdistancing all his fifty-five years of predecessors. It mattered because in his deepest heart was the sure knowledge that the public now recognized what the game's old lions—in front of their stuffed jockstraps in their trophy rooms and from the broadcasting booths—had declined to recognize for so long: He belonged with the masters. It wasn't a revelation to the football public from the critics or the ghosts of Walter Camp and Vince Lombardi. It was the evidence of fifteen years on their television screens. They had once colored him fluky. Wind up the little quarterback and see him run. Blitz the linebackers and watch him scramble.

But line him up with a team of quality and let him quarterback.

Tarkenton not only preferred it that way, he also insisted on it. He always believed that the choice of the team he quarterbacked was much too important to be left to general managers and the operation of the Rozelle rule. And so he returned to the Vikings in 1972, the result of what was called a trade but was really closer to a personal ultimatum. A quarterback could stage-manage a choice like that if he had the brains, the testicles, and an independent income.

The fact that the cup of recognition was now filling for him did not lift Tarkenton into trances of self-glorification. He had proved. He had made much money. And he had achieved. They were goals for which no professional athlete need blush. But among all the commandments by which the athlete lives (or is made to live), he recognized one of unshakable truth: The really unforgettable moments are the ones he shares with the men he plays beside.

He had a private credo he lived and played by, stapled to a wall of his business office in Atlanta:

I have come to really believe that the people who make it in the world aren't the most talented ones or the smartest or the luckiest, or necessarily the bravest. The ones who make it are the dogged ones. Just plain tenacity. Those are the ones who take the jolts and get up and look at the sky. And no matter what's there they'll say, "well, I've got to do it; so let's go." The athletes have an expression for it—suck it up. Other people do the same thing, in their own fashion. And whether they realize it or not, that's the real serenity of living. Coping in some civil, meaningful and positive way with the problems that come.

Today the problem was the Dallas Cowboys. He was ready, controlled, at ease. All the auguries were right. It could be a day he would remember above almost all others because it had been a season in which so much success had coalesced around him: a ten-game winning streak for his football team, the personal satisfactions, the enlargement of his life through the deepening joy of watching his children grow. All of this suggested it might, and probably would, be the year for the surmounting deed of his competitive life, the winning of the Super Bowl.

The thought exhilarated him, although he had made no such announcements when the telephone rang at 8 A.M. that Sunday morning in the Holiday Inn, where the Vikings were sequestered for home games. Mick Tingelhoff, the center, was not the kind of guy to whom you said, "Let's hear it for a good, good morning!" Buddies and old heads, they lost count of the guffaws they had milked from the other jocks with stories about their special kind of relationship: one spending the better part of his professional life with his hands on the other's crotch.

Tarkenton never ate breakfast. Others wolfed steak; he drank black coffee. It wasn't nerves; it was his modest digestive powers. There was a chapel meeting thereafter, attendance strictly voluntary among members of the Fellowship of Christian Athletes. Jeff Siemon, Nate Wright, Chuck

Foreman, Fred Cox, Terry Brown, Roy Winston, Paul Krause, and Tarkenton sat around exchanging thoughts low-key, considering a passage from the Bible, reciting a brief personal testament. Tarkenton's father was a preacher in the Pentecostal Church. In the newspaper stories about his son, the Rev. Dallas Tarkenton was usually transformed into a Methodist minister, which is not quite the same. But it was close enough and also considered more respectable in some places in the South.

From the earliest moments of his professional career, Tarkenton's religiosity had attracted the sports authors as magnetically as his statistics. And it was probably correct that he was measured for heaven on the sports pages far earlier than he was for the Hall of Fame. He tried not to make a display of his beliefs. From the beginning, his Christian witness was probably more casual and chummy than that of the born-again Fundamentalists who made up most of his father's congregations. After a while it became something of a weight, the swarms of requests—even demands—for his speaking services at father-and-son meetings and the full spectrum of benefit programs.

Only a saint could or would have wanted to deliver on all of them.

Since Tarkenton admitted his mortality early in the game, he found himself withdrawing from that kind of public witness. Some saw this as sophistry. Tarkenton preferred to call it privacy. But his alleged sainthood was retreaded when he was traded from the Vikings to the New York Giants in 1967. The impresarios found it impossible to resist the metaphor of matching the apostle who quarterbacked the Giants against the Jets' Joe Namath, who had managed so far to avoid canonization.

Friends of both would explain wearily that neither completely deserved the casting, but what chance does accuracy have against poetry?

Tarkenton's perception of what constitutes A Good Christian had undergone change over the years. It might partially explain his rise from the streets and alleys of Richmond, Virginia, and Washington, D.C., to the level of a net-worth millionaire by the time he was thirty-two. He tended now to define goodness more humanistically than he did in the days of the hallelujah commitment of his youth. What was godlike now, he decided, were qualities like loyalty and truth and understanding among human beings. Some people said he ran too hard in too many directions and was a conglomerate frantically capitalizing himself; they said he was a smoothie as a politician, plausible and adaptable. But you didn't have to be a pauper or a 'round-the-clock psalm singer to be a Christian. Tarkenton cared about people in the abstract, all right, but far more inquisitively when he was face to face and could establish something in human terms, not on a jock-fan basis, which sometimes he hated.

But in all his modification of values he never let himself forget the message—and more importantly, the simple inspiration—of the little preacher he sometimes called Squat: his father, Dallas Tarkenton. And so in his reflections three hours before a playoff football game Tarkenton remembered his daddy, and Frances, his mother. They were part of the thanksgiving of this day, in this year of years for their quarterback son.

His mother was an authentic fan. The last week of November she flew up from Georgia to attend the game in which her son broke Unitas' career record for most completed passes. Francis asked his wife, Elaine, to outfit her in suitable polar equipment for the game. Dressed in snowmobile boots, a half-dozen sweaters, an overcoat, and a Viking stocking cap, Mrs. Dallas Tarkenton witnessed her first game on the icecap, and was enchanted. The reverend wasn't there. He arrived a day later at the Tarkentons' seasonal home on Lake Minnetonka fifteen miles west of Minneapolis. His ignorance of football was deep and impregnable. It resisted television, the press, his wife's enthusiasm for the game, and table conversation with a houseful of his middle son's beefy friends. It wasn't that Dallas Tarkenton objected to football or was indifferent to it, he just never had the time to understand it. He had been born in the slums of Norfolk, Virginia. His policeman father died when he was five, and his mother when he was seventeen. From his adolescent days he had had the urge to preach. He was going to be a Pentecostal preacherman, and that, together with the rearing of his three sons—Dallas, Jr., Francis, and Wendell—would be enough to occupy a man who in 1950 was willing to serve the Lord and support a family of five on fifty dollars a week.

He was a little man in constant motion as a herald of salvation. He was one of those unapologetic strict constructionists who didn't believe in using aspirin and didn't allow the shining of shoes in his house because these were quackeries or frivolities. So were motion pictures, none of which Francis Tarkenton saw until he was a freshman at the University of Georgia when he was already a campus figure. On reflection, movies were worse than frivolities. They were the flashcards of the devil.

While he was rough on the devil and implacable on shoeshine, the parson Tarkenton was essentially a man with a friendly heart and a bounding style in his pursuit of redemption for the souls around him. He was the kind of man, his son remembers, who really saw no wickedness in other human beings, only confusion now and then. Dallas Tarkenton would rise at 6 A.M., read his Bible, and pray. Then he would stroll the neighborhood, shaking hands and socializing. The minstrels would have called him a man who liked to smell the roses, which he did. He also enjoyed his music but avoided controversy because he connected conflict with destruction, and perhaps this is why football sometimes befuddled him, although he never discouraged his sons from playing it.

A few days after his arrival in Minneapolis, Dallas Tarkenton did watch his son in a practice session. Standing on the sidelines at Metropolitan Stadium in midweek of late November, the little preacher had a difficult time releasing his eyes from his quarterback son. They had filled out the reverend with a Viking sweatshirt, a big purple jacket, and oversized boots. Somebody from the defensive line squawked a warning that Grant might fine him for wearing his shirtsleeves longer than prescribed. On the practice field even Bud

Grant, the expressionless Sheriff Iron Eyes of football coaching, was hazable. This time the coach smiled a ton. It would have been a scene for CBS. The parson stood in the cold for two hours, and it was a reasonable surmise that he did not have the foggiest clue to what he was watching. Did it matter? This was his boy's world, and these were Francis' friends. The parson had the normal gratifications in his son's long-standing celebrity, but it was more important to see him in his true environment: bantering, working, enjoying, getting ready for a game millions would see. There was no intimation that the young man was consumed by tension over the significance of it. Francis never was.

A few days later, the family had dinner at the Radisson Flame Room downtown. Francis would treasure that night because his mother and father seemed so graced by the relaxed pleasure of this interlude. It was a vintage hour for his daddy especially, a night out with his son and daughter-in-law, and his twelve-year-old granddaughter, Angela. Francis' longtime teammate and closest friend, Grady Alderman, and his wife, Nancy, sat across the table. The Radisson had a big violin ensemble called the Golden Strings, which spun rich Viennese mosaics and Hungarian gaiety. The parson beamed. He talked about his other grandchildren back at the Lake Minnetonka home, Matthew, six, and Melissa, five. And he confided to Alderman that it was a delight knowing there were still places where a family could be entertained without apologizing to heaven. He talked about his little church in Savannah, where he would return in a couple of days with his wife. He admitted not knowing much about the mathematics of the playoff system, but he expected the Vikings to be on television on December 28, and he would be manning the galleries in front of the living room set. Smiling, Francis lightly squeezed Elaine's hand. It seemed to him that all the work and praying his father had done for others, his cheerful sacrifices as a husband and father and parson, had reaped for him the surmounting contentment of a night like this.

For that and all the other gifts the year had provided, Tarkenton gave unspoken thanks at the brief pregame chapel meeting. There was time enough for his game face. The motel room was not the place. Laurel and Hardy were on the tube. It was the only act in show business, the quarterback observed with baffled respect, that would outlast George Blanda. The telephone rang: Cowboy Nelson, the trainer's assistant, was making his usual Sunday morning summons.

Cowboy always taped Tarkenton. Cowboy fended off insults with a fine blend of martyrdom and contempt and, therefore, was perfectly suited to minister to Tarkenton. Francis rarely solemnized the pregame hours of a football game. He turned himself on an hour before. They might have gone through walls at Alabama and in South Bend and Texas, but Grant discouraged such behavior as unbecoming and probably dangerous.

Tarkenton stuck the telephone under his pillow and let Cowboy strangle a little.

At the team meeting in the motel, Grant spoke for a few minutes. He was a tall man with dissecting blue eyes and a bristle haircut unchanged since the 1950s. His language, typical of all of his personal habits, was thrifty, disciplined, and functional. As a consistent winner in pro football, he ranked with Don Shula of Miami and Tom Landry, his rival today. In ten years at Minnesota Grant had become sanity's fixed beacon at Metropolitan Stadium, nerveless and impregnable, an emotional Sahara. When he spoke to the players it was usually to remind them in broad outline of their purposes, to focus them. The assistants handled the tactical briefings. For games of special importance he tried to impart some sense of the occasion without delivering an oration, which was as foreign to him as a sideline cartwheel or an upraised fist.

He could not remember another game that he personally had looked at with such anticipation, he told his players. From the first day of training camp they had expected to win their division championship. It was a judgment that reflected both the quality of their team and, the players conceded, the beneficence of the schedule. The organization would never admit it, but the only easier recorded schedule in recent years was Richard Nixon's in the 1972 election.

That aside, Minnesota had played well and consistently in the 1975 season. It harvested swarms of team and individual records in winning twelve of fourteen games. Now, in the playoff, it confronted a team that always stimulated Grant because Landry, and therefore the Cowboys, approached the game in the same tenor and with the same respect for untheatrical professionalism.

"It's here today," Grant said. "It's a new season. Three games long. I think you've looked forward to it as much as the coaching staff has."

Tarkenton, the quarterbacking sophisticate and mahogany-office tycoon, hung on Grant's every syllable in a way that might have startled the television fan whose own image of Grant was not so flattering. Some of Tarkenton's teammates themselves were not overpowered by Grant's terse wisdom before the games, regarding it as pro forma vapor like any other coach's. But Tarkenton didn't see it in those colors. Grant impressed him in a hundred different ways. He did it with his perceptions, his control, his understanding of the athlete's nature. Grant recognized strengths that could be appealed to, vulnerabilities that could be healed or outflanked, hungers that could be appeased, and, above all, doubts that could be cleared with straightforward talk.

Standing next to Grant on the sidelines, even in the midst of a critical football game, was invariably a learning experience for Tarkenton. The multitude could be in tumult. The hostilities on the field might offer all the prospects of a riot. And Grant could say aside, "Their quarterback has thrown five straight balls seventeen to twenty yards." It was a remark that might have no special profundity except to reveal that his mind was working deductively while everybody else in the joint was ready to come on with broadaxes and hand grenades. Tarkenton recalled a couple of years before when the Vikings played in Los Angeles in a game widely advertised as a collision of defensive goliaths. The Rams got off to a 17–0 lead. Grant gazed out on the proceedings in characteristic posture, resembling a displaced face from Mount Rushmore. He then spoke to his quarterback: "I don't think we are going to beat these people by running." Tarkenton nearly collapsed in giggles.

Restored, he charged onto the field to start throwing against the Ram's quarterback, Roman Gabriel. It was one of the great javelin contests of the decade. The Vikings won it, 45–41. They considered giving the game ball to their trainer, Fred Zamberletti, for keeping the wide receivers conscious between sixty-yard downfield sprints.

Grant's brief pregame speech at the Holiday Inn demanded no mass decimation of the Cowboys in memory of Hiawatha or Leif Ericson. Grant believed that a manageable kind of emotionalism was a cardinal part of winning football. But he, like Landry, expected each of his players to generate his own passion in accordance with his own disposition and glands. With this Tarkenton agreed. But if the quarterback had one reservation about the Minnesota football team, it was in the scarcity of let-'er-rip swashbucklers, the kind who could infect football teams with the fever of their mission. The team had a few emotional players by Tarkenton's definition. Wally Hilgenberg, the snarly, curly-haired linebacker, was one. Alan Page, the great defensive tackle, sometimes played in a frenzy, particularly when he saw himself as the victim of an unforgivable screwing by an official. Carl Eller once rescued a helplessly taut football team by smashing a blackboard at half time so wrathfully that Tarkenton had to duck into his locker to escape the shrapnel.

Tarkenton considered himself an emotional player in spite of his reputation as a cool dude and august head. It was a thought, however, that scarcely concerned him an hour before kickoff. He drove into the Met Stadium parking lot with Fred Cox and Mick Tingelhoff, through the acres of quilt-suited tailgaters. Some of the tailgaters were still sober. Tingelhoff had borrowed a housekeeping van in which they planned to spend a post-game hour unwinding with their wives, watching the second half of the Oakland-Cincinnati game and waiting for the traffic to thin.

The subterranean corridor leading to the Vikings' dressing room was drafty and chilly, like the tunnel of an iron ore mine, Tarkenton imagined. It never changed—the condition and the temperature never seemed to vary much from the Fourth of July to the end of December. Outside it was a jewel of a Minnesota day in December. The temperature was twenty-six degrees, and a ten-mile-an-hour wind was blowing out of the southwest. Somebody had plowed off a tiny rink fifteen yards from the end zone for a half-time figure-skating exhibition. In Los Angeles they paraded bikini girls at half time, and in New Orleans they refought the battles of 1812. In Minnesota they held dogsled contests and snowmobile races.

At the doorway to the Viking dressing room Unitas said hello. Johnny U., with his blazer, overcoat and lumpy smile. "Good day, considering," he said.

"I'll take it, John," Tarkenton said convivially.

351

"How yah been?" He had an impish temptation to say, "How yah doin', Avis?"

Unitas was now a licensed oracle, an expert analyst on the CBS Sunday afternoon telecasts. By no coincidence whatever he had been assigned to the Viking games when Tarkenton verged on breaking his career record of 290 touchdown passes. But to the sorrow of the network choreographers, Tarkenton broke the record when Sonny Jurgensen was doing the masterminding. The nation was thus deprived of a carefully plotted poignancy wherein the old king would lay anointing hands on his successor—or wrap them around his throat, if the old king felt aggrieved.

Unitas' evaluation of Tarkenton's quarterbacking had aroused some indignation from the Viking audiences two and three weeks before. Unitas didn't intend any slurs. They happened to be two different quarterbacking creatures. Unitas flourished when it was the emblem of honor and an assertion of the American way to stand in the pocket and get disemboweled if it came to that. In addition, Unitas couldn't beat an egg as a runner. Tarkenton was spontaneous and adjustable. He was cunning and, in his fashion, great. Unitas was methodical, precise, brave, and, in his fashion, great. His usual public assessment of Tarkenton was something on the order of "a really outstanding quarterback; the best thing he does is scramble." Tarkenton heard that often enough to have a stomachful. And when Unitas disclosed a few weeks before in midgame that "Francis didn't throw with much precision on that play," Tarkenton simmered in the aftermath, primarily because Green Bay's Alden Roche had just rapped him in the crotch before he threw, disturbing the precision.

But nobody in football had much anger for Unitas; Tarkenton had none that clung for any length of time. Unitas was earnest and likable, a clubby guy. He might not electrify television on Sunday afternoon, but who did? In their occasional encounters, Francis and John always hit it off with the conventional hazing. And because Tarkenton construed himself not only as a celebrity jock but also as an interpreter of the whole phenomenon of pro football, from the huddle to the grandstand, he could not resist probing the life cycle of the Tarkenton-Unitas relationship. . . .

"Congratulations on the record, Fran," Unitas said. "Good luck today."

Tarkenton nodded, and cuffed him on the shoulder. Neither one of them had any identity problems.

Tarkenton ducked through the locker room doorway, and inside said hello to Bob Berry and Bobby Lee, the reserve quarterbacks and his locker room neighbors. Also anybody else within range. Some ballplayers arrived at work with a prefabricated grimness, a kind of opaque absorption that was their armor for the pain and pressure. For some it involved an actual change in character. Tarkenton accepted that. Each by his own devices. But Francis was a social animal, and his temperament didn't change much despite the largeness of the event. He rapped a little with Jimmy Eason. Jimmy was the veteran equipment man who was simultaneously the hard-butt quartermaster, confessor, and mother hen of the expensive wards in his custody.

Tarkenton trussed himself in some of his gear and reconnoitered through the thin smoke camouflaging the outlying commodes, the only habitation allowed for smokers by Bud Grant. Grant firmly believed that both hell and the waiver lists are overpopulated with smokers. Tarkenton walked to the training room to heft a six-pound shot-put ball for a couple of minutes, in the fashion of a baseball hitter swinging the weighted bat. The therapy had been part of his routine since his arm nearly went dead a couple of years ago. But now it was restored. If John Gilliam got out there fifty-five yards today, Tarkenton would find him. As a matter of fact, the quarterback was planning on it. . . .

The field was slow. Gilliam informed Tarkenton of that after running three or four downfield patterns in the pregame warmup. It was an informal briefing, part of a pro football game's intelligence operation that begins the moment the players leave the tunnels and continues until the final play. Much of it was funneled to the quarterback, the kind of information a military commander receives from his scouts: effects of the weather, condition of the terrain. Is a weak point ready for exploitation?

The slowness of the field bothered the quarterback because he *was* a quarterback and he lived on the forward pass, and forward passes had to be caught. All right, so it was just as gloppy for No. 12, the Cowboy quarterback, Roger Staubach, and for Staubach's deep receivers, Drew Pearson and Golden Richards. But the quarterback had to file the information. His receivers would have trouble making precise cuts. It was critical information, but Tarkenton really didn't know what he was going to do with it. If he was throwing on rhythm or the rush was staring down his throat, somebody better make the right cut at the right time. . . .

Tarkenton was not all that festive about the game. But he did expect the Vikings to beat the Cowboys. Dallas had football players, but it missed the commanding presence of a Bob Lilly on the defensive line and the power and recklessness of a Calvin Hill in the backfield. In running situations and especially on first down, the Cowboys' defensive front would align itself in the so-called flex, dropping two of the heavyweights a yard off the line. These placements were intended to snag the enemy ground game by giving the co-ordinated Dallas defense better angles of pursuit once the direction of the play was established. Two years ago the Vikings scrambled it early by introducing a couple of influence or misdirection plays. Their intent was to dupe the middle linebacker, Lee Roy Jordan. Lee Roy was savvy and spry, a dynamic fellow Dallas liked to unleash to roam the field. But in the 1974 playoff Lee Roy was railroaded, and the Vikings won the game. With it they won the National Football Conference title. It is *de rigueur* for all professionals, winners and losers, to deny that tactics or trickery in any form influence the result of a game. All hands dutifully made their denials after the 1974 playoff. But the misdirection plays did terrible mischief to the Dallas defense early in the game, and the Cowboys never regrouped.

No misdirection plays would beat the Cowboys

355

today, Tarkenton understood. Landry long ago found ways to neutralize or at least minimize those. Minnesota had some new material in for the flex today, altered blocking, a little different emphasis on some of Chuck Foreman's plays. Tarkenton was certain he could throw against the Cowboy zone, in spite of the menace of Cliff Harris, who was wise and shovey back there. Mel Renfro, although a convalescent, also had to be respected on the Dallas right corner, and Charlie Waters was okay at strong safety. Mark Washington on the left corner was less experienced. Would Tarkenton snipe at the cornerback, fling the heady speedster, John Gilliam, against him? Of course he would.

Quarterbacks never admit that anymore. They consider it lowbrow and unethical to finger the enemy. It also makes your offense sound simplistic. But Tarkenton had not played pro football for fifteen years to ignore the fascinating possibilities of a meeting between Gilliam and young Washington. He planned such a meeting on the Vikings' first possession of the ball.

The introductions were delayed by the verdict of the coin flip. It came up Dallas, and Freddie Cox, kicking off for the Vikings, flopped the basic Freddie Cox kickoff. It was short and treacherous. Dallas, almost mishandling it, had to start from the nineteen. The Cowboys intended to surprise nobody. Landry's over-all concept of offense was essentially no different from Grant's or anybody else's in pro football. You didn't plan beforehand to throw forty times, or to run on three out of four plays. Events determined that. The controlling conditions in the opening minutes were the high stakes of the game

356

and your field position. The Cowboys were starting from a long way out, in a foreign arena. So they ran.

Roger Staubach directed, via Landry's messenger service from the sideline. Like Tarkenton, Staubach had to stand off the sour prophets early on in his career. He ran too much. He could disorganize his own offense. But he could also compete, passionately and without much thought of personal safety. A Heisman trophy coverboy when he played for the Navy, he was forgotten during his service days by almost all save the Dallas scouting system. Landry believed in him, saw in him genuinely heroic qualities, strength under fire, willingness to sacrifice, the ability to deliver the climactic play. With him, Dallas had won a Super Bowl. If Dallas was going to win today, Landry understood, Roger Staubach would have to be the instrument of it, throwing the football. From your own nineteen, though, you better run.

It didn't surprise Grant to see Dallas move out on the ground early, but the Cowboys weren't going to beat him running. They held the ball for six minutes and came up with nothing. Mitch Hoopes punted into the end zone, and Tarkenton trotted on with the Viking offense.

How about something a little rakish early, to let Dallas know the Vikings were not chary about taking risks? Tarkenton threw to Stu Voigt, the muscular tight end. Not too rakish, Grant might have suggested. It wasn't. The completed pass cost Tarkenton a yard. Show the run, he thought. Foreman for one. Throw some more, get them loose. He hit Gilliam for fifteen. And now he would maneuver Jimmy Lash against Cliff Harris, the violence-loving safetyman, in the hope of springing John Gilliam one-on-one against Mark Washington. Gilliam cut once and broke free. Tarkenton threw deep, a touchdown special.

It missed by four inches.

A few minutes later Tarkenton gunned with another pass that oozed through Gilliam's hands at the same range, fifty yards.

The Vikings' own ground game was moving with no noticeable destructiveness. Tarkenton was annoyed and puzzled by that, because the Dallas defense, while sound and statistically impressive, did not seem that good to him.

So in the absence of a quick-strike touchdown to Gilliam, it was becoming a struggle. What else is new? Tarkenton asked himself. He felt strong and confident despite the blanks on the scoreboard. Like any other veteran player, he had a total respect for Murphy's law when applied to the football field: "Anything that can go wrong, will." He lived with that kind of wariness. But he was a man of elemental optimism from Day 1 as a professional football player. He believed with the force of the evangelized that the man who made things happen was the one who won.

At the quarter no one had made anything happen yet. Tarkenton would be startled if this turned into one of his team's memorable hours, but they were going to win. He felt too good and assured to consider any alternative. In December of 1975, all the planets were in order for Francis Tarkenton.

The self-acknowledged hillbilly of the team, rookie Neil Clabo from Tennessee, punted from midfield for the Vikings. Neil was mustached and twangy, and took a large pride in being able to drop the ball near the goal line in situations like this. The Cowboys' Harris was waiting just outside the end zone. As the ball descended, the Vikings' rookie defense back, Autry Beamon, stared squarely into Harris' tonsils as the Cowboy safety tried to field the ball. Autry, in fact, nearly had him garroted. He gave him no room at all. It was very intimidating and quite illegal, although somehow ignored by the officials. It was also unsettling to Harris, who never touched the ball in its downward flight. It bounced around at the four-yard line and would have been given to Dallas there except, in the judgment of the officials, it touched Harris as it was flopping around. Or maybe it was Pat Donovan, one of the Dallas blockers. The touchee was never clearly identified. Whatever the ball did beforehand, it wound up in the embrace of the Vikings' Fred McNeill, and was awarded to Minnesota. Three plays later, Foreman smashed into the end zone, and the Vikings led, 7–0.

Nothing that happened in the remaining twelve minutes of the half ignited either the blimp-suited thousands in the arena or the millions in front of their television screens. It was stolid football, not always cautious football, but uneventful football. It did not offend the Met Stadium audience, which was unaccustomed to the rhapsody of easy winning. Grant's formulas militated against it. Get a lead, make the others pass, force a mistake, lead comfortably, and then *don't do anything stupid*. The Viking offense in 1975, ironically, was one of the most versatile in recent football history. But playoff games are not necessarily the times to showcase versatile football.

Tarkenton frowned. The Vikings weren't moving on the ground as well as they had programmed. The passing was mixed. Their problems had something to do with Harris. He could have played the heavy in a Gay Nineties melodrama, with his mustache and all the consternation he was causing. He tackled, loused up passing patterns, and in general raised hell. Offensively, Tarkenton calculated on the sidelines, Dallas was running better than a team with Robert Newhouse, Preston Pearson, and Doug Dennison in the backfield should run against a prospective Super Bowl defense. He wasn't downgrading anybody, least of all the Viking defense. The Vikings led, 7–0, but a deflected punt was responsible for that, not the Minnesota offense.

They jogged into the locker room, awaiting the arrival of the muses in their coaching caps. The professional teams didn't squander half time with hot-breathed elocution. Jerry Burns, the Vikings' offensive coach, led the contingent down from the press box observatory. The offense assembled at one end of the locker room, the defense at the other. Burns always salted his technical talk with punchy four-letter connectives. Plays 37 and 57 ought to go. He wanted Foreman running off tackle, to take advantage of the pinching-down tactics of the Dallas defensive ends, Too Tall Jones and Harvey Martin. They had pretty well killed the Viking inside running game. Also, Fran, Burns was saying, the bootleg and sprint-out actions are open for the passing game.

Burns didn't have an immediate antidote for Harris, nerve gas and grappling hooks being illegal.

Bud Grant brought the squad together. To win, he said, the team would have to play better, execute better. But he wasn't going to sound alarmist. Hardly. He reminded them they were leading, 7–0, and they knew they were capable of playing better. Trailing, Dallas would have to come to them.

At about the time the Vikings clattered back through the tunnel, the half-time conversation ebbed in the Dallas Tarkenton living room in Savannah, Georgia. The preacher draped his leg over the arm of an easy chair and listened to Wendell and Dallas, Jr. He conceded they had cleared up all the first-half mysteries to his satisfaction. His wife, doing something busy in the kitchen, prepared to join them.

On the field in Minneapolis, his third son decided to discard the long bomb in deference to Cliff Harris. It was back to the beanbag offense on the third quarter's first play. Tarkenton lobbed the ball to Eddie Marinaro to explore. Marinaro hustled it forty yards. *Now.* They were at the Cowboy thirty-five, and Tarkenton's filaments told him that Dallas was prepared to be disorganized. He remembered Burnsie's briefing. He would hammer them off-tackle with Foreman, where Yary and White and Chainsaw Voigt lived, on the Viking right side. Tarkenton could see the opening widen and Foreman churning. He might go the distance. But Too Tall Jones slipped off Chainsaw's

361

block with an acrobatic movement when he had only an eyelash of time left.

At the Viking bench, John Michels, the offensive line coach, gasped. It was an incredible play.

Two lousy yards, and they had a touchdown in their pocket. All right, same guy, same place. It was open again. Foreman was barreling. He had it broken. Tarkenton lifted his arms and he wanted to cheer. But Jones came off Chainsaw's block again.

Michels was stunned. The Viking execution had been perfect.

Five bleeping yards. So third and three. Would the Cowboys blitz? Probably. Tarkenton squinted out to Gilliam on the flank. Here they come. Dallas was blitzing. Somebody fouled the blocking assignment, but Gilliam was cutting for the sideline. Too Tall lunged, too late. Tarkenton got rid of it. Gilliam caught the ball for a first down, bobbled it, caught it. He was doing some of both, going out of bounds.

Incomplete. The Cowboys were ready to go over the cliff, but nobody obliged them with a shove.

Freddie Cox came in and methodically missed a field goal from forty-five yards out.

Zero points.

"The hell with running on the first down," Tarkenton told the gray eminence on the sidelines. The quarterback wasn't rebellious or mad at anybody except the Viking offense, Francis A. Tarkenton included. Dallas allowed him adequate stewing time. The Cowboys labored seventy-two yards. From the Viking four on third down, Landry opted for Dennison smashing the line. The Cowboy staff beside him nearly fainted. Dallas *never* ran on third and four in that situation. Not only did the Dallas staff know it, but Jeff Siemon and the Viking defense knew it. Dan Reeves, one of the Cowboy assistants, was so unsettled he wanted to call a time-out. But Dennison was a quick accelerator, an obsessed, straight-ahead runner in critical situations. This was the moment, Landry decided, for some deviousness.

They came off the ball, and Siemon flew out from his middle linebacker position, looking for the pass. Who could blame him? Certainly not Reeves. Dennison rammed straight up the middle into the end zone.

Almost at that same moment, a little sixty-three-year-old preacher in Savannah, Georgia, groaned softly and closed his eyes. His head fell backward in the chair, and he breathed deeply.

In a moment he was gone, dead of a heart attack.

His sons tried to revive him by breathing into his mouth. One of them went into another room, where their mother must be told why they were calling the doctor, must be comforted, offered some hope, although they knew there could be none.

In Minneapolis, the fourth quarter opened with a Toni Fritsch field goal that sent Dallas into a 10–7 lead.

Nobody had to hold up bulletin board maxims for Tarkenton, or Yary, or Tingelhoff. About sucking it up. They had been there a hundred times. If you've got the insides, and if there is any excuse for calling yourself a championship football team, you do not die there.

A procedure penalty sandbagged them. Clabo

punted. The defense stopped Dallas. With eleven minutes to go, the Vikings were seventy yards away. It doesn't matter how, Tarkenton told himself. This time we get in. Drive on them. Throw the ball fifty yards, kick them in the balls. Nobody is going to ask how you did it.

Yary was downfield on first down. It was a tribute to his hustle but a stain on his discretion. He wasn't supposed to be downfield. So it was first and twenty. The heroics can wait. Be patient.

Foreman for seven. Tarkenton was a hard man to amaze. But Foreman amazed him a half-dozen times a game, with his spontaneity, his guts, his hands, whatever he needed to advance the ball. Throw now. Sixteen yards to Foreman. Foreman for seven more. Now to Marinaro. How about McClanahan? When are they going to give me *all* the tools? Tarkenton would puzzle. Nobody on the team ran quite like McClanahan. Heedless, driven, and productive. So in came McClanahan.

Tarkenton ran him on a reverse. The quarterback had been holding the play face down in his little pile of hole cards. You save the reverses for the other guy's twenty to forty. In his own territory he has to react to any movement to protect the goal line, which makes the deception of the end-around or backfield reverse all the more potent. McClanahan went for thirteen.

Now they had it going. For the ballplayer, when he feels it in his marrow and groin, a touchdown drive becomes an ecstatic, Freudian ride on the wind. The men in his huddle are more than teammates. They are kin, united by the zealotry of the moment and the shared sacrifice. It sometimes heightens the euphoria, nourished as it is by violence and pain, to have swatches of blood on the uniform—an opposing player's, your own, it doesn't matter. The Vikings' Ed White explained it: "No matter what your mentality is, and how you sublimate the game and make it an intellectual as well as physical experience, you play it—or at least you used to—in mud, on half grass, half scrabble, on frozen dirt. There's no way you can get around the objective of the game when you're slugging it out on the line of scrimmage. It's force against force. You're hammering each other. And as long as you're doing it that way, you may as well do it on God's good earth, or frozen earth, whatever he gives you on Sunday afternoon. The artificial rug just doesn't seem like the right environment for all the mauling you have to do. You come out of it with the uniform looking pretty, and you wonder why you have to shower. I'm no bloodthirsty beast. But when you cut your knuckles lining up in the stance and you've got red streaks on your jersey, it makes the game seem a helluva lot more believable." . . .

Tarkenton would have wagered his four-hundred-thousand-dollar manor back in Atlanta that they were going in. He had felt it a thousand times. Vince Lombardi maintained that Paul Hornung could smell the goal line. The biographers of Patton said he could sense the presence of an ancient battleground. Tarkenton felt a tingling in his insides when a long drive was going to make it to the end zone. It was like rising cadenzas in the orchestra hall. The whole team felt it. The big people on the line couldn't wait for him to call the play, roll the cadence on the line. They wanted him to go for it on the ground. We can beat them running. Us against them. We've got it together. The Cowboys felt it. Old Lee Roy Jordan was jacking around in front of Mick Tingelhoff, and Lee Roy would bust his tubes chasing Foreman, but Lee Roy must feel it, too.

They were on the sixteen, first down. Half the game they had run on first down, half of it they had passed. Jordan knew they were going to run, all right. Tarkenton would never screw this up with four downs to work on. Foreman dipped to the outside. Somebody had a leg at the scrimmage line, but he was powerful and possessed. Harris finally got him at the five. Foreman again? Who else? He was all legs and moves, and he faked himself into slipping, as he often did. But he recovered at the five and bored to the one. The Cowboys anchored for the Vikings' double-flyover, Jerry Burns' jabberwocky for the Sam Bam Cunningham play, the helmet-first dive over the line of scrimmage. The upback flew in first, the ball carrier next. The play had the delicate nuances of an earthquake. They stacked in on Foreman, but it was McClanahan, blasting the left side. Stopped once, he blasted again through Lee Roy Jordan into the end zone.

Tarkenton trotted off briskly.

The professional's trot. Seventy yards and six minutes in eleven plays. It was 14–10, and the gin-laced snowmobile pilgrims in the gloomy tiers of Met Stadium screeched and stomped and clutched their Thermoses in the air.

The Cowboys were dying. A veteran ballplayer

can sense that as acutely as he can sense the irresistible momentum of a touchdown drive. They were not only dying, Tarkenton told himself on the sidelines, they looked terrible doing it. It was no judgment of the Cowboys' effort or their performance. For much of the game Dallas looked like the stronger team. Its play was smoother, and its statistics were more impressive. Yet heading into the final minutes, the Cowboys seemed uncoordinated and lost. Centering deep to Staubach in the shotgun formation, John Fitzgerald rolled the ball on the freezing turf and dirt a couple of times. Staubach groused the second time. Marshall and Page heightened his distemper by racking him for an eight-yard loss. With 3½ minutes to go, Mitch Hoopes punted for Dallas. It was short and almost abject. To compound the unsightliness, the Cowboys had an illegal man downfield. You could almost hear the air going out of Dallas.

The Vikings had possession. Their tactical situation was almost unbeatable. It was third and two on the Dallas forty-seven when Lee Roy stopped the clock. With just over two minutes left, and two yards to go, the Vikings could put it away right here. But Tarkenton needed more than a short-yardage play. The Cowboys were going to stack enough people on the line to hold the levees at Galveston. He wanted a rollout option to keep the Dallas secondary loose.

Tingelhoff snapped it, and Tarkenton rolled right. The strong safety, Waters, *had* to respect a possible pass there. It was in capital letters in the defensive playbooks. But Waters didn't. "They're not going to throw that thing on third and two at midfield," he counseled himself. Waters flew up to the line. Tarkenton tried to step inside, but there wasn't room. He couldn't throw because there wasn't time. He held the ball and got nailed. And Clabo punted one more time.

The pros sanctify the big play, which sometimes takes a very prosaic form. In all the shock waves ten minutes later, nobody remembered how Charlie Waters defied the manuals and buried the quarterback on the play Dallas needed if for nothing more than the usual doomed thrashings at the finish.

With Dallas in possession, Fitzgerald bowled the ball back to Staubach, who responded by barking and fuming. The Cowboys were disordered. On fourth and sixteen from the twenty-five, Drew Pearson told Staubach, "Me, throw it to me on the sideline. I can beat Wright with an out ball." Staubach lofted it amid a flutter of "Ave Marias," and Pearson leaped to spear it at the fifty as he was going out of bounds. Nate Wright nudged him while he was descending. Even without Wright's assistance, Pearson was likely to land out of bounds. The official, Jerry Bergman, could have seen it that way, but didn't. The catch was allowed. It was a marginal play, and not many officials want to decide a playoff game with a penalty call in the final minute. Bergman was under an even larger gun. He had been wounded by all the recriminations following the Mercury Morris fumble play in the Miami-Buffalo game a few weeks ago.

The hairy-chested tycoons would decide this on their own. Flags are okay early in the game. In the last minute of this one, Dallas and Minnesota were going to police themselves.

Tarkenton's view of the midfield pass was obscured. There was some bitching around him, but he couldn't join because he didn't really see the play. Staubach had thirty-seven seconds left from midfield. Tarkenton didn't visualize Tarkenton calling the play in this circumstance. He rarely looked at the other quarterback that clinically. All he wanted Staubach to do was get wiped out by the Viking rush. From the shotgun Staubach threw to Preston Pearson, who dropped the ball. Now thirty-two seconds left. Staubach set up again. The Viking rush was urgent but a half-second off and a half-yard late. Drew Pearson was flying shoulder to shoulder down the sideline with Nate Wright. It was a prevent defense, all right. But still, it wasn't preventing the Cowboys from loosing the jackrabbit flanker one-on-one against Wright. Krause was coming over, but Golden Richards was on the other side, and Krause had to worry about that. The ball was nosing down through the wind. Underthrown. Pearson had to slow down. Aware, Wright tried to adjust to the changed rhythm. They made contact, and Wright fell. Striding over him, Pearson hooked the football on his hip with one hand. It was a kind of catch only heaven could understand, or ordain. But Pearson had the ball and was stepping into the end zone in astonishment, almost in guilt, because even the professional flankers with all their big talk about catching anything in sight don't catch a football like that.

Pearson looked at the official slackly. Was it all right? Any flags? There was something yellow on the field. Pearson could have sworn it was a flag, but it was nothing more accusatory than a tennis ball flung from the stands.

Wright got up and charged the official with Krause. On the sidelines Tarkenton screamed and swore. He ran onto the field with a half-dozen others. The crowd was comatized in silence. The sounds were from the players, not the spectators. "You dirty son-of-a-bitch," Tarkenton yelled cross-field to the official. "It was interference! Call it!"

The culminating year. The season of seasons for the conglomerate quarterback, and the year of the Super Bowl championship for his football team. They were going to beat the Steelers somehow, and all the old derisions and neglects would be wiped away. And now a hotdog, cocksure official, which is the way Tarkenton characterized Bergman, pulled the plug on Tomorrowland. The screen went black.

And it all came tumbling down.

Tingelhoff got Tarkenton back to the sidelines. The Vikings couldn't stop yammering. These were the good, disciplined, mechanical men. Calculating professionals. And in this ugliest, wrenching moment of their football lifetimes they were acting like deranged dockyard toughs.

Grant restrained his players, but he couldn't blame them.

Page was chewing out one of the officials. "Take it," he said, "and stick it up your ass."

They docked Minnesota fifteen yards for that on the kickoff. Fritsch hammered the ball deep, and McClanahan brought it out to the fifteen. Tar-

kenton ran on with the offense, looking for Bergman.

He cursed the official from cap to shoelaces,
accused him of losing his guts and blowing the
ball game. Bergman flung his replies, then told
the quarterback to play football or he was going to
run him off. Tarkenton called a pass play, and
Too Tall Jones ripped him on the one-yard line
for a loss of fourteen. Tarkenton got up and renewed his assault on Bergman. Christ, he couldn't
believe it. Six months down to this. The day of
days for the quarterback and his football team.
Bergman told him to stop or he was out. "Go
ahead," Tarkenton railed. "You already took it
away from us." Bergman wasn't going to run him
in a championship game. But he might as well. As
they were arguing, the official nearby, Armen
Terzian, grabbed at his head, struck by a bottle
thrown from the stands. Other bottles were falling. Foreman raced to the railing. A week before,
other dues-paying morons in Buffalo threw rock-
hard snowballs and ice chunks at the Vikings and
caught Foreman in the eye. He had double vision
for three days. "Knock it off," Foreman pleaded.
"You already hurt one guy."

Tarkenton closed his eyes. It was degenerating.
It was a living horror. The day that began with
sunbeams and gold dust, with the intimations of
Jubilee ahead, was winding down with a cruelty
and vindictiveness that made the whole progres-
sion of events seem like a mindless mockery. They
were losing the football game in a way they couldn't
possibly lose it. The season was in ashes. And now

an official knelt bleeding from a missile flung from the stands by some drunken fan.

The pain was still too raw for Tarkenton to yield any remorse. He knew later he would experience that. But at the moment he could not summon compassion for Terzian, the fallen official. The officials had lost their nerve and changed the verdict of the scoreboard, he felt inflexibly. In the back of his head he understood the evil and cowardice of the bottle-throwing. He even remembered talking to a newspaperman three hours after the game in Buffalo. Minnesota liked to congratulate itself on the civility of its athletic crowds. Alongside the bleacher jungles of Boston, Baltimore, and Philadelphia, theirs had a drawing-room restraint. But Tarkenton maintained there were just as many brainless spectators at Metropolitan Stadium as there were in Buffalo or at Shea.

It did not occur to him at the moment that the anarchy could also spread to the field.

A game. Tarkenton himself insisted football was a game too solemnized by the American public, its true purposes and values perverted. Yet in the final moments of this game, animalism, shock, and frenzy took possession of the stadium—and the field.

There were still ten seconds remaining when Page and Eller started walking off the field. Their act was a violation of the most rudimentary codes of the solidarity of the team. But it was over, and the two saw no need to observe some sepulchral formality.

At the gun the quilted multitudes in the stands headed wordlessly for the corridors. The Cowboys danced and howled, and the Vikings moved stricken, like armored zombies, toward their tunnels.

Grant left them alone in the locker room. What was he going to tell them? That they had had a great season, but you can't win them all? That they had had the game won but were jobbed by an official? Nothing the coach could say to them was going to lift the big round rock in their stomachs.

Tarkenton lingered in the locker room long after the others left. He had been obliging in the postgame inquisition, responsive to all of the questioners, the incisive ones as well as the dullards. He was composed and articulate. The four-letter words belonged to the combat. This was the epilogue. It deserved some contemplation. His judgment hadn't changed. The Vikings were beaten, he said, by the failure of an official to make an interference call that was obvious to anyone with eyes.

But his responses were quiet and measured, even when a young eastern journalist asked him, "Does a game like this bring back the old ghost, that you still aren't able to win the big one?"

An explosion might have followed in another locker room, or even from Tarkenton himself in an earlier year. But in Tarkenton's eyes the Big One syndrome was now so old and so discredited that it required no militant rebuttal. Tarkenton turned slowly, smiling. He was not amused, rather resigned, to a familiar penance.

"I don't play football for the adulation of the fans or to survive their boos," he said. "I don't play it to achieve somebody's conception of greatness. I play it because I enjoy it. The opinion others have of you may be interesting and important, but the one that is the most important is the honest feeling you have about yourself. Have you done your best, have you conducted yourself as well as you can as a competitor, allowing for your human mistakes?"

He talked about the Dallas defense, which he said was sound and powerful, about the dedication of the Vikings' fourth-quarter touchdown drive. He talked slowly, until he was talked out. He rose, but he could not leave. Even on the days of the worst disappointment, he could shake it off and head for the parking lot with lift in his stride. But today the barrenness of the locker room seemed to imprison him. He couldn't bring himself to walk out, although by now all but Stu Voigt were gone. He paced slowly among the discarded towels and strips of tape, the trunks Eason and his helpers were filling with the soiled garments of a beaten football team. The locker room is sometimes the athlete's playpen. Sometimes it is his sanctuary, and sometimes his limbo.

He was oblivious of a far deeper grief ahead.

Tarkenton walked over to Stu and dropped a hand on the curly-haired outdoorsman's big shoulder.

"A nightmare, Fran," Voigt said, "the way the game ended."

Tarkenton walked back to the washroom, pretending to himself he had to clean some dirt off his hands. He stared into the bowl, making an examination of himself. He had never wasted much time in depression, over defeat or bad news generally. At the moment he couldn't remember having experienced such a foul sequence of blows. The defeat, the hysterically bad ending, the bottle-throwing, the ranting. Hideous. But he wasn't especially depressed now. Puzzled. "Why and how?" nudged his brain. He understood now why he wasn't leaving the locker room. He didn't really want to accept the finality of it. It was as if postponing his departure kept open the possibility of some made-in-heaven recount or, even more miraculously, an official's admission of error.

"Come to," he said. "Get out of here."

His daughter, Angela, was waiting in the corridor. An eleven-year-old girl with a mature woman's wisdom about the vulnerability of heroes.

They talked calmly, about this and that. He didn't want her to sense his futility, and she preferred not to let on that she did. Angela led him to the van where Elaine and his son Matthew were waiting, with Grady and Nancy Alderman, Mick and Phyllis Tingelhoff.

They had done this before. But for the first time Tarkenton could not find the handle to join the conversation, with Elaine and the kids, let alone with his friends. He was uneasy and un-hinged, palming a soft-drink glass as he stared at the television screen. It was half time in Oakland. The talk from Grady and Mick came to him in distant gutturals, halfhearted and indistinct. They tried to bring him into the conversation. He was appreciative, but the talk didn't interest him. He didn't want to be in the van, but he didn't want to be anyplace else, either. It was a kind of half stupor that was new to him and bothersome. A voice on television was saying something about wanting "to express our sympathies." He heard the name Tarkenton, and he looked at the screen again. Why the sympathies to Tarkenton? Jack Buck was talking. He said Mr. Tarkenton was sixty-three years old.

Mr. Tarkenton was dead.

He died watching the Minnesota-Dallas game with two of his sons.

Tarkenton put his hand to his face. Please turn the television set off, he wanted to say.

Elaine's hand gripped his. The others' eyes were moist. Other hands touched him. Lips.

Tarkenton rose. He wanted to go home. He put Matthew's coat on and took the boy by the hand to walk him to the car. Nancy Alderman was weeping. Grady and Mick offered to drive them home, but Tarkenton said he could handle it. In the car Elaine said she could drive. He shook his head and turned the key.

They were on the freeway going west, toward Minnetonka. When did I see him last? Tarkenton asked himself. His father was at the Minneapolis-St. Paul airport, big grin and all because he was glad to have spent an eventful week with his quarterback son, but he was going back to work for the Lord. Daddy was like the good soldier that way. Pastoring was what his life was all about. The little church in Savannah had pleaded with him to help out. It didn't have much money, and it had only seventy-five members. So Dallas Tarkenton came out of his semiretirement and went back to pastoring.

Tarkenton had another picture of his father. He

saw him by the big coffee urn in the Viking dressing room during practice week before the Washington game. He was listening attentively while Grant made a little testimonial of his own: "I never take anything addictive when I'm working," Grant said. He spoke mischievously, but it was the truth. The parson said he liked that, really liked it. He was wearing those oversized boots and the long-sleeved purple jacket. He looked ready for a rummage sale, but they all liked him, and that pleased his son.

He died watching his son play football. A game. The parson never understood the game but his son loved it, and that made it all right. His other sons, Dallas and Wendell, had tried to reach their brother at the stadium, but they missed him. NBC was unaware that Tarkenton did not know about his father.

"He's gone," Tarkenton said. He could think of nothing else to say. He wanted to speed home to talk to his mother, but the day needed no more tragedy. The blows had come with a terrible, concussive cadence. The grossness of the last minute, the end of the season and the Super Bowl mirage, the loutish bottle barrage, the official bleeding, and now the death of his father.

Even that seemed physically laden. Dallas wins. Dallas dies.

And five hours before, the world whirled brightly and beautifully, all synchronized. What better than to be Francis Tarkenton and playing a big football game with millions watching on December 28, a game that had no more surprises for him, no mysteries?

He asked Angela to hold his right hand.

Matthew slid his own hand into it.

Tarkenton drove the rest of the way silently. Five-year-old Melissa was home with the baby-sitter. "Granddaddy's dead," she said. Her mother hugged her, and her father went to the phone. In a few minutes he had talked to all of them in Savannah. He would fly there tomorrow.

Grady, Mick, Bill Brown, and Mike Lynn, the general manager, visited later in the evening. He needed them, almost as much as his family, because he wanted to talk about the parson and what a lovely, unselfish man he was. And he wanted to explain some of the things he had said that afternoon. He didn't apologize for his competitiveness, but he was ashamed of some of his hard rhetoric. His father's forgiveness? He would have that. The parson would have said it's just a game. But sometimes it's more than just a game, even when you deny it. It's your blood and dreams, Freud, Midas, God, and the big down. Tarkenton had chided apoplectic fans for transforming a football game into something larger than reality. But in the final minute at Metropolitan Stadium that afternoon, the accidents of luck, an official's decision, time, and even nature's wind had perverted the orderliness of the six months of his team's careful planning, and the aspirations of years. It all blew up capriciously, a blind disintegration.

Daddy didn't know about football, so he might not understand how it could become that desperately important to a civilized person. But he did know humanity, and therefore he would not have seen it as anything evil.

The parson, as much as any man he had met, Tarkenton now recognized, grasped the most enduring realities. He had sought to be a good person and to encourage others to so strive. He had expended all the energies God gave him, and he had never really slowed in his pursuit of goodness for those willing to listen. But he had still had time to smell the roses and to enrich daily the imperishable reality of his life, his family.

Tarkenton drew his wife and children to him, and said his father was the wisest man he knew.

EPILOGUE

BILL LITTLEFIELD
Sportswriter's Defense

Sportswriter Ring Lardner's contemporaries, F. Scott Fitzgerald among them, used to ask Lardner when he was going to stop scribbling about Alibi Ike and the rest of his bush leaguers and write something of conse-quence. Roger Angell has said that he's had friends who have assumed that each baseball season would be the last to consume him, and so far they've been wrong. Sports commentator Bill Littlefield has some answers for those who wonder why people who write about sports don't get serious.

I don't know if those who write about nature ever get letters from people who want to know why they don't write about economics; or if people who write about foreign markets and the dancing dollar are asked why they don't explore science and medicine. But people who write about sports are frequently challenged to take on subjects of more substance; to turn their appetites for detail and their analytical powers to areas which deserve their efforts; to stop chasing after boys and girls, some of them half their own age, just because the boys and girls can run or jump or hit a ball or put a ball into a basket dependably and with grace. In short, they are asked—we are asked—to put away our toys and grow up.

And sometimes the suggestion seems to have merit. Writing about sports sometimes means listening with a poker face to pompous nonsense, such as when a twenty-four-year-old ballplayer explains how he had to jump the team paying him half a million dollars a year for the one that offered him three-quarters of a million for the sake of his family's security . . . while a bunch of sportswriters, most of them family men, making far less than a tenth of the salary of the ballplayer rejected take notes and solemnly nod. It means being stood up by a preoccupied hockey coach for an interview in a freezing arena, stamping first one foot, then the other, as peewees and mites and midgets hammer each other in imitation of their heroes in the NHL and then look over their shoulders at you because you are not father to any of them, so maybe you are a scout.

But people who write about sports stick with it for all kinds of reasons: some because after stunted athletic careers of their own, they can't kick the habit and need the ticket to ride; some because, while politicians lie and accountants cook the books, athletes are either safe or out, in bounds or out of bounds, winners or losers, and in that there is the illusion of blessed order; some because in the arc of a perfect jump shot, or a perfect spiral, or the downward snap of a perfect curve ball, they find art and derive art's satisfactions as surely as others find them in sculpture or painting or poetry—moments of sustaining beauty that surprise and delight us and lift our spirits. And some philosophers, serious academics, have even said that play came before work; that to truly understand ourselves we'd better know something about the games we invent and value.

All this is not really by way of excuse, or even explanation. It's just thinking out loud because this is the time of year for it. Midway through the basketball and hockey seasons there's leisure for quiet, though it's time to tote up points and see who's made the play-offs. The Winter Olympics haven't captured the nation's attention yet, and baseball's equipment trucks are still rumbling down the road to spring training. In busier seasons there's less opportunity for measured thoughts, so it's necessary and important to review things now and to come—for whatever combination of reasons—to the conclusion that sports is still the right baili-wick; that you will leave the sniping and snarling of the candidates and the hocus-pocus of the stock market to the people who find those things more compelling than the brief, bright moments of the athletes whose struggles and folly and triumph we sing.

Acknowledgments

Ted Vincent, "Democratic Era of Sport," excerpt from Chapter 1 of *Mudville's Revenge*. Reprinted by permission of the author.

Andy Rooney, "Breaking Sports Records" originally titled "Of Sports and Men." Reprinted with permission of Atheneum Publishers, an imprint of Macmillan Publishing Company from *Pieces of My Mind* by Andy Rooney. Copyright © 1982, 1983, 1984 by Essay Productions, Inc.

John Ed Bradley, "Jock of Ages," appeared originally in *Esquire*, June 1986. Reprinted by permission of the author.

Red Smith, "One of a Kind," from *Strawberrries in the Wintertime: The Sporting World of Red Smith*. Copyright © 1974 by The New York Times Company. Reprinted by permission.

Russell Baker, "Idylls of the Kid." Copyright © 1984 by The New York Times Company. Reprinted by permission.

John Updike. "Hub Fans Bid Kid Adieu." From *Assorted Prose* by John Updike. Copyright © 1965

A note on the text
Large print edition designed by
Pauline L. Chin.
Composed in 16 pt Plantin
on a Xyvision 300/Linotron 202N
by Marilyn Ann Richards
of G. K. Hall & Co.